GLORY DENIED

Glory Denied

The Story of Association Football in Keighley

VOLUME TWO

Rob Grillo

Manchester
EMPIRE PUBLICATIONS

First published in 1999

This book is copyright under the Berne Convention. All rights are reserved. Apart from any fair dealing for the purpose of private study, research, criticism or review, as permitted under the Copyright Act, 1956, no part of this publication may be reproducedm stored in a retrieval system, or transmitted, in any form or by any means, electronic, electrical, chemical, mechanical, optical, photo-copying, recording or otherwise, without the prior permission of the copyright owner. Enquiries should be sent to the publishers at the undermetioned address:

EMPIRE PUBLICATIONS LTD
62 Charles Street, Manchester M1 7DF

© Rob Grillo 1999

ISBN 1-901746-05-4

Set in 9 point Book Antiqua by
Michael Hubbard
and printed in Great Britain
by MFP Deign &Print
Longford trading Estate
Thomas Street
Stretford
Manchester M32 0JT

CONTENTS

	INTRODUCTION & ACKNOWLEDGEMENTS	2
	FOREWORD by Mike Hellawell	5
	FOREWORD by Peter Jackson	7
(1)	KEIGHLEY TOWN RE-EMERGE	9
(2)	OTHER WAR-TIME COMPETITIONS	15
(3)	NEW HEIGHTS...AND FAILURES	19
(4)	SQUARE ONE AGAIN	26
(5)	NEW LEAGUES – LIMITED SUCCESS	32
(6)	WHARFEDALE SUCCESS – Silsden & Keighley Central	39
(7)	CHANGING FORTUNES	43
(8)	SUNDAY FOOTBALL COMES TO KEIGHLEY – THE DEAN SMITH & GRACE STORY	49
(9)	CENTRAL FLY THE FLAG	56
(10)	LOCAL LEAGUE HIGHLIGHTS – the mid and late 60's	63
(11)	SILSDEN & THE 70'S	71
(12)	MAGNET AND THE SUNDAY ALLIANCE	84
(13)	HOCKEY'S DREAM – Keighley Town '79 & the County Amateur League	90
(14)	INTO THE 80's – Saturday & Sunday highlights	101
(15)	THE MID AND LATE 80's – Saturday & Sunday Highlights	109
(16)	THE 1990's – Cross Hills & the Craven League	127
(17)	...AND INTO THE FUTURE	143
	KEIGHLEY'S SOCCER LEGENDS	144
	Tables	153
	KEIGHLEY SOCCER - WINNERS LIST Saturday competitions	204
	ABOUT THE AUTHOR	206

INTRODUCTION & ACKNOWLEDGEMENTS

The main difference in writing a more up to date volume on the history of soccer is that there are more people with first hand knowledge of events and happenings than were around for the first volume, which covered the pre second world war era. In addition it is far easier to lay your hands on photographs from private collections or the files of local newspapers and the like. I am therefore indebted to several individuals named below for their help and support in compiling this second volume of the history of soccer in Keighley. In fact I've been more than slightly surprised by the willingness shown by these people. I have added the prefix *'and district'* to the title to reflect the fact that sides from the surrounding villages such as Sutton, Silsden and Oxenhope are well represented in the book, and therefore to give a more accurate title to the work.

Once again my main problem was in editing the piles of information gathered. It would have been possible to produce a volume twice the size as this, so apologies to any individual or team who feel they have been unfairly omitted, particularly regarding cup finals or league results from the lower divisions of local leagues. Apologies also for any errors found in the book – please do not hesitate to contact me with any corrections.

Trying to find final league tables, and in some cases cup final results, has proved frustrating to say the least. I have included all of those available as originally published. It is important to note though that during the early 1960's there was a change from the W-L-D to the now conventional W-D-L format illustrated in league tables, which is reflected in this book. Another slight ambiguity is in the name of Crosshills / Cross Hills F.C. – the latter spelling has been used throughout. Likewise with Magnet F.C – known variously as 'Magnet Joinery' & 'Magnet Southerns' in their early years, reflecting the official title of their parent company, I have referred to them simply as 'Magnet' until their official name change to Airedale Magnet.

Many thanks to: **Peter Pamment, Bryan Pamment, Mike Breeze** (all Keighley & District F.A), **Alan Feather** (Keighley Sunday Alliance), **Bob Moye** (Wharfedale Sunday League), **Kevin Hopkinson, Bob Smith** (Keighley News), **Peter Marsden** (Craven & District League), **Clive Pratt** (Telegraph & Argus), **Roger Ingham, Jeff Cummins, Les Storton, George Walker,** the staff of Keighley, Bradford and Skipton reference libraries & **Andy Searle** and the team at Empire Publications in Manchester.

STILL AVAILABLE:

CHASING GLORY
THE STORY OF ASSOCIATION FOOTBALL IN KEIGHLEY
volume 1 – the early years to 1940

£7.95 from all good bookshops, or £6.95 from Empire Publications (see offer on page 207), or the author at 3, Spring Wells, Holme House Lane, Oakworth, Keighley, West Yorks, BD22 0QZ

The following sources were more than useful in compiling this book:

'A Pick of the Best of Bradford Amateur Football', Ronnie Wharton
'Sunday, Sunday: A History of Keighley Sunday Alliance', Roger Nowell
'Rothmans Football Annuals', various years
'Non-League Club Directories', Tony Williams pub, various years
Bradford City A-Z, Dean Hayes
Keighley News, 1876 to date
Bradford Telegraph & Argus / Yorkshire Sports, 1940 to date
Keighley F.A. minute books, (thanks to Peter Pamment)
West Riding County F.A. handbooks, various years
Craven & District, Keighley Sunday Alliance, West Riding County Amateur & West Yorkshire League handbooks, various years

Soccer in Keighley missed the boat in the early, developing years of the game. By the 1940's towns with half the size of Keighley had well established, and successful football teams. Following World War 2 several more sides in the area would come within a whisker of establishing themselves in wider circles, defeated in the end by facilities, finance, support or indiscipline – the first two of which still stand in the way of a successful football team from Keighley plying its trade in the higher echelons of non-league football. The introduction of Sunday football has allowed local sides to excel in the various county and national competitions, and for a while the local Sunday league was a revered competition. As the millennium approaches we can look at the past and consider how our locals fared in the years between 1940 and 1998, a period that had it all – drama, excitement and a fair deal of controversy.

MIKE HELLAWELL
Photograph of the England international taken in 1961.

FOREWORD

by Mike Hellawell, ex-England international footballer

My first recollections of football in my home town were of the Keighley Town team of the late forties, who played at the old greyhound stadium down Dalton Lane. When they gained promotion to the Yorkshire League, which at that time contained several Football League reserve sides, just after the war I was so proud that in footballing terms Keighley had 'arrived'. Unfortunately things did not work out for them, support was poor, the town's rugby league team claiming the support of most of the townspeople, and eventually Town folded. Being nine years old at the time, little did I think that fourteen years later I would be donning an England shirt to play against France in my first international. I suppose dreams sometimes do come true!

Rob Grillo has done a wonderful job in tracing the history of football in Keighley & district for the last few decades. He has obviously done a tremendous amount of research and many will surely enjoy this second volume.

Football, as we all know, has changed dramatically over the years, but one thing remains the same; enthusiasm at grass roots level, the unseen heroes, the ones who do all the work to keep their teams functioning. All Keighley seems to need now is a Rupert Murdoch who can inject much needed funds the way of aspiring Keighley clubs such as Phoenix. Rob has that same enthusiasm for the details of local soccer and I am sure that you will enjoy this book.

PETER JACKSON

FOREWORD

by Peter Jackson, Manager of Huddersfield Town

The earliest memory I have of playing football was at around ten years old when my brother and I would get together around the streets of Keighley using any available open space to throw down our coats and get a game going. The freedom and simple pleasure from an impromptu kick around stays with you forever. Even now in my capacity as Manager of Huddersfield Town Football Club I can honestly say the best part of the week is when I put on my boots and join in the training. Despite this there comes a time as you approach adolescence when the call of organised League football just can not be resisted. It is these experiences, good or bad, that stick with you for life. The 15 - 0 drubbing, the parents flagging for anything near to offside, the time when only eight players showed up. Memories treasured forever.

Keighley Boys played at the Marley Stadium and, through one of the most important times of a young boy's life, fourteen to sixteen years old, gave me the structure and discipline I needed to catapult me into a life of professional football.

Rob Grillo has really caught the essence of amateur football in his volume two of football in the Keighley area. He has researched and detailed places and events that to someone from the area, like myself, has brought back so many happy memories.

The enthusiasm and love I have for football is something I have always tried to pass onto my teammates and of course now my players. This same passion is shared not just by people in professional football but thousands involved at amateur level. Rob is one of these people. I hope you will enjoy this book as much as I have.

(1)
KEIGHLEY TOWN RE-EMERGE

The outbreak of World War Two put a hold on organised sport as we knew it. The Football League hastily reorganised the structure of its competitions and relaxed its rules on player registration, and sport everywhere was decimated by the young men enlisted to fight for their country. Most of the amateur footballing clubs in Keighley, along with those of other sports, made the decision to suspend normal activities until the the cessation of hostilities. Likewise the Keighley & District league, formed in 1905, shut down, as did the local District and Charity cup competitions.

As sides such as Sutton United, Steeton and Silsden, who had dominated proceedings in the town in the years leading up to the war lay dormant, Keighley Town made the decision to continue playing. The side, formed prior to the first world war as Parkwood F.C., had risen through the ranks of the Keighley & District, West Riding Senior and County Amateur leagues during its early years of existence, and at the height of its powers had achieved an Airedale & Craven League title. By the late 1930's however, the side's fortunes had gone into decline and by the outbreak of war they were struggling in the Keighley & District League following an unsuccessful stint in the Bradford Amateur League, despite the fact that they had the best facilities of any local side in their fine Beckside ground.

It was the Bradford Amateur League to which Keighley Town returned for the duration of the war. The league operated a single senior division from 1940 -46 and Town were the only side to play in each of the six war affected seasons. The locals embarked on a successful run in this company that would lead them to Yorkshire League status, a standard of football in excess of any league that a side from the town had yet played in.

Although the Bradford Amateur League was rated lower in standard than the Bradford based West Riding County Amateur League, the 14 teams that began the 1940-41 season contained several renown Bradford sides. Town's first two seasons in such company could not have been bettered – a league and cup double in each, and a hatful of goals in the process!

The 1940-41 campaign could not have started in more dramatic fashion for Keighley Town. Trailing 0-2 at Calverley at half time, Town

Chasing Glory

stormed back to win their opening game 3-2, thanks mainly to Brayshaw's brace. A run of victories followed, taking them to the top of the league, their superiority underlined with a 14-0 thrashing of Thackley Amateurs in October, when leading scorer Hindle scored six. Title contenders Idle Celtic and Wilsden were also overcome before the only points dropped before the new year came in a 1-2 defeat at Slackside (Wibsey) at the end of November, when Town had a seemingly good goal disallowed late in the game.

A friendly was played at the Beckside ground against the league's Army side just before Christmas, with proceeds for soldiers comforts – half to the army team and half to the home team's players who had enlisted. The most bizarre game played on the ground, however, was when struggling Victoria Old Boys travelled from Morley seriously depleted. Town 'lent' their opponents four of their own players for the match – one of them, Bayliss, actually scoring the lone Victoria goal. This was the only occasion in which a Keighley Town player scored a bona-fide goal against his own team! Luckily, Windle was on form during the game as he grabbed three of Town's five goals. At least their opponents had turned up though – the same side had failed to show for the fixture on its original date three weeks earlier!

The first match of 1941 was a disaster for Keighley Town as Bingley Amateurs romped to an 8-2 victory. Hindle missed a penalty, he had replaced Sutcliffe, who had already missed two spot kicks that season as penalty taker, and basically everything went right for the Bingley side, represented strongly by army based players, on this occasion. Strangely, Bingley's title challenge faltered over the remaining weeks of the season, whereas Keighley Town went from strength to strength. Only one more defeat was endured throughout their campaign, and double figures were achieved on several occasions – including another hammering of the hapless Thackley Amateurs side. Even Slackside, eventual runners up to Town at the season's end were on the end of a ten goal town rampage!

Slackside were again easily overcome in the league cup final at Park Avenue. The Keighley side's 6-0 victory was described in the Keighley News as *'a great victory and fitting reward to Town's brilliant football this season'*. On this occasion Windle was outshone as Wilson netted four of the six goals. W.E.Tetley, president of the Bradford association, presented the cup to Peel, the winning captain, while league president Mr.Dodgson handed the championship shield and prizes to the side at a private end of season social evening.

The Keighley Town squad for the league cup final was:
C.Murgatroyd, J.Thornton, H.Peel, J.Leonard, J.Taylor, Rifleman Baxter, Cpt Butler, F.Jenkinson, T.Hindle, Rifleman Napier, M.Sugden, T.Wilson, S.Brayshaw & W.Hewitt.

Keighley Town Re-Emerge

Town's amazing season had seen 151 goals scored, of which Tom Hindle scored around 40. It was a dramatic turnaround for a team that had struggled at the foot of the Keighley & District League the previous season. Hindle himself would go on to greater things, playing for Halifax Town and York City, amongst others, after the war.

Success was to continue the following season, which opened with a 'Youth Soccer Football Day' at the end of August. In charge of the 'training' day for under 18's were West Riding F.A. secretary Mr. Winterburn, J.H.Frew (former Leeds United defender & now a F.A.coach) and E.Royland (amateur international defender). Forty boys attended what was heralded a success at Town's Beckside ground.

The first match of Keighley Town's campaign saw a 4-4 home draw with Idle Celtic – a team they were to thrash 14-2 much later in the season. Despite losing several more players to the war effort, many of the previous season's team had been retained, and despite the disbanding of the reserve team, the locals looked as strong as they were in their previous campaign. Once again victories became the norm, their only defeat before Christmas coming against one of the army sides in the division. Unfortunately a 12-2 defeat of Park Rangers, when Taylor scored five, was expunged following that team's withdrawal from the league, but a further run of victories after the new year ensured that Town retained their league title despite strong competition from the army sides. Although far less goals were scored during this campaign, the side still managed to top the hundred mark again for the season.

Keighley Town also made some progress in the County Cup competition. Victories over the R.A.F.(6-3) and Illingworth (8-0) set up a plum tie with the renown Yorkshire Amateurs side. Despite an early strike from Kirkley, Town's more experienced opponents eventually took control and were well worth their 8-2 victory. The Keighley side would encounter better fortunes against this side in years to come though.

The Bradford Amateur league cup competition proved more successful and it was retained thanks to a late Sugden goal at Valley Parade against Army side number 2. It was a fitting end to another season of success for Keighley Town.

The following three seasons in the same league were to prove frustrating for Town, coming close to winning both league and cup competitions in each, yet finishing all three campaigns without any silverware.The 1942-43 season started badly for the locals as by the new year they were 'struggling' in mid table, despite a 15-0 victory over newcomers Hollybrook Sports, when Lingwood scored eight times. Another strange incident occurred in November 1942 when the scheduled game with Ingleby Magnets failed to go ahead when, through a misunderstanding, both teams arrived at their opponents' grounds!

Chasing Glory

The new year saw Keighley Town back to winning ways as they climbed back to the top of the table in a run that saw another thrashing of the hapless Hollybrook team, this time to the tune of 14-0, and during March and April 1943 a run of seven straight wins brought in a haul of 55 goals. Despite war calls affecting continuity of the team, it looked as if the side could again retain their league title.

The bubble burst in mid April however. A Bradford Cup semi final was lost at Manningham Mills to County Amateur side Bradford Rovers 0-5. Town held their own early on, but a missed penalty by Hodgson proved the turning point and their higher placed opponents scored four without reply in the second half to add to a single strike in the first. A week later saw Town lose their grip on the league cup when a depleted team went down to Ingleby Magnets.

It was still possible for the Keighley side to win the league though, as long as they won their remaining three fixtures, but the army number 5 team, based at Cottingley Bridge, beat them 1-0 on the 1st of May to clinch the title themselves. The same team failed to show at the Beckside ground the following week and Town successfully claimed the points then. At the season's end, a mere two points separated the locals from their third successive league title, but they had certainly not lost their reputation of being high scorers as both Dixon and Tatton had scored thirty goals during the campaign.

The team could now boast two proud records. Firstly, no side had done the 'double' over them in their present company in the three war seasons, and secondly, not one player had been sent off during this time. This was a superb disciplinary record to have and a message to all who thrive for success – and particularly impressive in the light of disciplinary problems that Keighley based sides have endured in recent seasons.

The 1943-44 season was another where Keighley Town came close to success. Runners up position in the league was again achieved, and a narrow league cup final defeat at the hands of new champions Butterfield's Sports Club followed. Despite losing Tatton, Windle and Stowell to Leeds United during the summer the side were always well placed in the league and could again have achieved the 'double' had Butterfields not achieved a 2-0 league victory and 1-0 cup final success in the final week of the season. Town's County Cup campaign saw an excellent 2-1 victory over the more illustrious Ossett Town in the second round, following a bye in the first. Interest was ended however in the following round as opponents Guiseley Celtic ran out 3-1 winners. There was no success in the same competition the following season as East Bierley from the County Amateur league ran out easy winners by 6 goals to 2, that after the original tie was abandoned after 55 minutes with the Bradford side leading 4-0.

Keighley Town Re-Emerge

Town's 1944-45 campaign was to be their worst since the onset of war. They finished fifth in the Bradford Amateur League, although the league cup final was again reached – and lost – when army side G.S.T & T.C. F.C. ran out 3-0 winners.

The 1945-46 season, the first after the war, saw football slowly getting back to normal. It wasn't until the following season when local, and indeed national, leagues were back in the normal swing of things and several pre war sides had still to re-emerge from their temporary hibernation. Keighley Town were joined in the Bradford Amateur League by Prince Smith & Stells, giving them local derbies for the first time since early 1940. Stells had won all before them in the minor wartime workshop competitions in the town and it was a big step upwards into their present company. The teams met for the first time in October, with Stells surprising their better established opponents in a 5-2 victory. However, once they found top gear a fine run, halted only by a 1-5 defeat to Selby Town in the County Cup and a surprise defeat at Salts Works in the League Cup, saw Keighley Town climb to the top of the table along with Sedbergh Old Boys.

January 1946 saw Town gain revenge over their neighbours with a 2-0 win, goals from Hewitt and Robinson being good enough to ensure victory. Prince Smith's also surprised Bradford Rovers in the County Cup, bowing out only after a replay, they did have the consolation of lifting the League Cup though with a 5-1 defeat of Salts Works in the final.

The race for the league title went all the way to the final 45 minutes of the season. Sedbergh needed to defeat Keighley Town at the Beckside ground to force a play off, and led 2-1 at the interval after Robinson had given Town an early lead. With the wind behind them for the second half however, Town overran their opponents and further goals from Robinson (2), Hewitt and Walker sealed victory and their third league title in six years. It was a fitting end to Keighley Town's Bradford Amateur league career, and a fine start to that of Prince Smiths. More local success was to to come in this league in the near future, although not from either of the two sides that played throughout the war – Prince Smiths could not repeat their successful season and Town were on their way upwards...

On 13th April 1946 the Keighley News reported; *'It is Keighley Town's intention to seek admission to a higher league next season in an endeavour to give Keighley a prominent place on the association map'*. Rather than opting for the West Riding County Amateur League, a league that had brought virtually no success for the club before the war, an even bigger step was to be taken. The club applied for, and were accepted into the semi professional Yorkshire League which was expanding its single division to twenty clubs. It was the highest accolade yet for a side from the town.

Keighley Town's final game before Yorkshire League status was a friendly at home to Huddersfield Town reserves, after possible fixtures

Chasing Glory

with Bradford City and Bradford Park Avenue had failed to materialise, the locals going down 2-5. The Yorkshire league would see Town competing with the 'A' (or 'third') teams of Football League sides such as Huddersfield.

KEIGHLEY TOWN 1941-42

Pictured at their Beckside ground, the side can be seen with the Bradford Amateur League and League Cup trophies.
BACK: J.Thornton, S.Dixon, J.Calvert, Butler,
MIDDLE: S.Brayshaw, M.Sugden, H.Peel, T.Hindle, W.Tatton,
FRONT: J.Wilson, – –, R.Banks, G.Ellis.

(2) OTHER WAR-TIME COMPETITIONS

Attempts were made in August 1940 to form an under 18 league in Keighley, but this did not come to fruition until the following campaign, although the local schools league did continue for the duration of the war. The local football association, with H.Ambler as president, was able to report a profit of £14 on the 1939-40 Keighley & District Cup Competition, but this competition, as with the Keighley & District League, would have to wait until 1946 before it could operate properly again.

The 1940-41 season also saw a charity match played at Keighley Town's Beckside ground, when night workers of Lund's Eastburn factory took on the day workers of the same company, one of many charity matches played mainly for war funds that season. It was the local schools' league that seemed stronger than ever this season, with the inclusion of the temporary Guernsey school, consisting of 'refugees' from the island. The side were too strong for the locals and romped away with the league and Brigg Cup double, the latter achieved with a convincing 3-0 victory over Parkwood in the final. The town's schools representative side were less successful, going down 1-9 on Easter Thursday in front of 2000 spectators at Valley Parade against their Bradford counterparts. The single Keighley goal was actually scored by a Bradford defender.

The Keighley Schools squad that day was;
Jehan, Durqumin, Martell, De La Mare (all Guernsey),
Pullin (St. Annes), **McGarry, Scott, Brook** (Highfield),
Jons (Eastwood), **Swift** (Morton), **Ingham, Driver** (Parkwood),
Metcalfe (National), **and Sugden** (Haworth).

The local schools league would continue throughout the duration of the war, but without their Guernsey guests and with a reduced programme of matches.

The under 18's Minor League was successfully launched for the 1941-42 season with St. Joseph's emerging victorious. A similar league for the Craven area was also organised, containing familiar names such as Cowling, Lothersdale and Crosshills as well as teams from Skipton, Gargrave and Barnoldswick.

St.Anne's would come to dominate the Keighley Minor League, with three successive league and cup doubles between 1943-46. Dropping only one point throughout their 1943-44 league campaign, they were

Chasing Glory

awarded a 'grant' of £4 5s for their success by the Keighley F.A. Their immense success at this level led to the core of the team staying together following the war and entering the reformed Keighley and District League, where they would eventually gain success.

Keighley Police came close to emulating their pre-war predecessors in the West Riding Chief Constable's Cup. They lost in the 1945 final at Altofts to Doncaster. Despite leading 5-2 with only ten minutes remaining, they allowed their opponents to force extra time and eventually sneak a winner.

The Keighley Inter-departmental League was formed also at the beginning of the 1941-42 season. Competition was confined to works teams and Prince Smiths were by far the most successful before their elevation to the Bradford Amateur League. Other works sides included; Haggas & Smiths, Dean Smiths, Smith & Browns (therefore a match against 'Smiths' could have involved a game with any of four teams!), Hattersleys, Dan Mitchells, Claphams and B.N.S.F.

The league was not affiliated to the English F.A and in its later years, just after the war, actually organised Sunday matches, which was against F.A. rules at the time. At the time of its demise the league had undergone several name changes, but it did run a wartime league cup competition for the Victory Shield, normally competed for by Keighley & District League sides.

A wartime Charity Cup was played for, mainly by sides in the Inter-departmental league. Prince Smiths defeated Dan Mitchells 4-1 in the 1943-44 final, thanks to strikes from Pilkin, Wilson, Green and Kirkley and they went on to successfully defend the trophy the following season. Likewise, a wartime District Cup saw Keighley Lifts defeat Dean Smith & Grace in a replayed final in 1944 in front of 350 spectators at the Keighley Town ground, and Prince Smiths romping home 7-2 in a 1945 replay against John Lunds. Neither competition ran during the 1945-46 season, and it was to be a considerable amount of time before a Keighley Charity Cup game would be played again.

The team that would eclipse all others in terms of goalscoring feats during the war was the Keighley Air training Corps team. Competing in the local A.T.C league, their 1944-45 campaign saw a league cup success, defeating the Otley squadron in the final at Salts F.C. This was merely a prelude to a remarkable season that followed. The side netted 182 goals in only a handful of games – with the Bradford 71 squadron routed on three occasions, to the tune of 28-2, 21-0 and finally 33-0! In addition, Pudsey squadron received hidings of 17-1 and 16-1. Not surprisingly, the Keighley side ran away with their league title, Otley squadron being the only side not to experience regular double figure defeats at the hands of the locals, for whom leading scorer Asquith netted 51 times. Other regulars on the

Other War-Time Competitions

scoresheet were Johnson and Smith (who were both selected for the Yorkshire A.T.C. team that played Durham in January 1946), Bower and Snookes.

Meanwhile Farnhill's Bob Wilson was making a name for himself in India. He was that country's number one referee, controlling many first class games as well as several cup finals. He was also asked to officiate in a wartime 'international' in Delhi between England and Scotland. On returning home, Bob went on to referee in the English Football League after the war.

Towards the end of the war, H.Ambler was awarded with a 'timepiece' and life membership by the county F.A. for his 21 years service. He had achieved some 36 years as a serving member of the Keighley F.A by now, of which he was still president! Harry died in 1954, a life member of the district F.A.

GUERNSEY SCHOOL 1940-41

These wartime visitors to the town achieved a Keighley Schools' league and cup double, several of the side appearing in the Keighley schools' representative side.

Chasing Glory

HATTERSLEYS 1941-42
The former Keighley & District League champions operated in the wartime Keighley League but failed to reappear after the war. Tom Hindle was obviously a very busy man, also turning out for Keighley Town the same season.
BACK: W.Storton, L.Flanaghan, J.Pickles, J.Simpson, J.Spink, M.Coward, E.Heaton, C.Newiss,
FRONT: Jack Emsley, E.Newiss, E.Worrall, Tom Hindle, C.Dovenor.

EASTWOOD SCHOOL 1944-45
Keighley Schools' League and Brigg Cup winners.

(3)
NEW HEIGHTS...AND FAILURES

The beginning of the 1946-47 season saw the many dormant sides in the region re-emerge. Silsden may not have played competitive football during the war years but the club's committee had been busy wiping off its pre war losses of £79, turning it into a profit of £77 through regular dances and other fund-raising activities. The Keighley and Craven leagues were also reformed, although their pre war roles were reversed as the stronger sides preferred to play in the latter of the two competitions. There was to be no revival of the Keighley Charity Cup though. Formed as a 'soccer' competition in the early years of the century after having previously been played for under rugby rules, the Charity Cup had been the region's longest running competition and it would never again be played for on a competitive knockout basis. Similarly, some pre war sides, such as Thwaites Brow, also failed to re-emerge.

Around this time, the Craven F.A. actually attempted to form a Sunday football league in the area, which would cater for shop assistants and railway workers who were unable to play on a Saturday. The idea was way ahead of its time and had it been successful would have been the first official Sunday league in the country. As it was, there would be another 14 years or so before Sunday football would kick off in the region.

Meanwhile, Keighley Town's step up to a much higher echelon of football was seen to herald a new dawn for the sport in the town. Unfortunately the side's brief, and ultimately unsuccessful, venture into the Yorkshire League proved anything but. The step up from the Bradford Amateur League was a huge one for the Keighley side. In effect they had jumped two rungs of the ladder, as they had leapfrogged the West Riding County Amateur League, where several unsuccessful seasons had been spent before the war.

The first match in new surroundings was on August 31st 1946 at home to eventual champions Thorne Colliery. 300 spectators were drawn to a rain sodden ground, but despite the heroics of Hardy in goal, the homesters were defeated 3-0. Three days later, and again in rain soaked conditions, only 100 brave souls saw Bradford United win 3-1 at the Beckside ground. Keighley Town's first league goal was credited to Ellis, who would go on to score in the following two games also. Following defeat at Heckmondwike against Huddersfield Town, a first league point was gained in an entertaining 3-3 draw at home to fellow newcomers Harworth Colliery. 300 spectators saw the Keighley side race into a three goal lead before being pegged back by their opponents. This was followed by a goalless draw at Goole where the attendance was around 3000, ten times the number present at Keighley Town home games.

Disaster was to hit the club at the end of September 1946 as, following a period of intense rainfall, the rivers Worth and Aire burst their banks and as a result the Beckside ground was completely flooded. The ground was declared unfit for use for a month afterwards, this after extensive improvements during the summer months. The playing area had been incorporated into a newly laid greyhound track and a covered stand for 2-3,000 spectators and clubroom for players were nearing completion. As a result of the floods, the scheduled home game with South Kirkby Colliery was switched to the ground of their opponents and it wasn't until the end of October that the next home fixture could be played, which turned out to be Town's only league victory before Christmas. The homesters romped to a 4-0 victory over Sheffield Wednesday, thanks mainly to a double strike from Stowell, back from Leeds United. The side were 19th out of 20 at the turn of the year although progress had been made in the league cup, where victories over Chesterfield and Hull Amateurs had taken them into the semi finals.

Things did improve after Christmas and the new year. Early league leaders Scunthorpe United were defeated at Beckside, although the crowd again numbered a pitiful 200, and Leeds United went away from the same ground well beaten. Comprehensive victories over the two teams that would finish below Town in the league, Hull Amateurs and Upton Colliery, were also achieved. Unfortunately eventual winners York City put paid to further league cup progress with victory in the semi final at Selby.

As if the enforced month away from home earlier in the season wasn't bad enough, Town were forced into a two month long break from competition caused by severe rain and snow during February and March. All of the region's sporting events were decimated during this period. With the break over, the Keighley side continued to show improvement, a home victory over the previous season's league and cup double winners Wombwell Athletic being the highlight.

At the season's end, 18th place had been attained. More worrying than the poor results however was the continued poor support that would prove to be the downfall of the club.

Keighley Town's reserve side had meanwhile taken the place of the first team in the Bradford Amateur League, although they struggled badly and disbanded. Prince Smith's also struggled, rather surprising in the light of the successful season they had experienced only one year earlier.

A reformed Haworth took the Keighley & District League title ahead

New Heights...And Failures

of Crossflatts and Cullingworth. They won 16 of their 18 league fixtures, including victory in their last twelve. Attendances in the league were often between 300-500, higher than those experienced at Keighley Town home games! It was a welcome return for the Haworth club, who had disbanded in 1932 following several lean years in the County Amateur and Airedale & Craven leagues.

Sutton United also returned to former glories. One of the district's oldest clubs, they swept to the Craven League title and would embark on a run of success that would see further league and cup victories. The 1946-47 Keighley & District Cup competition went Sutton's way, Silsden defeated 2-0 thanks to a strike from Greenwood and an own goal. Earlier, 2000 spectators had been present for a Victory Shield (Keighley & District league cup competition) semi final at Oxenhope between Cullingworth and Haworth. The former emerged victorious 5-3 and went on to beat Oxenhope themselves in a replayed final.

Keighley Minors defeated their Halifax counterparts 6-2 in that season's County Minor Cup. Atkinson, of Denholme Clough, bagged five of his side's goals, but was unable to repeat his feat after that as no further progress was made in the competition.

The 1947-48 season saw several new faces with football league experience arrive at the Beckside ground, among them ex-Bradford City goalkeeper Ken Teasdale. During the season, Alec Hastie, who had played professionally in Scotland as well as for Huddersfield Town and Bradford City, also joined the club, as coach. The season started brightly for Keighley Town as Brodsworth Main, returning to the Yorkshire League after several years absence, were defeated by a single McKenzie goal. However, regular defeats followed, several of them heavy – 1-7 at Bradford United, 1-6 at Selby and 2-9 in the return at Brodsworth. It was obvious that the side were weaker than ever and with ever dwindling gates they hit rock bottom of the league. Highlights proved few and far between and the scheduled County Cup game at home to Goole had to be switched to Goole's home ground in the hope that extra revenue could be created from a larger attendance there. The side's penultimate match was probably their best of the season, coming from 1-3 down at home to defeat Yorkshire Amateurs 4-3, with recent signing Walker scoring twice.

Town did well to actually reach the end of the season. Early in 1948 the club secretary, through the pages of the '*Keighley News*', had appealed to the general public of Keighley to get behind their team. Much needed funds were called for, the chronic lack of support and the financial burdens of the previous season's floods cited as the main reasons for the club's financial problems. The recently formed Parkwood Greyhound Company, although better off financially, were not in a position to help their fellow tenants and following a poor response to the appeal a letter of resignation was sent to the Yorkshire League secretary in March. League officials were anxious not to lose a side from a town the size of Keighley and persuaded club officials to at least see through the remainder of the season. This they did, amid negotiations that would see Bradford Park Avenue taking over the running of the side, renaming them Park Avenue 'A' and using them as a nursery side. This possibility became closer when the Football Association gave the Football League club permission for the takeover and their 'A' team were accepted into the Yorkshire League for the following campaign.

Ultimately, the finer points of the agreement could not be agreed upon and instead Park Avenue located their 'A' team at Bradford United's ground at East Bierley (used now by Dudley Hill Athletic in the County Amateur League). Keighley Town chose instead to play again in the Bradford Amateur League for the 1948-49 campaign but before the season had begun had disbanded. The final ignomy for the club was when a local poultry keeper bought the dressing room and committee hut. Other local clubs, led by the newly formed Worth Village Albion, bought Town's existing stock and although the committee had not yet officially disbanded Keighley Town were dead.

Playing alongside established sides such as Goole Town, who could regularly command four figure attendances, Town found to their cost that without adequate support they could not hope to be successful in a semi professional competition such as the Yorkshire League. For a side that would be watched by no more than 300 paying spectators, and who would be plagued by bad luck, there was no real hope that Keighley could at this time make a mark in non-league footballing circles. However, no side from the town has since scaled the heights of the county's premier league, and Keighley Town remain the highest placed team the town has yet produced.

Sutton United, meanwhile, were on a roll. Following their Craven League success the previous season, they swept to the Bradford Amateur title this time around. The league had replaced their Senior Division with a new Premier Division to cater for sides such as those from the Keighley area and for the first time the Bradford Amateur League champions came from this side of the valley. Sutton led the league all season. Nearest challengers Haworth, the Keighley League champions the previous season, were trounced 6-0, and only two league defeats were attained throughout their campaign. Progress was also made in the County Cup, where the fifth round was reached, Manningham Mills and Lightcliffe being overcome before defeat against Burtons Sports ended local interest. A second successive Keighley & District Cup final also went Sutton's way, this time the new Keighley League champions Guardhouse were defeated by two goals from Fisher in front of 3000 spectators at Keighley Town. Sutton had actually thrashed improving Silsden 11-1 in the semi final of

New Heights...And Failures

the same competition, the 'Cobbydalers' having risen from the foot of the Bradford Amateur League Premier Division to a position in the top half of the table during the early months of 1948.

Fourteen sides had started the Keighley & District League season, among them the reserve sides of Sutton United, Silsden and Haworth. Unfortunately, St.Annes, formed from the successful school side during the war, failed to complete the season although they would return the following year. Guardhouse actually achieved a league and cup double. They were awarded the Victory Shield after opponents Haworth (reserves) failed to appear at Oxenhope for the replayed final. Meanwhile, a reformed Cononley were pipped for the Craven League title when Gargrave defeated them 5-2 in the deciding match.

KEIGHLEY TOWN – COMPLETE YORKSHIRE LEAGUE RECORD 1946-47

Date	Opponents	Ven	Score	Scorer(s)
31.08.46	Thorne Colliery	(h)	L 0-3	
02.09.46	Bradford United	(h)	L 1-3	Ellis
07.09.46	Huddersfield Town 'A'	(a)	L 1-3	Ellis
14.09.46	Harworth Colliery	(h)	D 3-3	Ellis (2), Stuart
21.09.46	Goole Town	(a)	D 0-0	
28.09.46	South Kirkby Colliery	(a)	L 3-4	Jolly, Patrick, Stuart
02.10.46	Chesterfield 'A' (lge cup)	(a)	W 1-0	Clarke
05.10.46	Bradford United	(a)	L 1-3	Robinson
12.10.46	Ossett Town	(a)	L 1-2	Patrick
23.10.46	Sheffield Wednesday 'A'	(h)	W 4-0	Stowell (2), Stuart, Clarke
26.10.46	Hull Amateurs	(a)	D 1-1	Stowell
02.11.46	Burtons Sports (Cty Cup)	(a)	L 1-3	Clarke
09.11.46	Chesterfield 'A'	(a)	D 2-2	Hodgson, Dixon
16.11.46	Ossett Town	(h)	L 3-4	Stuart, Clarke, Steel
23.11.46	York City 'A'	(a)	L 2-5	Stuart, Clarke
30.11.46	Hull Amateurs (lge cup)	(h)	W 5-1	Futter (3), Clarke (2)
14.12.46	Gainsborough Trin (Res)	(h)	L 1-2	Futter (pen)
21.12.46	Harworth Colliery	(a)	L 1-5	Marshall
25.12.46	Goole Town	(h)	L 1-3	Patrick
26.12.46	Leeds United 'A'	(a)	L 0-1	
28.12.46	Selby Town	(a)	L 1-2	Patrick
04.01.47	Scunthorpe United (Res)	(h)	W 3-1	Futter, Clarke, Patrick
11.01.47	Halifax Town 'A'	(a)	D 1-1	Stuart
18.01.47	Leeds United 'A'	(h)	W 4-1	Clarke (2), Futter, Stuart
25.01.47	Wombwell Athletic	(a)	L 1-2	Futter
29.03.47	York City 'A'	(h)	L 3-4	Clarke (2), Hirst
05.04.47	Upton Colliery	(a)	W 5-2	Patrick (3), Hodgson, Clarke
07.04.47	Selby Town	(h)	L 1-4	Emsley
12.04.47	Hull Amateurs	(h)	W 4-0	Futter (2), Clarke, Hodgson
19.04.47	Sheffield Wednesday 'A'	(a)	L 0-1	
26.04.47	South Kirkby Colliery	(h)	L 0-1	
01.05.47	Halifax Town 'A'	(h)	L 2-3	Futter, Webster

23

Chasing Glory

07.05.47	Wombwell Athletic	(h)	W	2-1	own goal, Webster
10.05.47	Gainsborough Trin (Res)	(a)	L	0-2	
14.05.47	Yorkshire Amateurs	(a)	W	4-3	Futter (2), Firth, Emsley
17.05.47	Scunthorpe United (Res)	(a)	W	1-0	Futter
22.05.47	York City 'A' (league cup)	(n)	L	1-3	Stuart
24.05.47	Chesterfield 'A'	(a)	L	0-2	
26.05.47	Upton Colliery	(h)	W	3-0	Walker, Flatley, Webster
31.05.47	Yorkshire Amateurs	(h)	L	2-3	Stuart, Futter
07.05.47	Thorne Colliery	(a)	L	0-4	
14.05.47	Huddersfield Town 'A'	(h)	L	1-6	

KEIGHLEY TOWN – COMPLETE YORKSHIRE LEAGUE RECORD 1947-48

Date	Opponents	Ven		Score	Scorer(s)
23.08.47	Brodsworth Main	(h)	W	1-0	McKenzie
30.08.47	South Kirkby Colliery	(a)	L	1-2	McKenzie
06.09.47	Sheffield United 'A'	(a)	L	1-3	Stuart
13.09.47	Chesterfield 'A'	(h)	L	1-2	Wayper
17.09.47	Bradford United	(a)	L	0-1	
20.09.47	Scunthorpe United (Res)	(h)	D	5-5	Halford (3), Patrick, McKenzie
24.09.47	Selby Town (league cup)	(h)	D	2-2	Halford, McKenzie
27.09.47	Barnsley 'A'	(a)	W	3-1	McKenzie, Taylor, Clarke
01.10.47	Selby Town (lge cup rply)	(a)	L	1-4	Taylor
04.10.47	Gainsborough Trin (Res)	(h)	L	2-3	Finnie, Doran
11.10.47	Huddersfield Town 'A'	(a)	L	2-4	Stuart, Patrick
18.10.47	Huddersfield Town 'A'	(h)	L	3-5	McKenzie, Halford, Stuart
25.10.47	Harworth Colliery	(a)	L	0-3	
01.11.47	Sheffield Wednesday 'A'	(a)	W	1-0	Brook
08.11.47	Goole Town (Cnty Cup)	(a)	L	0-4	
15.11.47	Wombwell Athletic	(a)	L	1-3	Doran
22.11.47	Bradford United	(h)	L	1-7	Doran (pen)
29.11.47	Ossett Town	(a)	L	2-3	Hirst, Taylor
06.12.47	Selby Town	(a)	L	1-6	Davis
13.12.47	Ossett Town	(h)	L	2-6	Doran, Davis
20.12.47	Halifax Town 'A'	(a)	W	1-0	Dobson
25.12.47	Halifax Town 'A'	(h)	D	2-2	Staples, Thornton
26.12.47	Leeds United 'A'	(a)	L	1-2	Taylor
27.12.47	Selby Town	(h)	D	1-1	Staples
03.01.48	Sheffield Wednesday 'A'	(h)	L	0-3	
17.01.48	Wombwell Athletic	(h)	L	3-5	Taylor (2), Binns
31.01.48	Goole Town	(h)	D	2-2	Taylor (2)
14.02.48	Goole Town	(a)	L	0-2	
28.02.48	South Kirkby Colliery	(h)	W	1-0	Hawthorn
06.03.48	Thorne Colliery	(a)	L	1-2	Dobson
27.03.48	Barnsley 'A'	(h)	L	0-1	
29.03.48	Brodsworth Main	(a)	L	2-9	Clapham (2)
30.03.48	Scunthorpe United (Res)	(a)	L	1-3	Sylvester
03.04.48	Yorkshire Amateurs	(a)	D	1-1	Brayshaw
10.04.48	Thorne Colliery	(h)	L	1-3	Walker
17.04.48	Sheffield United 'A'	(h)	D	1-1	Pulling (pen)
19.04.48	Chesterfield 'A'	(a)	L	0-4	

New Heights...And Failures

21.04.48	Harworth Colliery	(h)	L 2-6	Taylor (2)
24.04.48	Gainsborough Trin (Res)	(a)	L 1-2	Foggon
27.04.48	Yorkshire Amateurs	(h)	W 4-3	Walker (2), Miller, Dixon
01.05.48	Leeds United 'A'	(h)	L 1-5	Powell

SUTTON UNITED 1947

The side are pictured following their Craven League title and Keighley & District Cup final victory over Silsden. Over the next few years United were to become by far the strongest side in the region.

(4)
SQUARE ONE AGAIN

With Keighley Town's departure from the Yorkshire League, the town was once again without a side in a higher standard of league. However, with the continual improvements in travel more Keighley sides were by now opting for Bradford based leagues, in particular the Bradford Amateur League, where Sutton United, Silsden and Haworth were already based, and to a lesser extent the Bradford Red Triangle. In addition the Wharfedale League was soon to become a hive for several of Keighley's top footballing sides.

Sutton United were left as the leading side in the district, although they were unable to recapture the Bradford Amateur League title during the 1948-49 campaign. Both they and Haworth were among the league leaders for most of the season but it was a rejuvenated U.S.M.P. Co, who had demolished the Sutton side 6-1 on the opening day of the season, who sped to their first league title. The same side also put paid to Sutton's County Cup hopes in the fifth round. Haworth had made it through to the fourth round, before going out in a replay to Normanton based Snydale Road.

Sutton did have the consolation of lifting the Keighley & District Cup for a third successive season following two thrilling games against Worth Village. 3000 spectators witnessed a 3-3 draw at Lawkholme Lane, in which Greenwood scored a hat-trick for Sutton. The Keighley League side were overcome by 3 goals to 2 in the replay – this time in front of 4000! How Keighley Town would have loved crowds such as this! The only dampener on what was a fine set of games was the unavailability of the old Beckside ground as a cup final venue.

The 1948-49 season also saw Guardhouse achieve a Keighley & District league and cup double. They managed to see off the challenge of Worth Village in the league and overcame Oxenhope 4-1 in the Victory Shield final.

The following campaign saw success return to local sides in the Bradford Amateur League. Sutton United lifted what was their third title in four seasons following the war as they proved themselves a class apart from their Premier Division rivals. Unfortunately it was also to be the last time that a Sutton side would achieve such honours. However, such was their domination during the 1949-50 season the title was sewn up well before the end of the campaign and at the season's end a successful application was made to the West Riding County Amateur League. The

Square One Again

season opened in tremendous style with a 7-0 rout of Wyke Old Boys. Fancied St.Josephs and Tyersal were also overcome as Sutton went straight to the top of the league, aided by the goals of Jack Hindle, brother of former Keighley Town stalwart, Tom. Frizinghall Rovers were also cast aside 12-1 before the first point was dropped in a goalless draw with struggling O.D.R.A. F.C. By the season's end, seven points separated Sutton from the previous season's champions U.S.M.P, and a measure of the side's growing credentials was another fairly successful County Cup run. Goole Shipyard were overcome 5-2 in the second round (a round in which Haworth went out 2-7 at Polish team K.S.Silesia from Huddersfield), before a tremendous 7-3 victory over former winners East End Park W.M.C. Sutton actually took with them to Leeds four coach loads of supporters!

The fourth round of the County Cup brought a tie with Kirkheaton Rovers, and again three coach loads of Sutton supporters were to arrive to cheer their side on in the tie at Huddersfield. A tough 1-1 draw resulted. Without key players Hindle and Waterhouse, and despite the presence of Cononley Brass Band to entertain the crowd, Sutton went out 1-5 in the home replay – their first defeat of the season. Sutton's only real 'off' day that season was in a surprise Bradford Senior Cup defeat against Dick Lane United. The locals had preferred to enter the Bradford cup rather than the Keighley & District competition which they had dominated since the war.

Haworth's fifth place in the final Bradford Amateur table was remarkable in that the side were bottom of the league at Christmas. In November 1949 the club appealed for donations to help improve the facilities at their Old Hall ground which were said to desperately need improving. The playing area at the time was uneven and badly shaped, and a 'Ground Improvement Committee' was set up to oversee any developments. The ultimate intention was to see a better class of football played in the village, but in view of the lack of success achieved by Keighley Town in their appeal to the public less than two years earlier it was never really likely that Haworth would come closer to their ultimate aim.

Ingrow United, in their second season in the Bradford Amateur League, gained promotion to the top flight. They were always among the leaders in division one and at the season's end third place behind East Ward L.C. and Crofts was enough to ensure that they would join Haworth and Silsden in the Premier division for the following campaign.

St.Annes took the 1949-50 Keighley & District League title. The league opted to run a single division again, but with a massive 18 sides – a number that would never be equalled. With so many sides in the league it was obvious that there would be a wide range of playing standards, and this was never more evident than in the matches between St.Annes and Riddlesden. The league champions' opponents, in their only season in the league, were routed 18-0 and 16-0, and were on the receiving end of several more hidings during the season.

St.Annes broke away at the top of the league along with Guardhouse, Worth Village and newcomers Addingham, whom they defeated 5-2 in January. They were actually the only side to complete all of their fixtures in the league and finished five points ahead of Guardhouse at the season's end, winning 32 of their 34 games. The strength of the leading Keighley League teams was evident in the District Cup, with neither Haworth or Silsden making it through to the final. The cup was actually shared as St.Annes and Guardhouse played out two inconclusive ties. The first game was abandoned due to bad light twelve minutes from time, with Guardhouse leading 2-1, although the cynics among those present suggested that the real reason was because of the poor gate receipts. The replayed final was also drawn, Spencer of Guardhouse drawing his side level with only 30 seconds remaining. It was decided that each side should keep the cup for six months each as another replay so late in the season was not a possibility.

Guardhouse did win the Victory Shield outright though, Addingham defeated 5-2 again in the final, but the major talking point of the competition was from an earlier tie between Sutton United reserves and Morton. Morton led 3-0 at half time, yet with twelve minutes remaining had allowed their opponents back into the game and were trailing 3-4. The side then walked off the field, disputing a refereeing decision, and refused to return – although in reality frustration may well have been the real cause of the problem. Other 'highlights' of the season included Keighley Minors' narrow 5-4 victory over their Craven counterparts, with Drake scoring four times for the victors, while Keighley Police went close to emulating their pre-war achievements in the Chief Constable's Cup, going down 1-2 in the final at Barnsley to Doncaster Police.

The 1949-50 campaign also saw a Keighley & District League representative side play at Lancaster against the North Lancashire League (where several North Craven sides such as Ingleton still play) for the first time. Despite losing 0-4 in heavy rain, league officials were confident that new friendships and acquaintances had been fostered through the match and a return was organised for the following season at Prince Smith's tiny Strong Close ground, when the Lancastrians again ran out winners, this time by 4 goals to 1. Keighley actually led in this game thanks to a goal from Anderton, but despite Peel's missed penalty they were described in the local press as putting up a *gallant performance*. The Keighley League side that played in the return was:

K.Preston (Morton), **J.Walls** (Guardhouse), **W.Hall** (Guardhouse), **H.Scott** (St.Josephs), **H.Peel** (Guardhouse), **R.Preston** (Morton), **J.Murgatroyd** (Oxenhope), **J.Holdsworth** (Guardhouse),

P.Anderton (St.Josephs), **J.Woollard** (St.Josephs), **F.Payne** (Guardhouse).
Reserves: **F.Walton** (Morton), **D.Meecham** (Haworth).
Trainer: **J.Sherlock**, Manager: **W.H.Lynch**.

Steeton defeated Central Y.C. in the Keighley Minor League championship play-off in two successive seasons (1949-50 & 1950-51), both sides having won each 'half' of the season in each case. The Central Youth Club would soon spawn a side that would be the toast of the town in years to come. Worth Village Minors, meanwhile, won the 1949-50 Keighley Minor Cup, defeating Steeton 5-3 in the final.

Cowling came close to the 1949-50 Craven League title, eventually finishing behind Settle United and Langcliffe Wanderers, although division two of the same league saw the first appearance of the Cross Hills Y.C.team, who would eventually drop the Youth Club part of their name and achieve great success in local footballing circles. The following season would see both local sides achieve their season's ambitions and lift their divisional championships. Cowling scored 101 goals in 22 league games en-route to the Craven First Division championship, their first title since before the war. The championship was sealed with a 13-0 rout of Settle late in the season, with Noble leading the scoring with eight strikes. Cross Hills lifted the Second Division crown to gain promotion for the first time. The Settle side had been the first visitors to Bradley United's new ground in October 1951, when league secretary J.O.Fairhurst performed the opening ceremony and kicked off.

Guardhouse regained the 1950-51 Keighley League crown. Reigning champions St.Annes surprisingly withdrew from the league before a ball had been kicked and it was left to the former champions to vie for the lead along with St.Josephs, Morton and Oxenhope. The latter did not drop their first points until December when St.Josephs defeated them 5-1 (the same day that Cowling lost their unbeaten record to Grassington in the Craven league), although St.Josephs themselves lost their chances of the title when thrashed 7-1 by Guardhouse, who wrapped up the title with a 10-1 rout of their own reserve team. Guardhouse's only league defeat came at the hands of Haworth reserves in their final fixture, although by then Haworth's first team had defeated them heavily, 9-1, in a District Cup semi final. Guardhouse had been expected to give the Bradford Amateur side a far sterner test in the tie, particularly as St.Josephs had come within a whisker of knocking out Haworth in the previous round. St.Josephs themselves had the last laugh as a solitary goal was enough for victory in a tight Victory Shield final.

Eldwick were surprise District Cup finalists, defeating Silsden, three Bradford Amateur divisions higher than themselves 5-4. They were no match for Haworth in the final though, the favourites recording a 5-2 success at the Parkwood Greyhound Stadium.

Chasing Glory

Sutton United's step into a higher standard of football proved as unsuccessful as Keighley Town's recent elevation. Despite a 5-1 opening day victory over Yeadon Celtic, the 1950-51 season was an immense disappointment for them, particularly in view of their fine form of recent seasons. Struggling at the foot of the table, and with an earlier than usual County Cup exit, the club made the decision to drop back into the Craven League for the following season. It was the start of the end for this renown local club and their demise would not be far away.

In contrast, Silsden played out their final Bradford Amateur League season in mid table before embarking on a run that would eventually see success in a higher standard of competition. They, along with Haworth and Ingrow United, made no impression on the league leaders, and by the following season of the three only Haworth would field a side in the league, Ingrow taking the place of their reserves in the Keighley League and Silsden becoming the first local side to compete in the now defunct Wharfedale League. Silsden had as their top marksman J.Wainright, and future years would see a number of top local strikers don the 'Cobbydalers' jersey.

In a late season friendly in 1951, Craven referees defeated their Keighley counterparts 3-2. It had been another busy period for local officials, with constant reports of barracking from spectators and players alike. A Craven cup tie between Lothersdale and Cononley was abandoned after 68 minutes that season following several pitch encroachments by over exuberant supporters that eventually resulted in a full pitch invasion.

Meanwhile the Sunday football debate was hotting up as two Craven district players, one from Sutton United, were suspended for having played in unauthorised Sunday games in the Keighley district. Other locals were reported as being treated a little more leniently during the season. Sutton were a trifle unfortunate with losing players during the season – three of them needing hospital treatment following a bruising League cup tie with Salts, who had Mike Hellawell among their scorers (more about him later).

Square One Again

KEIGHLEY & DISTRICT MINORS
Pictured before a County Minor Cup tie at Salts F.C. in the late 1940's.

KEIGHLEY & DISTRICT LEAGUE XI 1950-51
The league's representative side played the North Lancashire League at Strong Close, losing 1-4.

(5)
NEW LEAGUES – LIMITED SUCCESS

Silsden's switch to the Wharfedale League in 1951 was the start of a sustained period of success for the local side, although a league championship would elude them for a little longer. The runners-up position was attained in their first two seasons in the league, on each occasion behind Baildon Athletic.

Their first ever game in the Wharfedale League could not have started in a worse fashion as opponents Menston Old Boys took the lead inside the first five minutes. The locals recovered to win the game 5-1 and were to achieve several high scoring victories throughout their campaign. The early months of the season coincided with the opening of a new dressing room block, constructed from an old air raid shelter, with bathing accommodation added. This was described by one official as *'undoubtably the finest in the junior district'* but it was not too long before this construction itself was replaced. At the season's end, despite the goalscoring prowess of messrs Emsley and Tillotson, a late season defeat against Baildon proved decisive in thwarting Silsden's hopes of a first league championship title since 1940.

Silsden's reserve side did have the consolation of lifting the league's second division title, as well as their league cup competition. Lecra Sports were defeated 4-1 in the cup final and Henshaw Amateurs 4-2 in a championship play off after the sides had tied on points, Ambler scoring a hat-trick in the latter game.

The Keighley Road side also won the Keighley & District Cup that season. Guardhouse, riding high in the Bradford Amateur League, were overcome 3-1 in the first round, Crossflatts 13-0 in the second round and holders Haworth 4-1 in the semi final. Sutton United, in their last ever Keighley Cup final were overcome in a tight replayed final, when Tillotson's header after 70 minutes was all that separated the sides (this following a 0-0 draw). The hardest fought ties of the competition came in the quarter finals however, when Sutton needed three games to dispose of eventual Keighley League champions Oakworth Albion and Silsden needed four games and 420 minutes to defeat Cowling!

Silsden made less progress than was hoped for in the County Cup when Halifax League leaders Queensbury United defeated them 2-0 in an early round.

New Leagues - Limited Success

The following season saw Silsden again take residence at the top of the league, and again a late season defeat against Baildon Athletic ensured that the silverware stayed put. County Cup success was more marked however as easy victories over Reynolds Rovers and Mirfield Athletic set up a 5th round tie with Harrogate Town. The 'Cobbydalers' never recovered from losing a goal in the first minute before any of their own players had touched the ball and eventually went down 2-0. Despite the 0-2 defeat by Baildon in the league, hopes were high that the champions could be defeated in the league cup semi final. Yet in an amazing game Silsden allowed a 5-1 lead to slip and eventually went down 5-6!

Despite their reserves retaining their title, Silsden lost their grip on the Keighley & District Cup as Worth Village defeated them 4-1 in the final. Silsden led in the game until an injury to right back Frank Mitchell forced them into reorganising, Village capitalising on this and winning with goals from Mahomet (3) and Payne. It was to be this side's only District Cup success, Leeds United legend John Charles presenting them with their prizes after the game. To cap a remarkable season for Worth Village as they ran away with the Craven League title, they added to this the league cup with a hard fought 2-1 success over Cononley in the final.

Silsden's third Wharfedale League season was something of a disappointment, although they did update their facilities again in 1954 as a new pavilion consisting of dressing and changing rooms replaced the war shelter facilities. Huddersfield Town sent a representative side containing several players with Football League experience to Keighley Road to mark the occasion, running out 8-1 winners. Past president Jerry Walton officially opened the new facility claiming that he knew of no other amateur club in Yorkshire with as fine a ground and splendid equipment as had Silsden!

By now the Keighley & District League was in dire straits. As more and more local sides opted for alternative competitions, the 1951-52 season kicked off with only seven sides – further reduced when St.Josephs resigned due to 'financial and playing difficulties' during the season. Ingrow United started the season in fine form, demolishing Oxenhope, who turned up with only seven players and had to 'borrow' two spectators, 15-2. Ironically this was Ingrow's last ever league success as they lost most of their remaining games, including a District Cup tie against 11 man Oxenhope only weeks later, and they disbanded at the end of the season. Oakworth Albion won both 'halves' of the championship to win the title outright, and sewed up the league's Victory Shield with a 3-1 defeat of Oxenhope in the final, thanks to goals from Broad (2) and Fleming.

There was talk of completely reforming the Keighley & District League for the following season, thus cutting down on travelling and expenses for clubs competing in Bradford based leagues and at the same time increasing the amount of local derbies for these sides. However, only four clubs signalled their intention to play in the competition for the 1952-53 season and it was decided that for the first time since 1906 (barring war years) there would be no Keighley League. Of these four sides, Oxenhope, Prince Smiths and Worth Village elected to play instead in the Craven League (the latter of course lifting the title), while Steeton decided not to join a league after all. The previous season's champions Oakworth Albion also remained dormant for the season.

Luckily this was not the end for the local league as 10 sides declared their intention to compete in a revived competition for the 1953-54 season. This number included the reserve sides of several former members, as well as Silsden's third ('A') team. Two sides did withdraw during the season, Airedale Sports and Silsden, the latter after having struggled with a tiny committee to run three sides, withdrawing late in the season and therefore not having their record expunged.

Cullingworth based Grippon Sports held off the strong challenge from former Red Triangle side Morton to lift the title, while Central Youth Club, essentially the nucleus of the successful Minor League side, lifted the Victory Shield with a 4-1 defeat of Worth Village in the final. Village, and a reformed Oakworth Albion fielded sides in both the Keighley and Bradford Amateur Leagues during the 1953-54 season, although both struggled to put out two teams and their stay in the latter proved unsuccessful and brief. Albion lost all of their Bradford league fixtures, several by high margins, but it was surprising to see Village struggle so badly in view of their phenomenal success the previous season.

Success at Bradford Amateur level was proving more and more elusive for local sides during the 1950's. Guardhouse came close to a Premier Division title in 1951-52, their only season in the league, but a late season loss to eventual champions Swain House proved decisive. Surprisingly the side did not reappear for the following campaign, neither did the league's Premier Division, reverting back to a First Division for its remaining years. Haworth continued in unremarkable style, finishing just above the relegation places twice in three seasons before folding themselves prior to the 1954-55 season. A lack of interest both from within the club as well as from locals was the club's undoing and a sad end to the efforts of the few committee men who sought to place the village team firmly on the footballing map.

Keighley Trico failed to win a game in their debut Red Triangle campaign, although things did improve the following season before joining the Keighley League. The town's most dramatic failure around this time though was that of Newtown Boys Club. Renown in local Boys Club circles, they were defeated 24-0 by Millbridge in their opening Red Triangle game in 1953 and, way out of their depth, they resigned from the league soon afterwards.

New Leagues - Limited Success

Despite Keighley's lack of success in these Bradford based competitions, the Keighley & District Cup would prove a successful hunting ground for West Bradford and Bingley based sides. Both Wilsden & Eldwick won the trophy twice, and Cullingworth Rovers, who shared their ground with Grippon Sports, also got in on the act with a 1956-57 final defeat of Wilsden, by now one of the top sides in the Bradford Amateur League.

Cowling came within a whisker of lifting the Craven League crown in 1952, pipped at the death by Gargrave, who defeated Sutton United in their final league game. Victory for Sutton could have given them the title themselves, but the side did have the consolation of winning the Craven Burton Cup with a 2-1 defeat of Rolls Royce in the final. Turning briefly to the Bradford Amateur league again for the 1953-54 season, Sutton's first team failed to complete the season, although their reserves completed their Keighley League campaign. The 1954-55 season saw United field a side only in the Craven Minor League (Sutton Textiles briefly representing the village in the Keighley League) before one final campaign in 1955-56, during which they reached the Victory Shield final. After that Sutton United were no more, the famous old team had faded away through lack of interest.

One face that refused to fade from the scene was that of referee Bob Wilson. He scored twice for Keighley & Craven Referees in a friendly against Heavy Woollen referees in 1954 and the following week was awarded with an inscribed plaque celebrating 21 years service to the local referees' association, at their annual dinner.

The 1954-55 Keighley & District League campaign saw 11 sides take part in the competition. Morton and Central Youth Club (the latter of whom had lost many of their players to national service) were conspicuous by their absence, although both were to return the following season. Steeton began the season in fine style with a 9-3 victory over Worth Village, Smith leading the scoring with seven, and a 12-1 rout of luckless Trico. A relentless march towards the title included a 24-0 demolition of Prince Smiths, who had only the previous week been thrashed 24-1 against Silsden reserves. In a remarkable game Silsden's Jackson had scored eight times – five of these headers from successive corners!

Steeton sealed the title with a 16-1 hammering of newcomers Sutton Textiles, although they were defeated in the Victory Shield final by Silsden, who included several first team players in their line up. For the first time the Shield competition was played on a league basis before the top four competed in semi finals and a subsequent final.

The 1955-56 season was in fact the league's silver jubilee year, and as a consequence a special Jubilee Trophy competition was organised. The winners received a rose bowl paid for from the proceeds of a 'Jubilee Fund'

Chasing Glory

which was initially slow in raising the necessary funds. Worth Village returned to form as they took the title ahead of the returning Central Youth Club and previous champions Steeton. Village were actually undefeated throughout their league programme, and added the Victory Shield to their trophy cabinet, overcoming Sutton United 6-2 in the final. The Jubilee Trophy, however, went to Central Youth Club who defeated Oakworth Albion 6-0 in the final, with Stan Storton – one of a number of talented footballing brothers – scoring five times.

Worth Village moved back to the Craven League the following season, and the nucleus of Central's side helped to form Keighley Central in the Wharfedale League – leaving the 1956-57 Keighley League title wide open. The new season heralded the return of a famous name from the past, particularly in local rugby circles, that of Keighley Shamrocks. The original Shamrocks soccer team had competed briefly in the local league, relatively unsuccessfully, prior to the first world war. The new Shamrocks were to last much longer and would achieve almost immediate success, racing to the league title ahead of Steeton and a reformed Haworth. With McCormack, the ex Silsden forward in fine form, the side were among the league leaders all season and in a close finish defeated their rivals in their final two games to clinch the title – Haworth, the only side to defeat them in the competition, 4-1 and Steeton 8-1. Shamrocks then defeated Central Youth Club 2-0 in the Victory Shield final to wrap up a league and cup double at the first attempt. Following this, a Keighley League XI defeated a Craven League XI 6-5 at Silsden in a charity match organised by Keighley Referees Association.

The Keighley League also played a series of representative fixtures against the Halifax & District League between 1956 and 1961. The locals lost on five occasions, three of them heavily, but won once in 1957, by six goals to two.

Worth Village's 1957 league title and Sutton United's lone Burton Cup victory apart, local sides were finding opposition from Craven league and cup sides tough nuts to crack. Bradley and Cononley were on the receiving end of 0-13 and 0-14 scorelines in successive seasons against Ingleborough in the Craven & District Cup and success in the Craven League was proving ever more distant, even Worth Village themselves unable to seriously challenge the top sides, led by Rolls Royce (Barnoldswick). Among goalscoring feats however were Bradley United, all but their goalkeeper hitting the net in a 20-1 rout of a poor Cononley second string and Noble of Cowling, who scored an amazing six goals in the space of 20 minutes in an 8-4 defeat of Skipton LMS reserves! The 1956-57 season did see Cononley achieve second division league and cup success, defeating Hellifield reserves in a championship play off and the league cup final in successive weeks.

New Leagues - Limited Success

As Oxenhope, Worth Village and Central Youth Club continued to monopolise the local minor league competitions, they were left to play in the Bradford Red Triangle junior division for the 1956-57 season as the Keighley Minor League failed to attract sufficient clubs to run a meaningful competition. Central finished runners-up to Eccleshill CC, but suffered a shock Keighley Minor Cup final defeat when Silsden defeated them 4-1, thus avenging defeat in the same final the season before.

The same season saw Prince Smiths seek pastures new in the lower divisions of the Leeds based West Yorkshire League. The switch proved a disaster for the club as they finished at the wrong end of the table, and despite a fine 3-2 victory at Pontefract in their opening fixture managed only a single home point – that in their final game of the season at Strong Close against Headingley Rangers.

Other talking points at this time was Keighley man Maurice Lindley, now managing Swindon Town in the Football League, and Mike Hellawell who made his full league debut at the age of 17 on February 25th 1956, for Queens Park Rangers against Exeter City in the old Third Division (South).

One big boost for local soccer was the re-development of Marley Playing Fields. The newly developed grounds, officially opened on July 14th 1956 thanks to a grant from the National Playing Fields Association, included what was then described as 'one of the finest running tracks in the U.K.' (!) At the centre of this was what would become the famous 'Marley centre pitch'.

Chasing Glory

WORTH VILLAGE 1952-53
The side had a great season, winning the Keighley & District Cup and Craven League championship. The side went on to win the Keighley League title three years later, but by 1957 were defunct.

CENTRAL YOUTH CLUB 1955-56
The Keighley & District League side won the Jubilee Cup, defeating Oakworth Albion 6-0 in the final. A young Stan Storton is pictured (fourth from the right, back row).

(6)
WHARFEDALE SUCCESS –
Silsden & Keighley Central

Silsden's first three seasons of Wharfedale football saw the side gradually re-emerge as the top side in the Keighley district. Despite losing this title to a bunch of new pretenders in the late 1950's, they were to embark on a highly successful period before rebuilding again in the Craven League.

Captained by ex-Keighley Town player Foggon, and with Brown and Emsley in fine form, Silsden swept to their first Wharfedale title in the 1954-55 season. Despite an early season loss to bogey side Addingham and an early County Cup defeat to Huddersfield YMCA, the team went straight to the top of the table again – chief rivals Guiseley swept aside 5-0 in the process in November. This time there was no stopping Silsden, fancied Esholt also being brushed aside, and by the time Burley Trojans had been routed 12-0 late in the season the championship had been sewn up. Brown's massive total of 60 goals proved priceless during the league campaign, although ex-Silsden player Tillotson was proving influential too at Addingham as his side again defeated the locals in a league cup semi final.

Silsden's 1955-56 league campaign proved to be possibly their best since their highly successful 1931-32 season. The new season started with a 19-1 rout of a poor Cragg Wood side and, with McCormack leading the front line, a hatful of goals were notched up. Esholt St.Pauls were again challenging for honours, until they were defeated in a league cup semi final one week and 7-0 in the league the next. Guiseley became the only to side to defeat Silsden that season with a 6-3 success in March, the 'Cobbydalers' gaining revenge in the league cup final only a week later, winning 6-1.

Steeton were the next victims, beaten 5-3 in the Keighley & District Cup final. Silsden took advantage of the fact that their opponents were without their first choice goalkeeper, racing into a 5-0 lead, with a hat-trick from Doidge before Steeton sorted themselves out and made a game of it in the second half.

By this time Jack Emsley had become Silsden's 'chief tactician and schemer'. His leadership skills were never in doubt, although the club's small committee, who generally selected the team, were growing evermore impatient with the fact that such a successful club could have so few townspeople offer to help run things.

Chasing Glory

The 1956-57 season saw Silsden again head the league ladder, but they were now joined by a new force – Keighley Central. An offshoot of the highly successful Central Youth Club's Keighley and minor league sides, the club were known in their early days as Keighley Central Old Boys, but officially became a separate organisation towards the end of the 1950's. Central opened their Wharfedale campaign with a fine 4-1 defeat of Ilkley, Colin Reddiough grabbing the side's first hat-trick at this level. Their first defeat came against the previous season's runners up Otley, when Reddiough was absent through illness, but nevertheless Central were among the leaders of the division along with Silsden.

Despite the attention inside left Leslie Wood was receiving from clubs such as Peterborough United, Silsden suffered from a period of indifferent form. During October/November 1956 the side's two year unbeaten home record was in tatters as they lost three cup ties in successive weeks – all at home. Eldwick shocked the locals with a 4-1 Keighley & District Cup victory, followed by a 1-0 victory for Menston St.Johns in the league cup, Thackley then leaving Keighley Road 3-1 winners in the County Cup. By February Silsden were back at the top of the league though, and a late season defeat of Central ensured that they held on to top spot. The Wharfedale League committee however had by now introduced 'top four play offs' to decide the destination of the championship and in the final Silsden were again to meet Keighley Central. Central went on to shock their more experienced rivals with a 5-2 victory, after extra time, with goals from Stan Storton (2), O'Hara (2) and Gallagher. It was a great end to Central's first season in the league, and the name Storton would appear in the headlines many more times in the coming years – not just that of Stan, who was attracting considerable attention, but from his equally talented brothers who would also achieve success.

The 1957-58 campaign saw Silsden make the 'top four play offs' again, unfortunately resulting in a semi final loss to Ilkley B.L. Despite the consistent scoring of Tillotson, who managed a double hat-trick in a 13-0 rout of Burley Trojans, Silsden were not quite the force they had been, and despite a Keighley & District Cup final appearance the following season the side replaced their reserves in the increasingly popular Craven League in 1959, where they were able to regroup before once more becoming a major force. Central won the league cup competition but they failed to reproduce their league form of the previous season.

Keighley Central again made the play offs at the end of the 1958-59 campaign. Despite a horrendous fixture backlog in the final weeks of the season, a great run of form saw them finish second behind Otley to earn a home tie with Carleton in the play offs. Much of their improvement could be put down to new signing Robert Hobson, who scored several hat-tricks for the club in his first season with them, and with players such as

Wharfedale Success

Creighton and Pamment on top form the future looked bright. Central dashed Silsden's outside hopes of a top four finish with a 3-1 victory over them in March, and they went on to beat Carleton convincingly, 6-1, in the semi final. Opponents in the final, Otley, had been well beaten by Central in an earlier league fixture, but the final was much tighter and Central went down to a late winner to finish runners up in the championship.

Central made no mistake the following season however. Despite a 1-1 draw in their first game with Shipley Town, the Keighley side made light work of defeating their rivals to head the table by Christmas. They regularly scored six goals or over in league fixtures, their first reverse being against Carleton in November. Nunroyd Sports were demolished 10-0 and champions Otley defeated 5-2, before unlucky Ilkley BL were thrashed 13-0 and 11-3 in successive weeks in league and league cup fixtures, the latter at the semi final stage. Central actually achieved a Wharfedale League record of 14 games unbeaten during the season until suffering a shock reversal to Horsforth Town. Defeating Otley again, 3-1, in the play off semi final, Esholt St.Pauls were then overcome in the final to see Keighley Central worthy champions. To add to a great season, Oxenhope were defeated in the Keighley & District Cup final, Hobson scoring both Central goals in a 2-1 victory.

Jack Bailey was added to Central's strike force for the 1960-61 season and he proved an immediate success. Captained by Dennis Widdop the side were as usual to the fore in the league, and the league cup was won with a 6-1 defeat of Esholt. In their 28 league games 134 goals were scored, and this time they managed a run of 18 undefeated fixtures between September and April, Widdop with 30 and Arnold with 27 the main contributors to the large number of goals scored. Unfortunately the championship and Keighley & District Cup just eluded them, Keighley Shamrocks surprising them 3-2 in the latter competition's semi final, and Burley winning a league play off 4-3. It was Central's goalkeeper, Lunn who was hitting the headlines by now though. He had saved 13 of the last 15 penalties his side had conceded, and had only been beaten from the spot four times over the past four seasons!

The 1961-62 season was the last for Central's first team in the Wharfedale League. They were by far the best team in the league but were victims of their own success, still having 16 league fixtures to play by March. Inevitably, the record books were rewritten again as the side were not defeated in a league match until 26th April – a run of 23 games! Their backlog of games was due not only to the poor weather that again affected the local season again, but their successful cup runs. Both the Wharfedale League Cup (Westfield defeated 4-2 at Guiseley) and Keighley & District Cup competitions were won, with a revenge victory over Shamrocks in the final of the local competition. Shamrocks led the game 1-0 at half time

Chasing Glory

until a double strike from Dugdale in the second half, his first a stunning overhead kick and his second from a long clearance by Hobson.

The competition that really put Central on the map though was the County Cup. In only their second season in the tournament they became the first Keighley side ever to make the semi finals of the competition. Following a 4-2 success at Eldwick, Central had to overcome a strong Altofts side in the second round at Normanton, doing so with a 2-1 victory. County Amateur League leaders Liversedge were dispatched 4-3 in round three, with Dugdale, Widdop, Anderson and Spedding on the scoresheet, before Old Holmevalians were easily overcome 5-0, Foster grabbing a hat-trick in the process. This put Central into the quarter final, and a tie against Thackley. In a tense game, Lunn saved yet another penalty as the Keighley side came from behind with goals from Spedding and Alan Hockey to win 2-1. Only in the penultimate round were the locals defeated, then only after a second replay at Swillington against losing finalists Rothwell Town, the side that had knocked them out of the previous season's competition in the fourth round.

Keighley Central's credentials were now such that a move upwards was inevitable. With their reserve side taking their place in the Wharfedale League, Central took the decision to join the West Yorkshire League for the 1962-63 season. Over the next few seasons, they would become what would arguably be Keighley's best ever Saturday football team.

Central's Wharfedale success was not quite over yet though. Their reserve side almost went through their 1962-63 league programme undefeated, with several high scoring victories to their name – not least 14-0 and 9-0 thrashings of Westfield. Unfortunately Carleton defeated the side 4-2 in their final league fixture and Otley defeated them in the play offs, but the league cup was retained with a 2-0 success against Ilkley in the final.

(7)
CHANGING FORTUNES

From 1957, the fortunes of Keighley and district clubs would change considerably in the Craven League. With league and cup titles being won in this competition and in the Wharfedale League then the appeal of the Keighley & District League became less and less, and the oldest competition in the area was to gradually fade away.

Cononley and Cross Hills, led by goal machine Kitson, were early challengers for the Craven title in the 1957-58 season. It was Oxenhope however who emerged from the pack to take their first ever championship, winning all but one of their first 15 games and defeating favourites Gargrave 5-3 (after trailing 1-3 at one point) in the process. Gargrave gained revenge in April, but it was too late as Oxenhope had enough points in the bag to ensure the title was theirs. Competitive football had been played in the village since 1913, it had taken 44 years for one of its sides to lift a league championship. The only negative aspects from what was a relatively successful season locally was Haworth's withdrawal from the league. Said to be 'lacking in support and finance' they were defeated 1-15 by Oxenhope in their final match (the same day as their reserves, who did see out the rest of the season, were defeated 1-12 by Steeton) before declaring their resignation from the league. Worth Village had meanwhile decided to call it a day at the close of the previous season.

Oxenhope showed even better form the following season as they ran away with the league title. Their second successive success saw Gargrave and Earby thrashed 11-0 and 12-3 respectively, and nearest challengers Cross Hills defeated narrowly twice. Poor weather conditions severely affected fixtures after Christmas, but this did not prevent Oxenhope from marching on, sealing the title with a 10-1 defeat of Skipton LMS. To round off a tremendous season for the club, Grassington were defeated 4-2 in the league cup final. Right winger Nixon was on form for Oxenhope, scoring in each of their final ten fixtures.

The Craven League committee decided to take a leaf from the Wharfedale League's book by introducing play offs for the top four sides at the end of the 1959-60 season. All 17 of the league's first teams were to compete in a single division, each playing 24 fixtures. With such a wide range of abilities in the league, it was obvious that there would be some high scoring and one sided games, as Bradley United would discover – having the misfortune of being way out of their depth and conceding 222 goals in their fixtures. However, the top half of the table could not have been tighter as only four points separated the top eight sides! Oxenhope, suffering a fixture backlog, failed to make the top four by two points, and Cross Hills, who were also challenging all season, missed out by a similar margin. Outsiders Steeton, meanwhile, were the division's top scorers with 135 goals, helping them to qualify on goal average. They then shocked everyone by defeating Hellifield 5-1 and then Grassington 1-0, thanks to a last minute own goal, in the final to lift the title in their first season in the top flight.

Oxenhope did have the consolation of defending the league cup successfully with a 3-0 win over Grassington in the final, before losing narrowly to a strong Keighley Central side in the Keighley & District Cup final, Frazer's strike being sandwiched by two Hobson goals for the winners.

Steeton's grip on the league title did not last long. The following season saw the side fail to match the previous season's goalscoring exploits and the side failed to make the play offs. In their first game as champions, Steeton found themselves three down within 25 minutes before coming back strongly to beat Settle United, and although early leaders Barnoldswick Park Rovers were defeated before Christmas the side never really looked like retaining the championship. Silsden and Cononley (who added the name 'Sports' to their name as the club became part of a village Sports Club in 1962) also challenged the leaders early on before fading, leaving the spoils to consistent Oxenhope, who defeated Hellifield in the Burton Cup Final and regained the championship with a 2-0 victory over Skipton L.M.S. in the play off final, after finishing at the head of the league table. The club became the first and only club to date to make a clean sweep of the league trophies as their reserve side also achieved a league and cup double, finishing well ahead of the remaining clubs in their division and narrowly defeating Grassington in the cup final.

Oxenhope again finished top of the league at the end of the 1961-62 season, despite another early season challenge from Silsden. Despite maintaining their position as the strongest side in the league, they were unable to win the title again, losing to Skipton LMS in the top 4 play offs. A shock District Cup defeat to Keighley League side N.S.F. was also experienced, although their reserve side again won their divisional title, but lost out in the league cup when Steeton defeated them in the first round of the competition.

It looked as if the club might again win all four Craven League trophies as the final weeks of the 1962-63 season approached. Cononley had been early leaders of the first division, but as they suffered a poor run of form once fixtures resumed after a 10 week 'weather induced' layoff, they were overhauled by those clubs with games in hand. Steeton briefly took over at the top with a 13-1 rout of Skipton Bulldogs (the home side's heaviest defeat since the war), but this was relinquished as Oxenhope hammered bottom club Hellifield to take over pole position themselves. Also creeping

Changing Fortunes

up the table were Silsden. Despite losing their opening four games, the side were defeated only once in their remaining 16. Only 20 league fixtures were played by each club, due to the poor weather during the new year, as the top 4 play offs in each division were dominated by local clubs. Oxenhope duly retained their title with a hard fought 3-2 success against Barnoldswick Park Rovers, Bairstow's late winner following a double from Stubley seeing off their East Lancashire rivals. Goals from Stubley and Winstanley then saw off Steeton in the Burton Cup final. Oxenhope's reserves again won the second division title, with a 3-1 success against Grassington, but were defeated in the league cup final against newcomers Keighley Lifts, who had a hat-trick from Brown to thank for their victory. Despite winning three of the four trophies on offer, and coming close to repeating their haul of 1961, Oxenhope were now well established as one of the Keighley district's leading sides, a 3-0 defeat of Bradford Amateur side Keighley Shamrocks in a second round District Cup tie underlining the strength of the club.

As if there weren't enough problems in reaching a respectable number of clubs in its fold, the Keighley & District League's fixtures were severely affected by the town's flu epidemic at the beginning of the 1957-58 season. Haworth, Silsden and St.Josephs were all unable to field teams early in the season due to illnesses. Once the league programme was in full swing however, Keighley Shamrocks were once again in front from the onset. Newcomers Parkwood Amateurs (not related to the earlier pre-war Parkwood side who were to become Keighley Town) were proving a force to be reckoned with too, holding Shamrocks to a 2-2 draw early in the season, and becoming the only side to beat the champions with a 3-1 victory in January. Shamrocks became the first side since Guardhouse to win the title in successive years though, an 18-2 victory over Haworth underlining their credentials.

Parkwood and Keighley Shamrocks were to meet each other twice more that season. Parkwood won the league's Victory Shield final (despite originally losing to Steeton, who fielded an ineligible player, in the semi final), and Shamrocks the District Cup with an emphatic 6-2 victory, McCarten scoring four times.

As Shamrocks turned to the Bradford Amateur League, where they were to experience two seasons in the league's second division, Parkwood became the Keighley League's top side the following season. They went through their 16 game programme with a 100% success rate – the first time this had happened in the league since Morton achieved a similar feat in the 1925-26 season – finishing seven points clear of Oakworth Albion. Albion's second place was something of a surprise as they had been last minute replacements for Harden and were forced to play their games at Haworth – the village side there failing to reappear this season.

By the time Parkwood had defeated St.Josephs in February, the league title was theirs, despite the inclement weather that again disrupted the league programme. The side amassed a total of 139 goals, nearly nine per game (!), of which Neil Storton, brother of Stan, grabbed 49. Both Storton and Neil McDonald were the key to Parkwood's success, and with the latter's departure 'down south' at the end of the season he was sorely missed.

At the season's end, the league's top five sides played a mini league competition for the Victory Shield, duly won by Parkwood, while the bottom four played each other for the Jubilee Trophy, in which newcomers Keighley Grinders proved successful. Prince Smiths 'B' were awarded a special sportsmanship award also, for their unwavering efforts and good behaviour despite losing all of their 16 league games.

It was Keighley Grinders themselves who became champions for the 1959-60 season. They too managed to avoid defeat throughout their league fixtures, although points were dropped in two draws. Parkwood were only defeated once, and therefore had the proud record of being beaten only twice in their three league seasons, a total of 46 games. Led by Bryan Whitham, Grinders finished just a point ahead of their rivals. Ilkley could not have asked for a better start in their new league, scoring in the first minute of their debut against Prince Smith & Stells. A decline in interest at Morton though led to their unfortunate demise late in the season, leaving only seven sides completing their league programme.

The Jubilee Trophy was again opened up to all clubs, Parkwood defeating Steeton reserves in the final after extra time, but the Victory Shield competition was thrown into confusion when it was discovered that both semi final winners, Oakworth and Parkwood had played ineligible players. In the 'replays' Grinders were able to exact revenge for their defeat by Oakworth, while Parkwood won again – Grinders winning the final thanks to goals from Robinson (2) and Smith.

It was Parkwood's turn to lift the title again, defeating Grinders 4-1 in the early months of the 1960-61 campaign. Improved Prince Smith's also challenged for the championship, inflicting on Parkwood their only league defeat of the season at the end of November. The champions elect gained revenge the following month however, and despite losing to Keighley Central in the Keighley & District Cup, finished well clear of Keighley Grinders at the top of the table. Grinders then shocked the league by resigning due to a lack of players before they had completed their Victory Shield fixtures, Carleton defeating Parkwood in the final of this competition.

It was nice to see Grinders back the following season, and with Parkwood very much out of sorts, it was they who took their chance to regain the Keighley League crown. The race for the title was a much closer run thing though, Grinders unbeaten until their very last league fixture when N.S.F. defeated them 5-3. This gave N.S.F. a chance to force a play off for the title if they could beat Carleton in their final game, unfortunately they lost and had to settle for the runners up spot. Better things were just around the corner for the N.S.F. side though, as they, along with fourth placed Keighley Central reserves went on to play in the Wharfedale League the following season.

When the Keighley & District League kicked off again in September 1962 with only five teams (two of which were from the Prince Smith & Stells club) it was what would prove to be its last ever season. The top four clubs from the previous campaign had all left the league for various reasons and it was clear that the competition was no longer really viable in its current state. In a low key campaign, Parkwood regained the title, sealed with a 3-0 success over Prince Smith & Stells 'A', but the lack of strength in the league was never more evident than in the District Cup – Central Y.C. defeated 0-15 by eventual runners-up Denholme United and newcomers Parkwood Y.C. routed 1-20 by a rampant Keighley Central.

Before the 1963-64 season had begun, it was announced that there would be no Keighley & District League for the following campaign due to a lack of interest in the competition. It was hoped to revive the league in the near future, but the district's clubs were obviously happy in their current competitions and felt that a move into a 'new' Keighley league would be a step downwards. The county's oldest league competition formally disbanded in 1968, and there have been calls to reform it ever since.

Keighley Shamrocks' fortunes improved in their third Bradford Amateur League season as they gained promotion from the second division during the 1960-61 season. This followed a generous offer of £500 they made to Keighley Council towards the £2,423 cost of a pavilion at what was to become their new home at Highfield playing fields. The side also had the satisfaction of two successive District Cup final appearances, despite both games ending in defeat. The first, where they experienced defeat against Eldwick, had seen the favourites Keighley Central beaten 3-2 in the semi final, with Shamrocks' goals from Thornton, Butler and Wood. Central gained their revenge in the following year's final, but Shamrocks had done more than enough to establish themselves as one of the town's top sides – something they were able to maintain for the next twenty years or so. Under the captaincy of schoolteacher Tony Bland, Shamrocks finished a fine fourth in their first season in the Bradford League's top flight, achieving a similar position the following year, and during April 1962 the club undertook a small tour, with a couple of friendlies, in Ireland.

Among the younger end of Keighley's footballers was Brian Wilson, who scored four hat-tricks in successive games for Highfield in the local school's league. Silsden Minors meanwhile managed a total of 224 goals during their 1957-58 Keighley & Craven Minor League campaign. Two of their side, Billy Arnold and Chris Stephenson, had signed amateur forms for Huddersfield Town, while 16 year old Maurice Tillotson also signed for

Chasing Glory

Huddersfield, on professional terms, in 1960. Cross Hills won the same league following Silsden's success, while Central Youth Club kept a side in the Bradford Red Triangle and another in the local league, defeating Haworth in the 1959-60 Keighley Minor Cup final.

Second division Keighley Police, meanwhile, defeated first division Bradford Technical College 2-0 in the Bradford Half Holiday league cup final, the first time they had won this competition since well before the war. They were unfortunately defeated by Police HQ (Wakefield) in the Chief Constables Cup semi final, after a second replay.

The 1962-63 season saw the birth of Woodhouse Rovers. Playing in the Bradford Nig Nog League (under 16's) they finished in the runners-up position at the first attempt, winning 12 of their 16 fixtures. Ousey and Storton monopolised the side's scoring, with 59 between them, Ousey scoring four in the side's final game of the season – a 13-0 victory against West Bowling.

The saddest note of this era though was the death, in April 1959, of England international Jeff Hall from polio. The former Wilsden man had competed for Keighley St.Annes for two seasons before going on to greater things in the Football League and for England. Married only the previous year, Jeff's name lives on today in the world of Sunday football.

PARKWOOD AMATEURS

The side dominated the Keighley & District League in the late 50's / early 60's before disbanding at the same time as the league.

(8)
SUNDAY FOOTBALL COMES TO KEIGHLEY – THE DEAN SMITH & GRACE STORY

The Craven & District F.A. first came up with the idea of Sunday football in this region just after the second world war. This idea was treated with contempt by the local soccer authorities at the time, yet less than two decades later the time was right to finally form a Sunday football competition in the Aire Valley. Officially recognised by the national body in May 1960, Sunday leagues sprung up everywhere around the country, one such organisation in Birmingham catering for over 100 sides within a year.

The 'pioneer' of Sunday soccer in this region was Wilsden's Jim Lockyer, secretary of the Keighley West Yorkshire Road Car club. His appeal for local clubs to help set up a 'Keighley Sunday League' appeared in the *Keighley News* in August 1961. The initial response was promising, particularly in the light of the problems the Keighley Saturday League was experiencing in attracting a viable number of clubs to participate in its competition. The idea of soccer on the 'sabbath' appealed to many young sportsmen denied the opportunity to turn out on Saturdays due to work committments, and to those who wished to play an extra game at the weekend, and by the October 28th deadline ten clubs had applied to join the new league. Eddie Kennedy, himself an active referee, was elected chairman at the league's inaugural meeting at Keighley Liberal Club and the 'Keighley Sunday Football Alliance' saw its first games kick off on 18th November 1962 (some two months after the opening of the season) when three games were played.

The ten clubs that were to constitute the league in its first season were a mixed bunch; Volts All Stars, Shoulder of Mutton, Fountain & Victoria Star all Keighley 'pub sides', such teams becoming synonymous with Sunday football; Keighley West Yorkshire & Wask United local 'works' sides; Gargrave & Skipton Town Sunday sections of established Craven League sides, and two 'out of town' clubs based at Marley, Bradford Moor and Bingley Holy Trinity.

The new league also had a league cup trophy to be played for. The 'Jeff Hall Memorial Trophy' was presented to the league by Percy Hall, a founder member of the league, whose son Jeff had been cruelly struck down in his prime by polio in 1959.

Chasing Glory

Volts All Stars were early pacesetters in the new league. Following an 8-0 'pre season' victory over Trico, the side won their first competitive game 7-3 against Skipton Town and went on to record victories in their first 10 league fixtures. They were clear favourites to win the title until defeat by Victoria Star saw them replaced at the head of the table. As Volts dropped further vital points, Star remained firmly at the head of the table for the remaining weeks of the season and became the first champions of the Keighley Sunday Al'iance. The 'double' was achieved by Star, who went on to defeat Shoulder 4-3 in a closely fought final.

Fourteen sides kicked off the second Keighley Sunday Alliance campaign, and it was Star again who were to lift the title. Silsden were the early pacesetters this time, defeating the champions 2-0 in October 1962 thanks to goals from Wilson and Quinlan, and maintaining a 100% record until Shipley's Woodside Rovers held them to a goalless draw at the end of the same month. Rovers shocked Silsden in the Jeff Hall Trophy however, with a surprise first round victory, Silsden then losing their first league fixture the following week to Halifax & District side All Stars. By the turn of the new year Victoria Star had taken pole position at the top of the Alliance, but they too were rocked when Woodside knocked them out of the Jeff Hall Trophy. Star had only themselves to blame however, missing two penalties in a 1-3 extra time defeat. Woodside went on to beat Beaconsfield 2-1 in the final, thanks mainly to a couple of blunders by their opponents' keeper, Mahomet scoring late in the game for the losers.

By the time the final games of the season were being played, Star led Silsden by just a point. Needing a victory to be certain of the title, Star defeated Bradford Moor 5-2 to again emerge victorious. The result was merely academic, as Silsden were beaten 1-4 by Keighley West Yorkshire, for whom A.Thornton scored 34 times during the season and was thus the league's leading goal scorer. The same works team reached the final of their parent company's Raworth Cup competition, losing narrowly to York Depot in the final.

The 1963-64 season saw the league introduce for the first time a second division – ironically in the same season that the Keighley Saturday League failed to reappear. Nineteen teams made up the two divisions; among the list for the first time Dean Smith & Grace, who had briefly operated a Saturday side at the end of the 1940's. League champions Victoria Star could hardly have made a worse start against two of the league's strongest sides, going down 1-4 to Bradford Moor and 0-3 to D.S.G.(who themselves had gone down 1-5 on their debut to Silsden).The side never recovered and by the season's end finished next to bottom of the first division and failed to reappear after that.

Sunday Football Comes To Keighley

At the other end of the table Bradford Moor and Keighley West Yorkshire fought a closely contested championship race, closely followed by D.S.G. The bus men threw away their chances in January when they were defeated by both of their rivals, but the real drama was saved for the following month when Bradford Moor and Dean Smith & Grace met on successive Sundays. Moor came out on top on both occasions, by 5-3 and 5-4 margins, both closely contested and dramatic games, and as a result sewed up their first and only Alliance League title (the side moved to the Bradford District Sunday League the following season but briefly retained a reserve side in the Keighley league).

Deans did have the consolation of lifting the Jeff Hall Trophy, when, after defeating Bradford Moor in the semi final, they went on to beat Woodside Rovers in a replayed final – thanks mainly to a hat-trick from Williams. Little did they know that this was to be the first of many successes for the Keighley works side, not least the first of five successive Jeff Hall Trophy triumphs. Sadly, Jim Lockyer resigned as league secretary towards the end of the campaign, but he could be proud of what he had achieved – his dream of a Sunday league in the area was well and truly established and the Alliance was on the verge of becoming one of the strongest and well respected of Sunday leagues anywhere.

The 1964-65 season kicked off with a single Alliance division. 'Newcomers' Clifton Driving School, who were in effect a breakaway from the Keighley West Yorkshire club (Jim Lockyer was in fact a proprietor of the driving school), became involved in a closely fought battle at the top with Provincial. Provincial lost their unbeaten record to improving Dean Smith & Grace in January and a week later Clifton's suffered their first reversal to the very same team, Stowell and Bob Hobson cancelling out Bibby's earlier strike for the losers.

Bibby hit a hat-trick the following month in what turned out to be, in effect, the title decider. Clifton's came from behind to beat Provincial 5-1 and clinched the Alliance title at their first attempt. There was no stopping Deans in the Jeff Hall Trophy though, the holders defeating Clifton's 4-1 in the semi final thanks to a hat-trick from Stone. Stone went one better in the final as he scored four times in an 8-1 rout of Parkwood United.

For the next seven years Dean Smith & Grace became the undisputed kings of Sunday football in Keighley as they took the Alliance League title six times in the next seven years, the Jeff Hall Trophy four more times, a host of other cup competitions and achieved tremendous success at County and National level.

The 1965-66 season saw Deans run away with the league title – winning all of their games. With McGowan and Dugdale in fine form there was no-one to touch them – closest rivals Crossflatts-based Park Rangers defeated 5-0 twice and several other sides on the other end of

Chasing Glory

hidings. Fell Lane proved more of an obstacle in the Alliance cup competitions though. Deans defeated Fell Lane 3-2 in the division one Kensington Cup final, but were given a real fright in the Jeff Hall Trophy Final. By half time Fell Lane led 3-0 through goals from O'Hanlon (penalty), Walsh and Riley and it looked as if Deans' unbeaten record would come to a surprise end. In a dramatic second half Deans pulled level with goals from David Hobson (2) and Boland before Stone hit a dramatic winner minutes from the end to see the favourites retain the trophy again.

The same season saw Clifton Driving School become the first Keighley side to compete in the English Sunday Cup competition. Unfortunately they were drawn to play top Bradford outfit Ventus United (future Alliance winners) in the first round and they went down to a 0-4 defeat. By the end of the season Clifton's were struggling to raise a team and they did not reappear the following season.

Dean Smith & Grace made the decision to enter the English Sunday Cup the following season. Their credentials were certainly good enough as they swept all before them in the Keighley Alliance again. Winning all twenty of their league fixtures, they were chased closely by Bradford side Shearbridge early in the season. The champions opening match of the season saw a 17-0 rout of newcomers Magnet. Magnet were also trounced 15-0 by Morton and were relegated at the end of the season – how different their fortunes would be the following decade!

Shearbridge proved no match for Deans in the 1966-67 Jeff Hall final, going down 9-1 to the Keighley side. Deans' English cup run proved to be the highlight of the season though. Clayton-based Drum Rovers were defeated 5-0 in Deans' first ever F.A. Sunday Cup game, and this was followed by a 3-0 victory over Wrestlers of Carlisle in December 1967. In what was described as the biggest crowd seen at Marley for many years, the Cumbrian side went down to strikes from Hodson, Bibby and McGowan as well as a penalty save by Spencer. Deans' next opponents were Ventus United. At the time their Bradford District League opponents had lost a match since going down at the semi final stage of the same competition the previous season, but they were no match for the rampant Keighley side who, with goals from Hobson, Riley, Bibby and McGowan, won easily, 4-1.

The quarter final of the Sunday Cup brought Birmingham side Bromford to Marley. After a great start, when Hobson and Bibby were again on the scoresheet, Deans came under increasing pressure from the Midlands side and, as their offside trap became more and more effective and their forwards took control, the Bromford side were able to break through. After 90 minutes Bromford had booked their passage to the semi finals with a 4-2 victory – where they were to defeat London side Carlton United – but things were to take a dramatic turn when it was discovered

Sunday Football Comes To Keighley

that Bromford had fielded an ineligible player in a previous round and were forced to replay their previous three games in the competition. Defeating their fourth round opponents again, Bromford again arrived at Marley to replay their quarter final – and this time things worked out differently. Once again David Hobson headed Deans in front, once again Bibby scored a second, but this time there was to be no Bromford fightback and the Keighley side were in the semi final in their first season in the competition.

Opponents Carlton United had already been defeated by Bromford before being reinstated, so the general opinion in Keighley was that Deans could reach the final. Unfortunately Carlton were always on top in the tie and it was they who swept into the final, where they went on to defeat Stoke Works 2-0. Deans went out, losing 1-3 (Walsh scoring their semi final goal), but had done the town proud and could lay claim to being the first side from Keighley to make it to the semi final of a national soccer competition.

Deans returned following their summer break just as hungry for success. The 1967-68 Alliance season went predictably the way the previous two had – with the works side again maintaining a 100% record – and Shipley-based Westfield Rovers, their nearest challengers for the title, defeated 3-1 in the Jeff Hall final. By now the Keighley Alliance had grown to four divisions, with many sides from Bingley, Shipley and Bradford as well as the Wharfe Valley wanting to take part in what was now regarded as the strongest Sunday league in the district. On April 1st 1968, Ventus United inflicted on Dean Smith & Grace their first defeat in the Alliance when they won 2-1 in the Kensington Cup. It was Deans' first Alliance defeat since November 15th 1964 and allowed another side at last to take one of the league's major honours, Westfield defeating Ventus in the final (incidentally Magnet won the league's second division title). Unfortunately the F.A. Sunday Cup saw Deans fail to repeat their success. Following victories over Eccleshill and Burmantofts, the locals put up a poor display against modest opposition, going down to a last minute goal to Leeds-based Seacroft. Spare a thought for Alliance division four side Stells United however. The F.A. Sunday Cup was well out of their reach, finishing bottom of the division, losing all 18 of their games and conceding 281 goals in the process – an average of nearly 16 per game!

The 1968-69 season was a poor one for Dean Smith & Grace. They were knocked out of the F.A. Sunday Cup in the first round when Drum Rovers gained revenge for their defeat two years earlier, with an extra time victory, and Ventus United took the Alliance title. Ventus had replaced their reserve side in the league during the summer and, with the acquisition of two other very strong Bradford sides in Pile Bar and Crag Road United, the division was now stronger than ever. Pile Bar themselves became the

Chasing Glory

first side since Clifton Driving School in 1964 to defeat Deans in a league match, going on to finish just behind the Keighley side in the final league table.

Deans' final foray into the F.A. Sunday Cup saw the fourth round reached during the 1969-70 season. Hull-based Hall Road Rangers (now well established in the Northern Counties East League) were defeated by a Jimmy Walsh strike in the first round, and a single goal, this time from Thwaites, was again sufficient to see off Bradford side Otley Road in the second. Cumbrians Wrestlers were seen off for the second time in four seasons in the third round – this time 4-1 – but Merseysiders Melrose put paid to any further progress for the Keighley side with a 2-1 victory at Marley. The works side did have the consolation of retaining the Sunday Alliance title, once they had caught up on their fixtures, and defeated Westwood in the final of the Kensington Cup. The real drama in the Alliance however came in the Jeff Hall Trophy final when Holycroft led Westwood 3-0 at the break only for their Bradford opponents to force extra time and eventually a winner. With goals from Hainsworth, Laycock and Bromley the improving Keighley side let slip their best ever chance of lifting the trophy.

The 1970-71 season was Deans' last. The same season also saw them become county champions when they became the first Keighley side to win the County Sunday Cup in only its third season. With new recruit Neil Storton scoring freely, the Alliance title was won with ease, with another 100% record. Westfield took runners-up spot but had the consolation of becoming the second successive side from the Keighley league to win the Bradford Sunday Cup (Westwood being the first the previous season). Odsal ran Deans surprisingly close in the Kensington Cup final, while Holycroft lost their second successive Jeff Hall final going down 4-0 to the champions, but it was the county's premier cup competition where Deans really made their mark.

Such was the strength of the Alliance that two other sides from the league were encountered in the competition's later stages, Ventus United and Westwood in the quarter and semi finals respectively, while Deans' final opponents were the favourites, Mere Athletic from Doncaster on a poor pitch at Swillington, where the Keighley side were forced to change in the cricket scorebox. This did nothing to harm their game however as they took the lead when Jimmy Walsh headed home a Danny McGowan corner. Deans doubled their lead when another McGowan corner was headed home by David Hobson and, despite a late reply from their opponents, the locals held on for a famous victory. The Dean Smith & Grace team that day was

Murray, Bland, Lister, J.Hobson, D.Hobson, A.Hockey, McGowan, Walsh, Thwaites, Butterfield & N.Storton.

Sunday Football Comes To Keighley

As the Dean Smith & Grace side broke up at the end of the season it was obvious that they would be a hard act to follow. Despite the lack of a top class senior Saturday side in the town, Keighley had established itself on the Sunday game, not only through Deans but also through the strength of the Keighley Sunday Alliance. Deans' players now became dispersed around the remaining sides in the town – several choosing to play for struggling works side Magnet, and that, as we shall see, is another story.

DEAN SMITH & GRACE 1966-67
The side that went on to defeat Bromford in a replayed English Sunday Cup tie.

(9)
CENTRAL FLY THE FLAG

Keighley Central's move upwards into the West Yorkshire League for the 1962-63 season saw them commencing battle in Division Two (South), one step below the league's top division. Widdop gave the side an ideal start in their new surroundings with the only goal in an opening day defeat of Airedale Athletic, and only one point was dropped in their first six games. In October, Glasshoughton were condemned to their first home defeat for two years by the locals as second spot in the 14 team division was attained. A disappointing 0-1 defeat against Turnshaw put paid to any County Cup success, although goalkeeper Lunn was in the news again, saving two penalties in a game marred by constant niggling and free kicks. By the end of the season, Central had won 20 of their 26 fixtures, losing on only three occasions, enough for runners up spot behind Fryston Colliery. In addition, the semi final of the league cup was reached, before defeat, in a replay, to eventual winners Britannia Works.

Central's Keighley & District Cup campaign underlined their supremacy over the remaining sides in the town – scoring 47 goals in only five games! Bingley Central were defeated 10-1 in round one, Parkwood Y.C. 20-1 in round two, Steeton reserves 9-0 (Hobson scoring five times in both round 2 and 3), Eldwick 3-0 in the semi final, before a comfortable 5-2 success against Denholme United in the final. Despite going behind to a first minute goal at Lawkholme Lane, strikes from Anderson (2), Widdop, Black and Spedding saw the cup retained.

Central did not step up to the first division of the West Yorkshire League the following season, as in effect they moved up two rungs of the ladder – accepted into the Third Division of a much expanded Yorkshire League. It looked as if the side, by now playing home fixture on Marley's 'centre pitch', might have been able to match the albeit brief heights that Keighley Town had reached in a single division Yorkshire League just after the war.

The move up could hardly have been more successful. Seventeen years to the day after Keighley Town had opened their Yorkshire League account, Central set their wheels in motion with an impressive 2-1 victory over Yorkshire Amateurs, a side Town had met in both of their Yorkshire League seasons. As well as a resounding 9-0 success at home to Ossett Town, when Thornton struck four times, Salts were defeated twice in the Division Three league cup competition. Ironically Central's first, and only, league defeat at the hands of Harrogate Railway in September coincided with the absence of Alan Hockey who was getting married.

Central Fly The Flag

A brace from Hockey helped Central to a 2-0 defeat of league leaders Farsley Celtic in January. In fact, only two points were dropped by Central from the end of September until the end of the season, and they hit top spot at the end of January when they came from behind to beat Ossett Albion 2-1.

Harrogate Town were the only side to take points off Central after Easter, the Third Division championship trophy being presented to the Keighley side by Mayor G.W.Dale after the sides had met at Marley in April. Unfortunately a league and cup double proved elusive as league runners up Farsley Celtic gained revenge with a 2-0 success in the league cup final at Salts.

Keighley Central were hoping for a successful County Cup run, but defeat by Doncaster based Pilkingtons in round two put an end to these hopes. Earlier, unbeaten West Yorkshire League leaders East End Park had been narrowly defeated 1-0 after extra time at Marley.

The Keighley and District Cup was retained however, but Central were made to work surprisingly hard in their ties. Craven League strugglers Oakworth put up a strong resistance in round two (Central receiving a bye in the first), and Cross Hills Y.C. came within five minutes of putting their more senior opponents out of the competition altogether at the semi final stage. The Youth Club side led in the first game, played at Silsden, through a goal by Ward and it wasn't until five minutes from time that Hockey popped up for the equaliser. Central won the replay at the same venue 6-0 but they had been given the shock of their lives by a side from the bottom half of the Craven League's First Division. Keighley N.S.F. were Central's opponents in the final at Lawkholme Lane. The works side had defeated a strong Shamrocks in their semi final but were denied a surprise victory by strikes from Hockey, after their keeper had been penalised for 'carrying', and Hobson, from the penalty spot.

Central suffered only three defeats in their 30 match 1963-64 season. In less than ten years they risen to become one of the County's top amateur sides yet they lacked a major asset that would have enabled further progress up the league ladder – a suitable ground. Reliant on the local council for the use of Marley's Centre Pitch, this field could not be guaranteed in the future, and as their rivals from the previous season found themselves incorporated into an expanded Second Division of the Yorkshire League, Keighley Central were forced to drop back into the West Yorkshire League. It was in the new Premier Division of this league that Central would spend the rest of their days – although their run of success had not ended yet!

West Yorkshire League success was not a formality and, in the company of names such as Guiseley and Thackley, several unsuccessful campaigns were endured before the title was finally lifted at the end of the 1969-70 season. Finishing 6th of 11 teams in their first season in the league, Central finished only three points above the bottom club. They improved to finish fourth and then third over the next two seasons, but on both occasions well off the pace at the top of the league. By now Central's position as the top club in town was under threat from sides such as Silsden, Oxenhope Recreation and Shamrocks. Both Silsden and Oxenhope surprised Central with Keighley & District Cup Final victories in the mid 60's, but the side recovered to win the cup three times over the next four years. Keighley Central began the 1966-67 season with several resounding victories, 8-2 & 5-1 v Altofts, 5-1 v D.P. & E. and 4-0 against Methley, before finally settling for third place in the league. Strong Huddersfield League outfit Bradley Rangers were defeated in the County Cup and the side became the first from the town for many years to compete in the F.A. Amateur Cup. Leeds Ashley Road defeated Central in this competition, although the locals were missing leading scorer Palamountain and Hockey was forced to play out the second half with what proved to be a broken arm. The Keighley & District cup was regained during the 1966-67 season when Cross Hills Y.C. were defeated 4-0 in the final at Marley. Central raced into a two goal lead inside the first seven minutes through Hodson and Bibby and never looked like losing the game, Riley adding two further goals. The Youth Club side were again defeated in the following season's final, but this time proved much sterner opposition. Central won 3-1, with a hat-trick from John Fay, but they were facing a much more important final tie only days later.

The 1967-68 season proved possibly the best ever for Central. Despite finishing well down the league table they became the first and only side from Keighley not only to reach the West Riding County Challenge Cup final, but to actually win the competition itself. Central had made the semi final of the competition as a Wharfedale League side six years earlier, and their season began to come to life when they were drawn against fellow West Yorkshire League side Methley United at the same stage. In a dramatic encounter at the Dudley Hill ground of Bradford Rovers, the locals were soon a goal behind until a Walsh equaliser and an own goal gave them the lead. This they held until just two minutes from time when a poor goal kick enabled Methley to equalise. Almost immediately Central attacked again, and when they were awarded a last minute penalty Fay coolly slotted the ball home to send Central into the final.

Former winners Brook Sports from the County Amateur League were Central's opponents in the County Cup final at East End Park in Leeds. The tie was drawn 1-1 necessitating a replay closer to home at Thackley. In the replay, Fay was once again on the scoresheet as he gave the locals the lead, only for the Heckmondwike side to again level the scores. It all turned sour for Fay when he was later stretchered off with a broken leg, but the injury did not distract his teammates who went on to win 2-1. A shot from Walsh was parried by the Brook Sports 'keeper and Danny McGowan followed up to score the winner. Presented with the trophy by County F.A. chairman E.Wilson, Central had at long last brought the County Cup to Keighley.

Central's reserve side capped a fine 1967-68 season for the club when they won the new Keighley Supplementary Cup, a competition designed for the second strings of local sides. Despite initially losing to Keighley Lifts reserves in the semi final, an objection regarding an ineligible Lifts player was upheld and Central won the 'replay'. Cross Hills were Central's opponents in the final, as they had been in the first team cup final, but were no match for Mervyn Beck who scored all of his side's goals in a 4-1 victory.

The following season saw Keighley Central come within a whisker of lifting the West Yorkshire League title for the first time. Despite dropping vital points to Keighley Shamrocks along the way, Central were always in a challenging position at the top of the league – missing the opportunity to lift the Premier Division title when they could only draw 1-1 with eventual champions Monckton Colliery late in the season. In their defence of the County Cup, strong Leeds Red Triangle outfit Farnley were defeated 3-1 in the third round. The holders surprisingly trailed 0-1 at the interval until goals from Magee, Cusker and Neil Storton saw Central through. Firth Sports were easily overcome to the tune of 6-2 in the quarter final. Beck, McGowan and Cusker shared the goals on this occasion in the absence of captain Alan Hockey who was playing for the County F.A. side (McGowan and Winston Butterfield were also selected to represent the County side during the season). Unfortunately another Huddersfield League outfit, Holmes Holset, prevented a second successive final appearance when they defeated Central 3-1 in the semi final, going on to win the competition themselves.

At his point news of Central's exploits all but dried up in the local press. Reliant on reports from league and club secretaries for much of the information, newspapers such as the '*Keighley News*' obviously had no-one at hand to do the job for Central. Despite the re-emergence of Silsden and that club's challenge to Central's mantle of number one club in Keighley, there was still a little more in the former youth club side's tank yet. A Danny McGowan goal three minutes from time was enough to defeat Silsden in the 1969-70 Keighley & District Cup final, this after a convincing 6-1 defeat of Denholme United in the semi final, and at last the West Yorkshire League title was won. The following year saw Central lose both the District Cup and league title, but the 1971-72 campaign proved far worse. For only the second time in eleven seasons Central failed to reach

Chasing Glory

the Keighley Cup final and an embarrassing 0-5 defeat was endured at home to Pontefract Collieries in the County Cup.

The 1972-73 season proved to be Keighley Central's last. Despite a fairly successful league campaign, their Keighley & District Cup campaign saw a 0-2 final defeat to Westfield Rovers, two divisions lower than themselves in the West Yorkshire League, who became the first, and so far only, Shipley based side to win the cup. This after Silsden had been defeated by the same scoreline through goals by Jimmy Walsh and John Hellawell en route to the final.

As Keighley Central broke up during the summer of 1973, the town had lost arguably its most successful side for many years. To this day Central remain the only Keighley side to have won the West Riding County Cup.

Keighley Central in action during the 1963-64 Yorkshire League third division cup final at Salts against Farsley Celtic.

Central Fly The Flag

KEIGHLEY CENTRAL COMPLETE YORKSHIRE LEAGUE RECORD 1963-64

Date	Opponents	Ven	Score	Competition
31.08.63	Yorkshire Amateurs	(a)	W 2-1	League
03.04.63	Salts	(h)	W 3-2	League Cup
07.09.63	Ossett Town	(h)	W 9-0	League
10.09.63	Salts	(a)	W 4-1	League Cup
14.09.63	Harrogate Railway	(a)	L 1-2	League
28.09.63	Farsley Celtic	(a)	D 2-2	League
05.10.63	East End Park W.M.C.	(h)	W 1-0	County Cup 1
12.10.63	Ossett Albion	(h)	W 1-0	League
19.10.63	Oakworth Albion	(a)	W 2-0	Keighley & Dist. Cup 2
26.10.63	Salts	(h)	W 2-0	League
02.11.63	Pilkington Rec	(a)	L 0-2	County Cup 2
09.11.62	Yorkshire Amateurs	(h)	W 5-0	League
07.12.63	Harrogate Town	(a)	W 1-0	League Cup
14.12.63	Harrogate Town	(h)	D 2-2	League Cup
21.12.63	Silsden	(h)	W 2-0	Keighley & Dist. Cup 3
04.01.64	Farsley Celtic	(h)	W 2-0	League
11.01.64	Salts	(a)	W 3-1	League
25.01.64	Ossett Albion	(a)	W 2-1	League
01.02.64	Harrogate Railway	(h)	D 2-2	League Cup
08.02.64	Slazengers	(h)	W 6-1	League
15.02.64	Cross Hills Y.C.	(n)	D 1-1	Keighley & Dist. Cup S/F
22.02.64	Slazengers	(a)	W 2-1	League
29.02.64	Harrogate Railway	(a)	W 3-1	League Cup
07.03.64	Harrogate Town	(a)	D 1-1	League
21.03.64	Cross Hills Y.C.	(n)	W 6-0	Kly & Dist. Cup S/F replay
04.04.64	Harrogate Railway	(h)	W 2-0	League
11.04.64	Ossett Town	(a)	W 5-0	League
18.04.64	Harrogate Town	(h)	D 2-2	League
21.04.64	Keighley N.S.F.	(n)	W 2-0	Kly & District Cup Final
31.04.64	Farsley Celtic	(n)	L 0-2	League Cup Final

KEIGHLEY CENTRAL 1967-68

Proudly displaying the West Riding County Cup. The first and only Keighley side to win the trophy to date.

61

Chasing Glory

KEIGHLEY CENTRAL 1966-67

BACK: D.Sturdy, C.House, M.Beck, S.Magee, R.Cox, D.Wellock, F.Bland, D.Palamountain, R.Lister, R.Butterfield, B.Spencer, R.O'Hanlon, R.Hobson, J.Bland, FRONT: P.Boland, T.Wilson, N.Creighton, G.Riley, T.O'Hara, D.McGowan, W.Butterfield, A.Hockey, J.Bibby, J.Parker, J.Clark.

KEIGHLEY CENTRAL 1972-73

Possibly the last team photo taken of the side before they disbanded at the end of the season.
BACK: R.Dugdale, J.Hellawell, J.Caulfield, C.Murray, B.McGuinness, R.Lister, J.Parker, FRONT: M.Hockey, C.Storton, A.Hockey, D.McGowan, P.Anderson.

(10)
LOCAL LEAGUE HIGHLIGHTS
– the mid and late 60's

With no Keighley Saturday League to play for after 1963, the area's local footballing sides became dispersed throughout a number of different leagues. Several sides opted for the Craven League while others turned to the Bradford Red Triangle, which was expanding at the expense of the better established Bradford Amateur League. The more ambitious clubs in the town turned initially to the Wharfedale League and then on to the expanding West Riding County Amateur or West Yorkshire organisations. Not since before the last war had more than one side from Keighley chosen to play at this level, and for the first time success was achieved.

Keighley Shamrocks' switch to the Wharfedale League proved instantly successful as they romped home to win the 1963-64 title. Finishing well ahead of their rivals in the league with a near perfect record, they went on to secure the title with victory in the end of season play offs. The side narrowly failed to recapture the title the following season. Faced with a huge backlog of fixtures the side were forced to play ten games in fourteen days at the end of the season, eventually going down 2-4 to Ives Sports in the play off final but defeating the same opposition 4-3 in the League Cup final, a competition in which they had finished runners-up the previous season. With such a fine record over their two Wharfedale seasons, Shamrocks turned to the West Yorkshire League for the 1965-66 season.

Success in this higher league was not immediate for Shamrocks, but at the end of the 1966-67 season they finished in what would have been a promotion place to the Premier Division behind Queensbury. Unfortunately promotion to the Premier Division was by invitation only and as this was not yet forthcoming then a third season would have to be spent in Division One. In a fine season, Shamrocks made sure that they would be invited the following year as they stormed to a league and cup double, defeating Fairburn 4-2 in the league cup final with goals from David Hobson (2), Richard Dugdale and right back Ken Heaton.

Despite continuing ground problems at their Highfield base, resulting in many of their home games being switched to Marley, Shamrocks took their rightful place in the West Yorkshire League's top division alongside Keighley Central for the 1968-69 season. Despite Central's push for the title, Shamrocks actually got the better of their great rivals during the season. Opening with a 2-1 defeat of champions Snydale Road and a 5-0 thrashing

Chasing Glory

of East End Park, Shamrocks went on to defeat Central 2-1 in December 1968. In a match transferred to Marley's frost bound 'tip top', Shamrocks weathered a strong Central attack to lead 2-0 through a brace of Bob Hobson breakaway goals. In the fading light Parker reduced the arrears but the scoreline remained 2-1 in the newcomers favour. The sides drew 0-0 in the return encounter in April before Shamrocks again defeated the holders Central in a Keighley & District Cup semi final. This set up a tie with Keighley Lifts, who had just completed their first season in the County Amateur League. In an entertaining game at Silsden, refereed by Jack Holmes, Shamrocks proved the stronger to win 3-2 with goals from Jack and Bob Hobson and Terry Boland, after Johnson had twice given Lifts the lead. Lifts gained revenge however in the Keighley Supplementary Cup, inaugurated a year earlier, when their reserves defeated Shamrocks 2-1 in the final.

Lifts' second string had actually reached the final of the same competition a year earlier after a surprise defeat of Keighley Central reserves in the semi final but had been forced to replay the game – which they lost – after it was discovered that they had played an ineligible player. Exactly the same thing happened in the Craven division two league cup competition the same season, when Lifts played another ineligible player in that semi final!

Keighley N.S.F. Rangers were another improving side. Despite finishing well adrift of Shamrocks in the Wharfedale League in the 1963-64 season they shocked their rivals with a 6-3 victory in a thrilling Keighley & District Cup semi final. The works side won with goals from Foster (3), Dovernor (2) and a Boland penalty, with replies from Pullich, Bland and a Dovernor own goal. N.S.F. went down to Keighley Central in the final, but went one better in the Wharfedale League Cup when they defeated Taylors of Shipley 3-1 in the final. A fine victory was capped by a spectacular individual goal from Peacock.

The following season saw N.S.F. competing in the B Division (in effect a second division) of the West Riding County Amateur League. They made a brave bid for honours, leading the division for most of the season and going through a long unbeaten run before being overhauled by Bradford based Cooperville White Star, who won their games in hand, at the death. Runners up spot was also achieved in the League Cup when the side fell to British Railways in the final. The side made amends the following season though with a league and cup double. With John Fay and Richard Dugdale in their line up, the side were rarely defeated – their first defeat, to Clayton, occurring when Mahomet was absent getting married and captain Dugdale poorly with flu. To cap a great season, their reserve side, coached by Tom Hindle, took the C (reserve) division League Cup. Unfortunately that was the end of the N.S.F. story as the side did not reappear the following season. Several of their players went on to further success with sides such as Central

Local League Highlights - The Mid And Late 60's

and Shamrocks. At the same time, the N.S.F. name was lost to amateur Rugby League, but the club re-emerged for the 1966-67 season under the now familiar guise of Worth Village A.R.L.F.C.

There was more success for local sides in the Craven League. Oxenhope lost their grip on the title but Silsden surprised everyone with their 1963-64 success. A great end of season run saw the side defeat the league leaders Grassington both home and away to clinch a place in the play-offs. After disposing of Skipton Bulldogs, who had earlier in the season put nineteen past a hapless Keighley Grinders side playing their final season of Saturday football, Silsden met Keighley Lifts in the title decider. Lifts themselves had defeated Grassington to reach the final but it was the Cobbydalers who won a dramatic game 3-2, the winning goal from Anderton coming in extra time. Silsden also won the League Cup with a resounding 5-2 defeat of improving Lothersdale. With Riley and Arnold both on top form, Silsden were back among the best in terms of local footballing prowess and their credentials were good enough to gain them election straight into the West Riding County Amateur League's top division for the 1964-65 season. The side had last appeared in this league over 40 years ago and it was a welcome return for one of the league's founder members.

After a poor start, Silsden began to climb the table, holding runaway league leaders Liversedge to a draw at the end of October. The side had risen to joint second place by January, their unbeaten run stretching to 14 games with a 4-1 defeat of struggling St.Josephs in February, and ended only by champions elect Liversedge. Silsden produced a dramatic fightback in the semi final of their League cup competition. Trailing 0-2 to Lightcliffe with only five minute remaining, the locals stormed to victory with three goals before the final whistle to set up a clash with Liversedge in the final. Unfortunately the heroics would not be repeated as Silsden's Heavy Woollen opponents sewed up a league and cup double with the only goal of the game.

Silsden did win the Keighley and District Cup for the first time in years when they broke Keighley Central's run of victories. Silsden led through an Arnold penalty at half time and went on to wrap the game up when Palamountain scored twice in three minutes in the second period. Despite a Bibby consolation late on, Silsden held on for victory in front of a fairly large crowd at Lawkholme Lane. Despite a bright start when they were defeated only once before Christmas, Silsden could not match their success the following season. The same year over £300 was spent on ground improvements at their Keighley Road ground.

Unfortunately Silsden struggled badly in the County Amateur League over the remaining years of the 1960's. Despite a reasonable run in the County Cup during the 1966-67 season – when victories over Ardsley Celtic (4-3) and East End Park (3-1) were achieved – the side found themselves at the wrong end of the table and endured a string of poor results, not least a 0-11 hiding by Brook Sports in the league cup. By the end of the 1968-69 season, Silsden found themselves as wooden spoonists, but thankfully spared relegation. How things would change for them the following decade!

Silsden ran a popular six-a-side tournament at the end of each season during the late sixties and seventies, among the winners were Colne Dynamos in 1967. The 1967-68 season was notable for Silsden only in that their president of many years Stanley Wass stepped down due to ill health.

Woodhouse Rovers were another side who tried their luck in the county leagues. Stepping up from Youth football the side applied successfully to the West Yorkshire League, where they were placed in Division 3 North. After a poor start, having to wait until Watsons Sports were defeated at the end of October for their first victory, the side lost only one of their final eleven games at the end of the 1964-65 season. Rovers were well supported by the Storton 'clan', with brothers Trevor and Carl starring in the team alongside their cousin, full back Les. Trevor actually managed a hat-trick in the space of four minutes in a fixture against Gibbs Sports in January 1966.

Haworth Youth Club were another side formed originally as a youth side. Success was not long in coming once they reverted to the open age ranks as they swept to the Bradford Red Triangle Division D title at the end of the 1963-64 season. Closest rivals Cottingley Dynamos were defeated 3-1 along the way, but the Bingley side gained their revenge the following season when both were competing in a reconstituted Division One – inflicting on Haworth their first home defeat for two and a half years in December 1964. Haworth were again among the divisional leaders and at the season's end joined the Craven League. Placed in Division One (below the league's new Premier Division) for the 1965-66 season, Haworth achieved a league and cup double at Oakworth's expense. Strengthened by the acquisition of three former Shamrocks players, Oakworth needed only a point from their final game against Cononley to win the Division One title. Earlier in the season they had defeated the same opposition 6-5 after trailing 1-5 with fifteen minutes remaining, but the South Craven side gained revenge with a 7-4 victory. This meant that Haworth and Oakworth would have to play off for the title, as well as compete in the league Cup final the same week. Haworth won both games to cap a successful return to Craven League football for the Brontë village.

Oxenhope returned to form in the 1965-66 season. Their third Craven League championship in six years was sealed with a 2-1 victory over reigning champions Skipton Bulldogs, with goals from Steele and Hopkinson. The side underlined their return to form as they inflicted on Keighley Central their second successive Keighley & District Cup final defeat. A lone 63rd minute strike from Greenwood following a weakly taken free kick was

Local League Highlights - The Mid And Late 60's

enough to defeat the West Yorkshire League side. Oxenhope had also defeated the cup holders Silsden in the semi final, Greenwood and Gillson scoring in a 2-1 victory.

Keighley Lifts were an emerging force in local circles, narrowly failing to lift the Craven League title three times in the early and mid sixties, they returned to take the 1967-68 title. Both Lifts and Haworth had broken away from the chasing pack by Christmas but as the season came to a close both sides started to drop points, enabling Skipton Bulldogs to ease their way back into contention. Late in April 1968 Haworth seemed to have the upper hand as goals from Brook, Knowles and Poynter enabled them to defeat Lifts in front of a large crowd 3-2, but when Lifts won their remaining games and Haworth were defeated by Bulldogs it meant that Lifts and the Skipton side would have to play off for the title, a game won by Lifts through a single headed goal by Spragg late in the first half. Led by two sets of brothers, David and Peter Spragg and Peter and Alec Ratcliffe, Lifts then turned their hand, briefly, to the West Riding County Amateur League. Their player-manager Harry Haddington, with his years of Football League experience with clubs such as Walsall, had built a fine, well disciplined side but County Amateur success was to elude them and by the end of the decade had returned to regroup in the Craven League.

Another emerging force was the Cross Hills Youth Club side, who ran Barnoldswick Park Rovers close for the 1968-69 Craven title and reached two successive Keighley & District Cup finals, losing on both occasions to the strong Keighley Central side.

Among the better known faces in the Craven League at this time was former Bradford City star John Hellawell, who was turning out for Prince Smith & Stells. Stells form was improving at this time, finishing as runners up to Cononley in the Craven first division at the end of the 1966-67 season they went on to win the divisional league cup, while their reserves achieved a league and cup double the same season in division two.

Probably the most bizarre match involving a local Craven League side in the mid sixties was that involving the reserve side of Cross Hills. In December 1964 they routed Skipton L.M.S. reserves 25-0, mainly due to the ineptitude of their opponents. L.M.S. fielded only seven players, and to make matters worse scored four 'own goals' during the game! For the winners, Walker scored TWELVE times. In another reserve team game in the same league three years later, Cononley walked off the field at half time in their game against Lifts and refused to play the second half on the grounds that there was 'no point in continuing' – they were trailing 0-10 at the time!

Among other sides at the time – albeit briefly – were familiar names in Guardhouse and Parkwood, (the latter of whom also operated a side in the Keighley Sunday Alliance) both competing in the Bradford Red Triangle. Guardhouse's Keighley Junior League side had been rampant during the

Chasing Glory

1963-64 season, finishing ahead of Woodhouse Rovers to win the title, but unfortunately neither Guardhouse or Parkwood survived very long, neither did Keighley A.F.C. in the same league.

Keighley Police continued their proud record in the Chief Constable's Cup, defeating Barnsley 5-1 at Sandal to win the trophy again in the 1963-64 season.

Ex-Keighley man Maurice Lindley, who had begun his career with Ingrow United in the old Keighley & District League was made assistant to manager Don Revie at Leeds United during the 1965-66 campaign after five years as chief scout for the club. Lindley himself had managerial experience in the Football League, having been in charge at several clubs, including Swindon Town. Another Keighley man on the move was Dennis Widdop, who emigrated to Australia with his wife and children during the same year. Widdop had been a key figure over the years in sides such as Worth Village, Silsden and Keighley Central. As well as a brief spell at Bradford City, he had also had spells with Farsley Celtic and Lancashire Combination side Nelson. Widdop had also sampled the delights of Bradford League cricket, appearing for the Keighley and Queensbury clubs in what is one of the country's foremost club leagues.

Several 'old timers' were in Keighley during the mid sixties. Keighley Lions organised a charity football match at Lawkholme Lane during the 1964-65 season between a Rugby League XI and an All Stars XI, led by cricketing 'great' Freddie Truman. Several other famous names from the world of sport were invited but for various reasons failed to appear. Not long afterwards, Silsden were hosts to a Burnley 'ex-Clarets' side, who won 1-0 in April 1966, and during the 1968-69 season Peter Blacks played host to a team of Northern TV stars.

Youth football was still producing talented young stars in the town. Many of those representing the Keighley Minor's and School's sides would become familiar names in the top local sides during the following two decades. During the 1967-68 season the Keighley Minor side again reached the semi final of the County Minor Cup, defeating Barkston Ash 3-0 at Kippax in the quarter final with second half goals from Joe Zieba (2) and Barney Maude. With other players in the side such as goalkeeper Bob Lee and England youth international Pete Turbitt (his three appearances against Wales, Scotland and Ireland), the side was the strongest for many years, but they failed to overcome a powerful Wharfedale side in the semi final. Despite leading 2-0 after 50 minutes through goals from Spencer and Rowan, the Keighley side were overrun in the final stages and went down 2-5. The same season a Keighley Minor side also reached the final of the Bradford Nig Nog League Cup in their first season in the league. Frobisher grabbed both of the Keighley side's goals late on in the game in a 2-4 defeat against Canterbury Y.C.

Local League Highlights - The Mid And Late 60's

The ladies also got in on the action during the 1960's, when in July 1969 two sides representing the West Yorkshire Road Car Company and Silsden played out a friendly at Silsden playing fields, the homesters winning 2-1 with goals from Harper and Bower.

The demise of the Keighley & District League was much lamented in local circles, and an attempt to form a new Keighley based league looked like becoming successful when in April 1966 it was announced that an 'Airedale Combination League' had been formed for the following season. Unfortunately the response from local clubs was less than encouraging and sadly the league disappeared as quickly as it had arrived. However, in March and April 1968 negotiations were underway to reform the Keighley League itself. Initially four clubs did express an interest in the reformation, but when others were not forthcoming the league formally closed down, handing its trophies and assets to the Keighley F.A.

KEIGHLEY N.S.F. 1965-66

The side are pictured following what was their final - and most successful season ever. The side had just achieved a league and cup double in the West Riding County Amateur League, and their reserves, also in the photograph, won their league cup competition. Upon their demise, many of the N.S.F. players went on to play for sides such as Central, Shamrocks and Silsden.
Among those in the photograph are coaches Roy Brook (front left) and Tom Hindle (centre, second left). Players include John Fay, Richard Dugdale, Vic Mahomet, Jack & Dave Hobson, Eddie Whitaker, Jimmy Walsh, Dennis Baxter and Pat Boland.

Chasing Glory

KEIGHLEY SHAMROCKS 1967-68

The side achieved a league and cup double in the West Yorkshire League. Several of the players, and the two coaches Brook and Hindle, had achieved a similar feat with the N.S.F. side only two years earlier in the County Amateur League.
BACK: T.Powell, R.Dugdale, T.Hindle, T.Fudge, B.Hanson, Jack Hobson (captain), V.Nutter, D.Thwaites, David Hobson, S.Brook,
FRONT: Bob Hobson, T.Boland, L.Pullich, K.Heaton, R.Peacock, R.Brook.

PRINCE SMITH & STELLS

Photographed at the end of the 1966-67 season when both first and second elevens won silverware in the Craven League.

(11)
SILSDEN & THE 70's

The 1970's began without one of the best known sides in local footballing circles. District Cup holders Shamrocks disbanded during the summer of 1969, problems with their Highfield ground among the reasons. Shamrocks players subsequently moved 'en masse' down the road to Silsden. It was a pity that such a well known club was left to die, but in contrast things could not have been much brighter for a Silsden side that was about to embark on their most successful, and controversial, era in the club's long history. Over the next decade the side would win the Keighley & District Cup seven times and lift both County Amateur and West Yorkshire league titles, yet despite their immense success events would transpire that would lead them to their self inflicted downfall by the end of the decade.

The 1969-70 County Amateur campaign saw a much improved showing by the Silsden side, as well as their first District Cup final appearance for five years when they were defeated 1-0 by Keighley Central. The 1970-71 season, however, heralded the return of Silsden as a major force in the region. The side enjoyed a fine season in the league, lifting the Premier Division league cup with a single Ian Patrickson strike against champions Luddendenfoot. Revenge was gained over Central in the Keighley & District Cup when a goal in each half from Jack and then David Hobson saw the favourites off in the final at Cross Hills.

The following year Oxenhope Recreation were routed 9-1 in the semi final before the trophy was retained with a 4-0 success against Cowling in the final. That same season saw Silsden become the first Keighley side to lift the West Riding County Amateur League championship, interrupting Luddendenfoot's run of three titles in four years. The reigning champions were held to a 1-1 draw in December 1971, Silsden racing to the top of the league courtesy of emphatic victories over Eccleshill United and Phoenix Park, both by 4 goals to nil, Pepper scoring two on his debut in the latter of the two games. Manningham Mills were routed 7-1 in April before two vital games against Bradford Rovers were both won, 1-0, thanks to an early Snowden strike and then 2-1 to ensure the league championship trophy came to Keighley Road for the first time. By this time Silsden's reserve side had wrapped up their second successive Reserve Division title, nearest challengers Liversedge defeated 7-1 in January when Derek Hobson netted all seven! The 1971-72 season also saw the reserves win their league cup competition too.

As Silsden embarked on their run of success, the name of Shamrocks was not gone for long. While their old base at Highfield lay dormant a new Shamrocks emerged in the early 1970's from the successful Keighley Minors side in the Bradford Nig Nog League. The minors raced to a league and cup double during the 1969-70 season – defeating St.Josephs 1-0 in their cup final thanks to a Brendan Gallagher strike, and Buttershaw St.Pauls by the same score courtesy of Ian Stewart. At the end of the season the improving side were presented with their trophies at a celebration dinner by Maurice Lindley. The 1970-71 season saw the side in the junior section of the Leeds Red Triangle, changing their name to Keighley Juniors and then the following year to Keighley Shamrocks Juniors. In a fine 1971-72 season not only did the young team enjoy a fine run in the Keighley Supplementary Cup, but became the only Keighley based side to reach a County Junior Cup final. With victories including those over Whitkirk Wanderers (3-0) and Ossett Trinitarians (5-2), when Greenwood, Howarth, Kryjnak and Shaw were among the scorers, a final spot against crack Leeds outfit Ashley Road was secured. Shamrocks' opponents were past winners of the competition but they were left trailing when Stewart gave the Keighley side the lead. Unfortunately Ashley Road equalised in the second half and then went on to win the replay, but the locals had put up a fine performance against a side that would go on to Yorkshire League success over the next decade.

Shamrocks had the consolation of lifting the relatively new Keighley Youth Cup that season, defeating Keighley Grinders 3-0 in a replay after having equalised in the very last minute of the original tie. The side continued their membership of the Leeds Red Triangle before reviving the Shamrocks as an open age team in 1976 when an entry was made into the County Amateur League.

Silsden meanwhile made a poor start to the defence of their County Amateur title in 1973, and had to settle for a spot behind Luddendenfoot in the final league table. Unfortunately this heralded the start of the club's problems as they were thrown out of the league at the end of the season for failing to play their league cup final against Lower Hopton on the specified date. Silsden were unable to play the tie on the day in question due to injuries, ineligible players and the fact that six members of the team were due to travel to Wembley to see the Leeds United/Sunderland F.A. Cup final – leaving the club with only seven players available. Despite giving the league management committee the required nine days notice, their appeals fell on deaf ears and when Silsden failed to appear for the final they were duly fined £10 and dismissed from the league. An appeal to the county F.A. proved unsuccessful and the club were forced to find new competition. It was hoped that a step up to the Yorkshire League might be possible for Silsden, but instead a place was taken up in the West Yorkshire League – albeit one step below the Premier Division, in the first division.

Silsden & The 70's

By now the club were also under fire from some quarters who argued that the side were not a true Silsden team, merely a 'Keighley lot' who had taken over the running of Silsden football club. This was something that was strongly refuted by Silsden F.C's management who claimed that the side did actually train in the village and that residents of Silsden were more than welcome to train with them. Meanwhile a new village side, under the name of Silsden United, and composed of Silsden residents, had been formed. The side used as their base Silsden playing fields and were accepted into the Keighley, and later Wharfedale Sunday leagues. This problem would resurface again later in the decade.

Controversy aside, Silsden proved far too strong for their opponents in their new league. Barney Maude hit a hat-trick in the side's opening 5-0 victory over Ardsley Celtic, while the reserves routed Monk Fryston United 9-0, Stewart Howarth scoring four times. The following week saw Natynczyk grab another hat-trick as Ferrybridge were defeated 5-0, while the reserves again outscored the first team with a 7-2 success against Allerton Bywater. The 1973-74 season could not have started in better fashion as both sides marched relentlessly to their divisional titles. A promising run was also put together by Silsden in the County Cup and by the time a strong Rawthorpe side were met, the quarter finals had been reached. Now under the leadership of Ian Patrickson following the untimely death of Roy Brook, Silsden took the lead against many people's favourites to lift the trophy through David Hobson. Rawthorpe equalised after 70 minutes and only minutes later, in a torrential downpour which wiped out several games across the region, the tie was dramatically abandoned. The replay turned out to be one of the most exciting games ever involving a Silsden side. Trailing 0-2 with only seven minutes remaining the locals late charge was rewarded with first a David Hobson strike and a dramatic equaliser from Smith to force extra time – during which time Hobson again and Natynczyk struck to send Silsden through to the semi final and a tie with Huddersfield side Brackenhall United. Despite goals from David Hobson and Alan Hockey, Brackenhall won a close game 3-2 to reach the final, going on to lift the trophy themselves.

Undeterred, Silsden wrapped up the league title with victory against nearest challengers Shaw Lane Sports, and the double was achieved with a 3-0 defeat of Ansons Sports in the league cup final at East End Park. Another double came in the form of the Keighley cup competitions when holders Westfield Rovers were beaten 5-2 in the final of the District Cup and Steeton reserves thrashed 8-1 (Maude, 5) in the Supplementary Cup final.

With such a successful season behind them, and in view of their past record, one would have expected Silsden to have received the invitation to join the Premier Division in the West Yorkshire League.

Chasing Glory

Unfortunately, as had been the case with Keighley Shamrocks years earlier, the side were forced to play out another season in division one. As expected, Silsden took no time in jumping to the top of the league, scoring 32 goals in their first seven games, including five in a ten minute spell in the 7-1 victory over Hemsworth. Their 49 match unbeaten run in the league came to an end when Ansons Sports defeated them at the end of March but by then the league title was something of a formality. County Amateur sides Yeadon Celtic and Crag Road were defeated in the County Cup before a disappointing exit was made to Seacroft W.M.C, who scored their winner through a hotly disputed last minute penalty, while Westfield Rovers, who had already taken two hammerings from Silsden in the league, were defeated 5-0 in the Keighley & District cup final (United Lifts were even more unfortunate, going down 0-12 in an earlier round to the rampant side). In all, it was another highly successful season for Silsden who at last gained their rightful promotion to the league's Premier Division.

The 1975-76 campaign did not signal the end of Silsden's remarkable run of success. With Ian Patrickson now being assisted with coaching duties by Trevor Hockey, the side carried on where they left off. Carlton Athletic were defeated 6-0 on the opening day of the season, and by the end of September Monckton Colliery and Altofts had also been hit for six, Patrickson himself hitting a hat-trick against Monckton. Another Huddersfield League side, Almondbury United scored a last minute winner to deny Silsden a good run in the County Cup and a poor run of four successive league defeats during an injury crisis briefly jolted Silsden's hopes of success, but a run of 12 successive victories took them back to the top of the league. Four teams who were also challenging for the title, namely Whitkirk Wanderers, Fryston, Robin Hood Athletic and Pontefract Collieries were all defeated during Silsden's winning run, the latter of whom ending the sequence by forcing a 2-2 draw late in the season. At the death, Silsden had completed their third successive championship and for the first time the West Yorkshire Premier Division title. To cap another fine season, Silsden then went on to defeat Craven League Bingley Juniors 3-0 in the Keighley & District Cup final, the star of the show being Jimmy Walsh who scored twice after being brought in to replace the injured David Hobson, and their reserve side were again champions of their division in the league.

History was to repeat itself at the end of the 1975-76 season though, when following incidents between Silsden and Fryston players at the league's presentation evening, Silsden were again expelled from their league. Whereas Fryston had already gained admission to the Yorkshire League, Silsden were forced to take another step downwards – back into the first division of the County Amateur League, the league from which they had been originally expelled three years previously. The club again

Silsden & The 70's

argued their case, and again professed a desire to move up to the Yorkshire League. At the time their facilities met the Yorkshire League's requirements, but unfortunately the necessary finance was not available and in any case the league would hardly have welcomed a team ejected from two leagues in such a short space of time.

So Silsden were left to start at square one again. Joining them in the 1976-77 County Amateur League were Keighley Shamrocks, albeit a step below in Division 1A, and both made bright starts. By the end of September Silsden's intentions were clear as Manningham Mills were brushed aside 5-0, while Shamrocks were also in the running thanks to the goalscoring exploits of Ian Greenwood, a product of the Shamrocks junior side who had recently returned to the club. Greenwood hit early season hat-tricks against Hepolite and Fields as well as against Wrose Rangers in November. The same day Silsden achieved their biggest victory for many years with a 15-0 thrashing of a poor Grattan side, Jimmy Walsh leading the way with five goals, backed up by David & Jack Hobson (3 each), Dicky Snowden (2), Derek Hobson and Cliff Kelly. The following week Greenwood hit four more, making his tally 14 in 6 games, as Salts reserves were thrashed 11-0 by Shamrocks, Silsden 'only' managing to defeat Eccleshill C.C. 8-1 that day. Silsden again made progress in the County Cup, defeating Harrogate League side Wetherby Athletic 3-0 and unbeaten Halifax Leaguers Sowerby Bridge 2-1. Unfortunately Silsden were drawn against Bradley Rangers, the cup holders, in the next round and went out 0-3.

By now Shamrocks had risen to second in their league behind eventual champions Dudley Hill reserves, a side they had actually defeated in the league cup. Greenwood grabbed another four in an 8-0 drubbing of Salem Athletic in the new year. Unfortunately both they and Silsden lost their long unbeaten league records on the same day in March – Shamrocks 16 game sequence ending in a 2-3 defeat to Trinity Athletic from Baildon and Silsden losing by the same score to Phoenix Park, the Bradford side pipping them to the first division title before going on to win the Premier Division title the following season, Silsden having the consolation of lifting the league cup instead.

With both Alan and Trevor Hockey in fine form, Silsden took the County Amateur title at the second attempt the following year, their fourth title in five seasons being supplemented by another league cup success and two further reserve section titles for their reserves. The Keighley & District Cup was won twice more, with victories over holders Cross Hills in 1977 and then Steeton in 1978. The latter game was reported as being ruined by Silsden's 'spoiling tactics' during the first half, but the criticism endured here was nothing compared with what was to happen.

Chasing Glory

Despite being officially promoted to the County Amateur League's top division, Silsden were once again thrown out of the league at a later management meeting for what league secretary Dave Brotherton described as ' violent and abusive conduct by players and officials both on and off the field'. As if a third expulsion in six years was enough, the same week saw the club's facilities taken from them by the ground trustees and Sunday side Silsden United installed as tenants instead. The argument here was that Silsden United were actually a side representative of the village and that the current Silsden F.C. weren't. The tenancy agreement stipulated that players should live within a five mile radius of Silsden and that several of the current players did not. In effect, Silsden United became the new Silsden F.C. (a condition of the tenancy being that the tenants must be called Silsden F.C), while the old Silsden had no name, no league and no ground! It brought to an end a remarkable run of success for a side that, but for its problems with discipline, had the potential to make it to a higher standard of football. While the ex Silsden players became dispersed throughout the region's remaining clubs, the village was temporarily without a Saturday side for the first time since the second world war. The Keighley district was left with only Shamrocks in a higher league, and it was not until the emergence of a new Keighley Town in 1980 that success at County Amateur level would return.

Of course Silsden and Shamrocks were only two of a number of clubs in Keighley during the 1970's, the rest of the town's sides operating in either Sunday football or the Craven League.

It was Lancastrians Barnoldswick Park Rovers who took the 1969-70 Craven title ahead of Cross Hills, who were actually the only side to defeat them in league competition that season. However, the following year saw Cross Hills sweep to the title themselves courtesy of the scoring talents of Jim Fenton and the influence of new player-coach Mike Hellawell, who scored a hat-trick in a 4-1 defeat of Park Rovers early in the season. Hills won their first 17 league games before held to a 2-2 draw by the Barnoldswick side at the end of January 1971, remaining unbeaten to the season's end and reaching the Keighley & District Cup semi final before going down to eventual winners Silsden.

Another Lancashire side, improving Colne British Legion, who finished the 1970-71 season closest to Cross Hills in the league, reversed their roles the following year to lift their first Craven title. It was due mainly to a poor end of season run by Cross Hills who saw their 18 month unbeaten league run ended by sides from 'across the border'. Gisburn defeated the locals 6-3 at the end of January 1962, and a week later Park Rovers emerged 4-0 victors. When Gisburn again defeated Cross Hills in March, the Colne side were able to sneak to the top of the table.

Silsden & The 70's

Prince Smith's spent the 1970-71 season chasing eventual champions Crossflatts in the Craven first division, but they made no mistake the following season when they ran away with the title, ahead of Haworth and Oxenhope, to earn promotion to the Premier Division themselves. The works team had goal machine Stuart 'Bert' Woolley to thank for their success. He scored five goals on three consecutive weeks during September/October 1971 (v Skipton L.M.S 9-1, United Lifts 7-1 & Oakworth 10-0) and by December of that year had scored his seventh hat-trick of the season in a 7-0 rout of Prince's nearest challengers Oxenhope. The side's success was remarkable in the light of the fact that following a takeover of their parent factory, Prince Smith's Sports club had actually been wound up, resulting in the demise of their well respected cricket side. The soccer club carried on for a few more seasons in the Premier Division of the Craven League before they too became defunct in 1974.

Oxenhope endured a decade of relative struggle during the 1970's following their successful era in the 1960's. Losing their top division status in both 1971 and 1979 they successfully regained their place the following season on both occasions, reaching the league cup final in 1971 when they went down 0-4 to Colne Legion (when at the same time another Colne club, Dynamos, were dominating Silsden's end of season 5-a-side tournaments before beginning their sensational rise to the top).

Cross Hills were back on form as the 1972-73 season opened. By Christmas they were back at the top of the league thanks to a 5-1 success against Grassington. Champions Colne Legion were held 1-1 at the end of the year before the local side eased away from the rest, despite losing to Colne in a league cup quarter final. Hellawell was again among the scorers as challengers Settle were brushed aside 4-0 and a 6-2 success against former County Amateur side Carleton late in the season sealed the title for the second time in three years.

Steeton, who spent over £5,500 on ground improvements in the early 70's briefly led the Craven league table the following season but it was to be Barnoldswick Park Rovers' year again as they regained the title, thrashing Oxenhope 6-0 before departing to pastures new.

Both Park Rovers and Colne Legion went on to compete in the higher West Lancashire League following their success in the Craven League, Colne moving up a year after the Barnoldswick side, a measure of the greater ambitions, or greater resources, of several of these East Lancashire clubs as opposed to clubs such as Oxenhope and Cross Hills, who despite great success in the 1960's and early 70's respectively chose to remain in the Craven set up (Cross Hills of course not moving on until the early 1990's). Both of the local sides were able to make progress in terms of their facilities however, Oxenhope opening their new pavilion during the 1973-74 season following the Cross Hills club's purchase of their own field.

The remaining years of the decade saw East Lancastrian sides dominate the league, Trawden Celtic becoming the dominant force before they too moved on. Steeton, with Neil Storton in their ranks, put up a strong challenge during the 1975-76 campaign before Trawden took the title for a second successive season, although Steeton did K.O. them in the league cup and Cross Hills inflicted upon them a rare league defeat thanks to a lone strike from Hargreaves.

Unfortunately there was bad news for the Craven League when its chairman John Brown died suddenly. The former Sutton United and Cononley player had been a founder member of the Cross Hills side. Another loss was that of Keighley greyhound stadium which closed down early in 1975, the former 'Beckside' ground of the old Keighley Town a victim of the uncertainty surrounding the proposed new Aire valley motorway. The most tragic loss of the era however was that of Mostyn Hockey, younger brother of Trevor and Alan Hockey. The 24 year old Silsden and Broom United player was killed in a road accident, leaving two young children and an expectant wife. A benefit game between a Keighley XI and Bradford City XI was held for his family later in the year.

Craven League sides, starved of league glory during the late 70's, went in search of success in the Keighley & District Cup. Cross Hills reached the 1976-77 final, as did Steeton a year later, but on both occasions favourites Silsden emerged victorious (Steeton's best cup result being a 5-1 County Cup success against Snydale Road in an early round in 1977). However, upon Silsden's demise, Cross Hills were able to take advantage by winning the competition two years in a row. The 1978-79 season saw them defeat County Amateur side Shamrocks in the semi final thanks to a Holmes header, going on to defeat surprise finalists Morton Village, in only their second season as a senior side, in the final. Shamrocks were again defeated a year later, this time in the final by two clear goals.

Morton had been formed as a junior side at the start of the 1975-76 season by Roger Nowell and his friends and had entered the Craven League two years later, playing on Morton Rec, once the home of former Keighley League champions Morton F.C. Despite lifting the league's second division title during the 1978-79 season, and possessing players of the quality of 16 year old Andy Gaughan – a star of the successful Keighley Schools team a year earlier, the new club failed to take their place back in division one, disbanding due to financial problems only days before the start of the new season. Another local club to disband were Oakworth Albion. The side had been forced to move out of Oakworth due to the unavailability of a suitable ground in the village and had instead played home games at Marley, resulting in a gradual loss of interest in the club and the loss of premier division status in the Craven League. Of their former grounds, the field behind Ghyll Clough farm is still accessible, as is their former sloping pitch behind Holden Park which is now a recreation ground. The Wide Lane field, adjacent to the cricket ground, which was used in the club's early years, was until recently used firstly by Bogthorn Juniors and then Oakworth Juniors before their move to Brontë Middle School.

Young talent continued to prosper throughout the 1970's, with many of the greatest footballing moments in Keighley coming from the junior ranks during this era. An 18 year old Pete Turbitt made an impressive Bradford City debut during the 1969-70 season, making four more appearances before returning to local football, while the same year the Keighley Schools under 15 side made it through to the national stages of the English schools cup for the first time. A record 7-1 defeat of Morley at Brontë was followed by a 2-1 replay success against a strong Sheffield line up – Brent Smith, nursing an injured leg, striking the winning goal in extra time. Progress was halted when Manchester ran out 4-0 winners at the last 16 stage in January 1970, but the side continued to perform admirably in Yorkshire Shield matches in this and following seasons.

The 1972-73 season brought victory for the local schoolboy side over Bradford for the first time since their reformation. A 2-1 win in the Yorkshire Shield was achieved with second half goals from Considine and substitute Haygarth, avenging a narrow defeat at the hands of the same side a fortnight earlier in an English Shield tie. Spurred on by this result, the locals went on to hammer Airedale/Wharfedale 6-2 before being brought down to earth with defeats to Halifax and Sheffield.

A spot in the later stages of the Yorkshire Shield was achieved for the first time in 1975-76, when, spurred on by a four goal haul from Simon Dalby in a 6-1 defeat of Spen Valley at Dewsbury, a strong Hull side were met in the semi final at Marley. Under the captaincy of one Peter Jackson, who had just signed for Burnley along with Dalby, the Keighley schoolboys were involved in a cracking cup tie. A Keith Bailey strike cancelled out an early Hull goal, Keighley then taking the lead through Rutter. There were only ten minutes remaining when Hull equalised to force a replay, which they duly won by a single goal. The same season saw Keighley Minors also reach the semi final of the County Minor cup where they were defeated by the eventual winners, Craven F.A.

The 1976-77 season saw the local schoolboys reach the fourth round of the English Shield, but this was only a prelude to a great run in the Yorkshire Shield the following year. In a quarter final tie, Sheffield, who had earlier knocked Keighley out of the English Shield, were defeated 3-1. The winners came from behind to earn a semi final spot courtesy of goals from Andrews, Grew and Patterson, the latter of whom scored a hat-trick in an earlier 3-2 defeat of Bradford. The semi final at York was drawn, necessitating a replay at Marley, and this time it was Grew's turn to score a hat-trick in a 3-1 victory, to send the side through to their first final. Unfortunately the game was marred somewhat by the first ever sending off of a Keighley schools player when Andy Gaughan was dismissed for fighting. The final brought Keighley up against Middlesbrough, and although the locals lost both legs 3-0, they never gave up the fight and were commended for their efforts by all involved.

The Keighley schools squad for the final was:
Hagyard, Clarke, Ashdown, Larkin, Smith, Gaughan, Patterson, Gilham, Andrews, Dlambulo, Grew & Brunskill.

Two years later, the 1979-80 season saw Keighley Minors go one better than the schoolboys had as the County Minor Cup was won for the first time. Defeating Castleford in an early round, their neighbours Wakefield were met in a thrilling semi final. The Keighley Minor League had been reformed for the 1977-78 season, and the Keighley squad composed of players playing in that competition, no less than seven of whom were in the Aire Valley side. Noticeably several of the team had also starred in the Keighley schoolboys team.

Keighley struck first in their semi final through Guest, only for their opponents to equalise just before half time and to take the lead soon afterwards. However, an equaliser came from Patterson following a goalmouth scramble, and the same player sneaked a dramatic winner in the dying seconds from an acute angle. The final against Goole was nowhere near as close. Keighley had defeated their opponents 2-1 the previous season when Goole were defending their title, this time the winning margin was 5-2 and Keighley were County Minor champions at last.

The winning squad was:
M.Andrew, S.Jagger, G.Harrison, S.Clarke, S.Miller (capt), **J.Patterson, R.Sattecto** (all Aire Valley), **A.Gaughan, S.Guest M.Guest, S.McNulty** (all Steeton), **E.Dlambulo** (Low Mill Lane), **R.Guy** (Cullingworth), **M.Revak**(Braithwaite), **D.Wiseman** (Greenhead).

Aire Valley, who supplied seven of the successful squad, not surprisingly won the Keighley Minor League that season, although Greenhead Youth Club defeated them 5-2 in the league cup final. Despite the withdrawl of the previous year's Craven Minor League champions Morton, the league could boast a strong line up, including a Bradford City side that was unbeaten until Low Mill Lane took both points off them in October. Greenhead Youth Club, who had previously competed in the now defunct junior section of the Wharfedale Sunday League, were actually the forerunners of today's successful Phoenix side. Formed by Mike Breeze in 1975, they had considerable success in five a side tournaments

Silsden & The 70's

throughout the 70's & 80's, reaching the National Youth Club finals on three occasions as North Eastern champions. Greenhead sides had the enviable reputation of staying together in later years as former Youth Club members formed the first Phoenix side in the 1980's, and later still, former Phoenix junior players turned out for the side's senior Saturday and Sunday teams throughout the 1990's.

Not all of Keighley's junior sides were successful. Guardhouse made their debut in the Craven Minor League in 1973 and were routed 0-28 by champions Nelson Stanley. A year earlier Bradley minors had lost all of their games in the same league – only to be awarded with a special sportsmanship trophy at the end of the season.

The late 1970's were notorious for fixture pile ups caused by the inclement weather. In 1978, Silsden United Juniors and Pendle Colts were forced to play three games in one! Fighting for Craven Minor League points, the sides also agreed to the match counting as both legs of their league cup tie too. There were several other odd events at local football games too. The power crisis and three day working week that almost crippled the 1973-74 season obviously became to much for one Cowling linesman. He was sent off for swearing at the referee in a game against Grassington! Referees were in short supply at the time, with the Craven League at one point considering scrapping a division due to the severe shortage of men in black. Those that were around to officiate were not always treated well – one referee abandoning a Craven League reserve team fixture at Crossflatts between the home side and Skipton L.M.S. after being snowballed by some of the players who disagreed with his decisions!

No such problems with the snow for Maurice Tillotson who was having a ball down under. The former Silsden and Huddersfield Town player was named New Zealand's player of the year in 1973. After having made a name for himself in Canada and Belgium before moving on to Gisborne City in New Zealand, Maurice had played in the national side in World Cup qualifiers against Australia, Indonesia and Iraq. He regularly coached the local youngsters and was much sought after by Australian clubs. By this time Trevor Hockey too was a seasoned international, having made his debut for Wales in a 1971 European Nations Cup tie against Finland at Swansea.

The 1970's saw the emergence of organised football for ladies' teams in the region. Brontë Ladies emerged in the early 70's to eventually become one of the leading women's teams in the country. Before their move to Salts F.C. and eventual demise in the 1990's, the side played their home fixtures at Marley and were very much a 'Keighley' side. The first reported match involving a Brontë Ladies side was in January 1971 when a charity fixture to raise money for the kidney unit at St.James' Hospital in Leeds was played against Sutton Ladies. Brontë won 2-1 and the proceeds of

Chasing Glory

£120 far exceeded expectations. Less successful was a later fixture between Brontë and a team of 'T.V. all-in-wrestlers' to raise money for the new Keighley Leisure centre sports hall, which raised only £40. Led by Marion Reape the side played several more fixtures during the year and had Marion Illingworth, Brenda Peel and youngsters Wendy Potter and Maureen Kelly regularly among their goal scorers. Early success was earned in a Bradford league 5-a-side tournament where Brontë's under 13 side finished as runners up. Joining Potter and Kelly in the team that day were Vivienne Cowman, Linda Seward and Debra Bentham.

The 1974-75 season saw Brontë reach the final of their league cup competition, Stocksbridge defeated 7-3 in the quarter final and the holders Ossett 2-0 in the semi final thanks to a double strike from Julie Turner in front of the England selectors. As a result, Reape and Potter were both invited to the England trials later in the year, both narrowly missing out on a place in the national team. The following year saw Brontë in the semi final of the Townsend Cup competition at Rotherham. From a field of 16 teams, the locals won through to the last four with victories over Woodbeck (Derby) 5-0 and Rangers (Nottingham) 1-0, as well as a goalless draw in their other group match against Star Inn (Rotherham). Brontë conceded their first goal in the semi final, which was enough for another Nottingham side, Car Fasteners to win through to the final. Later in the season both Brontë Ladies and Brontë Girls won their respective 5-a-side competitions at Parkside Sports Centre with 2-0 victories over Fairfax and Sutton respectively in their finals. In total 64 goals were scored by the two teams, Maureen Kelly leading the way with 11, with only a single goal conceded.

The senior side established itself in the Lancashire League throughout the remainder of the 70's, playing on Marley's centre pitch, a privilege denied men's teams except for cup ties. County 5-a-side tournaments were dominated by Brontë too. Wendy Potter scored 11 of her side's 28 goals en route to a 2-0 final victory over West Park Rangers in the 1976-77 competition, Denholme routed 13-0 in the semi final. The girls retained their title with a 7-1 success against St.George, Lorraine Kennedy and Alison Hall leading the scoring. Two weeks later Ulverston Dynamos were thrashed 22-0 in a league fixture, double figures also being achieved against Stakepool (18-0 & 17-0), B.A.C. Warton and Lancaster. Unfortunately Preston North End's two convincing victories over Brontë gave them the league title instead. As consolation, the North East Regional 5-a-side competition was won instead, with an emphatic 6-0 defeat of Sheffield in the final.

Several ex Brontë players helped to form Nab Wood Ladies in 1977, the same year Brontë defeated their own girls' team in the final of the Sunblest 5-a-side at Parkside. The new club joined Brontë in the Lancashire League, the locals at last lifting the title at the end of the 1978-79 season when, again, double figure victories were not uncommon – Cumberland coming off worse, on the wrong end of a 15-0 scoreline. The title was sealed with a 3-1 victory over Preston North End. The same season saw Brontë reach the last 16 of the Womens F.A. Cup for the first time, going down narrowly to Queens Park Rangers at Otley after Christmas, while the Brontë Girls took the Lancashire League's second division title. To cap a great season, Robin Hood were demolished 11-0 in the final of the County 5-a-side's, Brontë Girls finishing in third place. By the end of the decade, there was no doubting Brontë's position of supremacy among women's football sides this side of the Pennines, and indeed their position among the top ladies' sides in the north.

SILSDEN 1971-72

The newly crowned County Amateur champions pictured before their Keighley Cup final victory against Cowling. It is interesting to note how many of the side had played for both N.S.F. and Shamrocks in previous seasons.

BACK: K.Heaton, Derek Hobson, A.Daniels, Jack Hobson, R.Ainsworth, David Hobson, J. Gallagher,
FRONT: R.Brook (coach), I.Patrickson, R.Snowdon, R.Dugdale (captain), D.Rowan, T.Hey.

(12)
MAGNET AND THE SUNDAY ALLIANCE

By the mid 60's, the Keighley Sunday Alliance had firmly established itself on the map and as the 1970's approached the league was still expanding. Despite the absence of Dean Smith & Grace following their all conquering 1970-71 season, the league was still as strong as ever, inundated with new sides wishing to join the competition and considering starting a youth section for junior sides. Yet by the end of the decade we would find the league struggling for clubs and in turmoil due to the immense success of one of its sides that threatened to undermine the viability of the league itself.

Magnet had lifted the Alliance second division title at the end of the 1967-68 season, but had finished at the foot of the first division the following year. By the end of the 1970-71 season they were pointless at the bottom of division two and their future looked in doubt. That is until a large influx of ex-Deans players joined the club (others going on to Broom United, Holycroft Y.C. and Tommy Holmes F.C.). Magnet were instantly transformed and swept to the second division title the following season. They were far and away the best team in the division, if not the league, double figure victories including a 20-0 hammering of Addingham and an even more emphatic 25-0 rout of the Young Christians. Magnet became the only Alliance second division side ever to complete a sweep of three trophies in one season. First division champions elect Ventus United were defeated in a replayed Kensington Cup tie, before Holycroft were beaten by goals from Farrington and Brown in the final, and the treble was achieved with a 5-1 success over Fieldhead in the Jeff Hall Trophy final.

The same season saw the Alliance organise a Keighley News sponsored 5-a-side tournament to mark the opening of the new sports hall at Keighley Leisure Centre. Tommy Holmes scrap metal merchants meanwhile were having a great season in the Alliance third division. With players of the calibre of Neil and Nigel Storton in their line up, the side, like Magnet, were far too strong for their opponents. In demolishing unlucky Knowle 22-0 in one game, Neil Storton grabbed no less than eleven himself!

By now the occasional Keighley side played in the much inferior Wharfedale League. Oakworth Wanderers were among the first before moving into the Alliance for a couple of seasons, as were Silsden United,

Magnet And The Sunday Alliance

who placed their reserve side in the Wharfedale set-up. The Keighley Sunday Alliance boasted five divisions at the start of the 1972-73 season, which hardly reflected the amount of football played in the town. Of the 47 sides in the competition, there was an increasing number from the Wharfe Valley, as well as those from further afield who had the option of choosing leagues based much closer than the Keighley Sunday Alliance. Within three years there would only be a single division operating in the Alliance, consisting mainly of sides from Keighley.

The 1972-73 season saw not only the Alliance at its peak, but the inauguration of the Keighley Sunday Cup, organised by the Keighley F.A. Magnet were to dominate the competition in its early years, winning the cup ten years in succession, the first a convincing 6-0 win over Alliance second division side Fleece (Haworth). The same season saw Fleece also lose out to Ventus in the Jeff Hall Trophy final, Magnet losing their first Alliance fixture for nearly two years when Shire Rovers knocked them out of the same competition in an earlier round. However, the Alliance league championship returned to Keighley when Magnet were crowned champions for the first time, ahead of Ventus United and Tommy Holmes, who had acquitted themselves well following their 'double' promotion.

Magnet remained unbeaten in all competitions the following season. With players such as Alan Hockey, Barry McGuinness and Barney Maude in fine form, not only did the side sweep all before them in the Alliance but they were able to emulate the feat of D.S & G three years earlier by lifting the County Sunday Cup.

Three goals in the final four minutes helped to see off Ventus 4-0 in the Jeff Hall final, and, as well as the winning the Kensington Cup, they defeated Grinders through two late Derek Hobson headers in the Keighley Cup final. But by far the biggest feat of Magnet's season was that County Cup. Defeated by Queensbury the year before, the side made no mistake in 1973-74. With what was virtually the Silsden line up on a Saturday, Magnet defeated Robin Hood 1-0 in their quarter final, and Rowley Hill (Huddersfield) 3-2 in the semis before a great 2-0 victory over Lidget Green Wanderers in the final at Thackley. In no time at all the name of Magnet had risen from obscurity in the Keighley Alliance to County champions, and despite going out of the competition at the third round stage the following year that was not the end of their success at this level.

Meanwhile the Alliance itself was having success in the Lancashire Inter-league competition which ran for a time during the 1970's. The 1973-74 season saw the league's representative team go down 3-4 to eventual winners Warrington, this despite a hat-trick from Neil Storton.

The first ever Alliance side that day was:
J.Sewell (Fleece), **B.McGuinness, A.Hockey, J.Hobson** (captain), **R.Snowdon** (Magnet), **P.Sharp** (Oakworth),

85

Chasing Glory

S.Vento (Ventus), **W.Butterfield**, **N.Storton** (Long Lee), **M.Thompson**, **J.Yeadon** (Shire). Sub: **P.Smith** (Magnet). Also in the squad: **Rowan**, **Hainsworth** (Magnet), **Spence** (Ventus), **C.Storton** (Long Lee).

The 1974-75 Inter-league campaign was far more successful, the Alliance also entering two sides in the Craven Inter-league competition too. Here the league's 'A' and 'B' teams met in the semi final, the former, comprising mainly of players from Magnet and Grinders winning 4-0 against a team made up of players from the 74-75 Alliance District Division. The final, with several of the top faces in the Alliance missing, was lost 0-1 to the Craven League, but it was the Lancashire competition where the greatest success lay. Goals from Storton and Rowan saw the South West Lancashire League defeated 2-1 in the first round before a 3-1 success against the Morecambe & Lancaster League when Patrickson, Snowdon and Lupton were on the mark. The semi final against Oldham proved a dramatic occasion. David Hobson missed a penalty, his brother Derek was sent off, and it wasn't until the last 17 minutes that the Alliance were able to break through with Patrickson, Hobson and an own goal setting up a 3-1 victory. The final pitted the locals against the Kirkby Newtown Combination (Liverpool) over two legs and it looked as if the Merseysiders would lift the trophy when they won 2-1 at Marley. Unable to accept defeat the locals produced a stunning performance away from home and with goals from Patrickson and Hobson, the latter with two late headers, the Alliance emerged 3-1 winners to win 4-3 on aggregate.

In defence of their title the Alliance selected their entire side from Magnet players, although several players from other clubs made the reserves list. The Magnet players were certainly a busy lot – turning out for Silsden on a Saturday, for Magnet on a Sunday and representing the Alliance in inter-league fixtures. Unfortunately the trophy was not retained as, following a 7-1 thrashing of the Rochdale League, Ashton won a controversial second round tie courtesy of a last minute strike that had more than a hint of offside.

Meanwhile the Alliance was experiencing its mass exodus of clubs. The league committee were forced to revert to two divisions for the 1974-75 season – a Town division, which contained Magnet, and a District division. Inevitably Magnet had scored 89 goals in only 11 league matches by Christmas as they won their section with ease ahead of Cross Hills W.M.C, the side they defeated 2-0 to win the Keighley Sunday Cup again. It was much closer in the District division where improving Silsden United gave Ventus and Saltaire County a good run for their money, before lifting the Kennedy Cup with a 4-1 defeat of Airedale Rovers in the final. Magnet defeated Ventus in a play off to win the overall championship.

Magnet And The Sunday Alliance

Only two of the previous season's District division applied for membership of the league for the 1975-76 season, the Alliance being forced to revert to a single division for the first time in eleven years. At the same time the Wharfedale League was rapidly expanding, Silsden United and Ventus elected to its Premier Division, and other former Alliance sides such as Airedale Rovers, Crossflatts, Cullingworth and Ilkley Phoenix amongst many others also playing in the competition. With many of the stronger sides leaving the Alliance it was no surprise to see Magnet way out on their own at the head of the table again. They saw off the early challenge from Broom United and Cross Hills W.M.C. again, and as usual retained their Jeff Hall and Keighley Sunday Cup titles (a nationwide journalists' strike preventing any of this reaching the local press!). The same season saw Magnet make a sortie into the English Sunday Cup, going out to a single goal in a closely fought contest against Brandon United of Durham, who now play in the Northern League.

Only ten clubs applied to join the Alliance for the 1976-77 season. Ten of the fourteen that had finished the last season left, and it was only through the applications of six new sides that the league was able to continue. Magnet's title seemed another foregone conclusion, but they were given a close run by Dog & Gun. With rising stars Keith Lowe and Ian Greenwood in their ranks the pub side won their first 12 games, and although Magnet also boasted a 100% record they trailed their rivals, having played fewer games. Magnet won a key encounter between the sides 6-0 in March, although Dog & Gun fielded a depleted side, but it was not certain that the champions would win the league again as they were so far behind with their fixtures due to cup runs and poor weather. The side were forced to fit in seven league fixtures in two weeks before the May 15th deadline (two games remaining unplayed), as well as facing Broom in the Jeff Hall Cup final, which they unwaveringly won to seal another league treble.

Again, Magnet's greatest feat came outside the Alliance when they became the first side to win the County Sunday Cup twice outright. They had some close games en-route to the final, beating Robin Hood (Leeds) 1-0, Glasshoughton 3-2, Lidget Green 4-3 and Tadcaster Y.C.O.B. 2-1 in the semi final before defeating Bradford league and cup double winners George (now known as Oakenshaw) in the final at Thackley.

The side's dominance over all Keighley sides continued too, Silsden United, despite playing well, going down 2-0 in the 1977-78 Keighley Sunday Cup final. Derek Hobson had opened the scoring before a 50/50 challenge between Dickie Lupton and United's David Hanson led to the ball drifting over the head of 'Keeper Kev Knappy and into the net for Magnet's second. The same opponents were defeated again one year later. Captained by Carl Storton and now known simply as Silsden F.C., the underdogs were this time defeated 3-0, with Trevor Hockey among the scorers.

Chasing Glory

Undeterred by their previous defeat against Brandon, Magnet were still pinning their hopes on English Sunday cup success, reaching the quarter finals in 1978 and 1979. The first occasion saw victories over Eagle (Liverpool) 1-0, Newton Aycliffe 1-0 following a 2-2 draw the previous week at Marley, and 2-1 against Willington Belle Vue, before another North Eastern side Rams Head (Newcastle) were defeated 1-0, thanks to a single David Hobson strike. Unfortunately Dibby Rowan was forced to miss the last of these games due to the death of his brother Brian, who played in the Keighley Sunday Alliance for Burlington. The quarter final pitted Magnet against Birmingham side Olympic Star, and through Trevor Hockey's 'connections' the locals were able to train for the tie at St.Andrews, the home of Birmingham City. Unfortunately the tie was postponed twice due to the weather, and at the third attempt the Keighley side played well below their best and had David Hobson sent off on their way to a 1-3 defeat. A year later Magnet were back in the quarter finals following victories over Hull Fish trades 4-0, Morton Community Centre (Carlisle) 2-0 and Hull Pipers Club 2-1 before Rams Head, now known as Langley Park gained revenge for their defeat twelve months earlier.

Such was Magnet's success that the very existence of the Sunday Alliance was being put into question. Cup games always took precedence over league fixtures, and this was leaving the side way behind the other clubs in the number of games played. Whereas Magnet were able to catch up on their games at the end of the 1976-77 season, they were unable to do so the for the next two years. Therefore Keighley Grinders were awarded the 1977 -78 Alliance championship, based on games played before the cut off date. Grinders defeated chief rivals Burlington 2-1 before Christmas thanks to a Steve Broadley double, and with Leo Heggarty also in fine form the side maintained a 100% record until Burlington forced a 1-1 draw in March. Magnet defeated Grinders 5-2 in the league cup final, and won the Jeff Hall Trophy again, but they finished the season way behind with their league fixtures and had to concede the title. The 1978-79 season saw Magnet again win both cup competitions, 6-1 against Grinders in the Jeff Hall and 3-0 versus Burlington in the league cup. However, they were way behind with fixtures again, and added to the problems of a particularly poor winter that affected all clubs, the Alliance were forced to scrap the league competition altogether. Burlington defeated Grinders 4-2 in a 'mini league' final (the losers losing three cup finals in a week) to become the 'unofficial' Alliance champions.

Magnet's membership of the Alliance was now in serious jeopardy. Despite signing on 33 players and offering to field a reserve side to complete their fixtures, neither the league committee nor the remaining clubs were satisfied, arguing that the league was far less attractive with all the best players concentrated within one club. It was also argued that any other

Magnet And The Sunday Alliance

side not completing its league fixtures would have been thrown out of the league. Magnet were the victims of their own success, and when their application for membership of the Alliance for the 1979-80 season was rejected, it signalled the end of an era for Magnet in the Keighley League. Luckily this was not the end for the club, for despite losing a few players during the summer, Magnet were accepted into the Wharfedale League's Premier Division instead.

Local sides had already tasted success in the Wharfedale League. By the time Magnet had arrived, Silsden White Star were already becoming a major force. Named after the side that had graced the old Keighley & District League following the first world war, they had struggled at the foot of division four during the 1977-78 season, but bounced back the following year to gain promotion (while their reserves became the first local team to try their luck in the Ilkley based Wharfedale Triangle). Druids and Timothy Taylors also competed, albeit briefly, in the Premier Division of the league, while Keighley Post Office delivered the best results with many high scoring victories in their runaway division four success during the 77-78 campaign, Steven Whittaker and Pat Redman regularly among their scorers. The same season saw Busfeild Arms' keeper Dovestone score a hat-trick against Ilkley Phoenix reserves, all from the penalty spot, in a 7-1 victory for the Morton side.

MAGNET 1971-72

The side had finished bottom of the Keighley Sunday Alliance the previous season, but thanks to the acquisition of several players from the defunct D.S.G, notably the Hobson brothers, the side began their haul of local silverware. Magnet are seen here collecting the Kensington Cup following a 2-0 defeat of Holycroft Y.C. in the final.

(13)
HOCKEY'S DREAM – Keighley Town '79 & the County Amateur League

Although Keighley still had no football team in the higher echelons of non-league football, the 1970's had seen success at county level from both Dean Smith's and Magnet on a Sunday and Silsden on a Saturday. It was hoped that those who carried the town's name then would continue to do so into the 1980's, particularly as plans were afloat to bring out the best of Keighley's talent at both grass roots level with youngsters and at senior level with the revival of the Keighley Town name.

The man behind these schemes was none other than Trevor Hockey. The former Welsh international was all too aware that for sport to thrive it must have firm foundations, and this is where he started. In August 1979 the first of his Sunday soccer camps for youngsters kicked off at Utley playing fields. The interest he managed to generate was immense, 160 children attending the first session and by the end of the month there were 300 youngsters on the soccer camp's books. Hockey had the support of several of the town's top footballers, noticeably David and Jack Hobson (the latter now being player manager at Crag Road United) who helped with coaching.

In October of the same year, a charity match between a Trevor Hockey managers' XI and Leeds United All-Stars side was held at Marley in front of a large crowd eager to see the skills of legends such as John Charles (who delighted everyone with a fine goal) and Jackie Charlton, as well as current stars such as Bryan Flynn and T.V. personalities such as Frazer Hines. Proceeds were shared between the soccer camp and the Spina Bifida association, and it was clear that Hockey had really fired the imagination of the Keighley public.

There was more. Hockey hoped eventually to field a junior side in the Northern Intermediate League, although he recognised that in order to do this he may have to go via a Football League club. The indoor facilities at Greenhead School were secured for the cold winter months and a monthly lottery was organised as a way of bringing more funds into the soccer camp. Attempts were also made to revive the old greyhound stadium as a football ground and family entertainment centre. Hockey hoped that one day the former Beckside home of the old Keighley Town would again

Hockey's Dream - Keighley Town '79

be a focus of public attention, and he actually organised a reunion of the former Yorkshire League side's players. Unfortunately the old ground lay, in part, on the line of the proposed Aire Valley trunk road, and although Hockey was offered the site on a short term basis there was no security and any buildings erected would have to be taken down within a few years.(Ironically Sandy Lane now use the current site for Sunday league fixtures).

And then there was Keighley Town 1979. Less than two months before the start of the 1980-81 season, Westfield Rovers withdrew from the County Amateur League. Hockey seized the opportunity and applied for a new Keighley Town to fill the vacancy. The new side were formally accepted into the league, playing their home games adjacent to the Keighley Technical College cricket ground at Utley, and this was to herald the start of a new era in the history of soccer in the town. Not only were Town to become a major force in the league, but they were to enjoy a fierce rivalry with neighbours Shamrocks, who had narrowly lost out to Ventus and Gascoigne United for the league's first division title in the previous two campaigns. They had built a formidable side and regular strikes from Dave Driscoll, Jeff Cummins, Ian Greenwood and Jimmy Caulfield had seen them consistently among the top scorers in their division.

Keighley Town assembled a squad for the 1980-81 season composed of many of the faces previously seen at Silsden, as well as several of those signed from Shamrocks during the close season, such as Ian Greenwood and Mark Ginley, and several other up and coming 'stars'. Following practice matches against Brackenhall and Menston Fieldhead they kicked off their first County Amateur season with resounding victories over Blakeboroughs and Rawdon, 3-0 and 4-0 respectively, before dropping their first point in a 1-1 draw with Brackenhall. The Huddersfield side led until a second half header from substitute David Hobson saved the Keighley side from defeat.The side was also boosted around this time when they were able to convert offices in Church Green into their official town centre headquarters, where Hockey was able to organise not only his County Amateur outfit, but could also oversee the progress of Town's junior sides in the Keighley Minor and Spen Valley Youth leagues.

Town led the County Amateur league after five games, but their first competitive defeat was endured when arch rivals Shamrocks defeated them 2-1. Jimmy Bland's second minute opener for the Highfield based outfit was cancelled out by a Greenwood header, only for Bland to pop up again half way through the first half to score the winner. A few days later Keighley Town played a prestigious match under Lawkholme Lane's floodlights against Northern Premier League champions Mossley. 1,500 spectators saw the more established side win 4-2, but the locals were far from disgraced, with Keith Lowe scoring both of their goals, the second late in the game from the spot.

A great run of successive victories saw Keighley Town established at the top of the league by the time the return match against Shamrocks was played. On a muddy Highfield pitch, a late Andy Isherwood strike saved Town a point in a 2-2 draw. The first division title was duly secured, ahead of a strong Civil Service side, and despite several injury worries – not least that of Cliff Kelly who broke his leg in a match against St.Blaize. Before the season had ended Westbrook had been defeated 2-1 at Eccleshill in the league cup final and Silsden 2-0 in the Keighley Charity Cup final, which was crammed into a crowded end of season fixture backlog (see chapter 14 for Charity Cup). A measure of the ability of the new Keighley Town came in the County Cup when, following a tight 2-1 victory over Leeds Red Triangle side Beeston St.Anthonys, they tackled County Amateur premier division leaders Dudley Hill Athletic. Andy Isherwood fired Town into an early lead which they held until the last quarter of an hour, and despite going down to a late extra time winner it was clear that they were a match for any of the sides a division above them. Unfortunately the side's first setback occurred when they were denied promotion to the premier division due to their inadequate facilities at Utley. Trevor Hockey was somewhat aggrieved with the situation, but they were to spend another year in the same company.

Keighley Town's junior sides also experienced successful campaigns. The under 17 Keighley Minor League side beat Greenhead Y.C. 3-1 in a mini-league final before going down 0-1 to Apperley Bridge based Stansfield Rovers in the league cup final. Hockey intended fielding this side in the Craven League the following season, but the venture fell through at the last minute, again leaving the Town manager slightly less than happy.

The 1980-81 Keighley & District Cup final turned out to be the first of several successive Town v Shamrocks finals. Despite finishing well behind their higher profile opponents in the league, Shamrocks had taken three out of a possible four points from them in head to head battles and were confident of lifting the cup for the first time since their reformation. It was Town who lifted the trophy for the first time however, with strikes from Malcolm Hagyard, David Hobson and Andy Isherwood. A late consolation from Jimmy Caulfield made the score 3-1, but it was not the first time that Shamrocks would be frustrated in a District Cup final tie. A year later Town won the trophy again, Isherwood twice on the end of Hobson free kicks as Shamrocks went down again 2-0, a game in which Alan Hockey marked his 19th District Cup final! Town's dominance over other Keighley sides was underlined by the fact that they had the defended the competition without conceding a single goal

Hockey's Dream - Keighley Town '79

By this time Keighley Town were back on top of the County Amateur first division and on their way to their second successive title – and with it promotion to the premier division. It had proved a hard struggle. Following an excellent pre-season victory over Yorkshire League side Guiseley, Town's first defeat of the season had again come at the hands of Shamrocks. St.Blaize caused a league cup upset during the campaign, but by the time Blakeboroughs were defeated 3-0 late in the season, with goals from Kelly, Isherwood and former soccer camp player John Mitchell, the title was on its way to Utley again. The emerging Ovenden West Riding pipped Shamrocks for runners up spot and the Halifax side too gained promotion to the top flight. Town's reserves meanwhile came close to a league and cup double, but had to be content with runner-up spots instead, behind Salts in the league and Littletown in the league cup. At the season's end both Keighley sides forwarded applications for promotion to the premier division, but while Town were at last accepted, Shamrocks suffered a severe setback when the club's management withdrew them from the league. Luckily a fresh application from Shamrock's 'go-it-alone' players, led by Paul Smith, to rejoin the league was accepted, but any hopes Shamrocks had of joining Keighley Town in the top division were now gone.

The 1982-83 season – Town's third since their reformation – proved to be their most successful ever. Strengthening his side with players of the quality of John Dembickjy and Peter Thompson, Trevor Hockey saw his side trail favourites Dudley Hill Athletic early in the campaign. At the same time a useful County Cup run was being put together. Harrogate League side Knaresborough Town went down in a tight game to a rare Alan Hockey strike early in the competition, before local rivals Cyprane were defeated 4-0 in the third round. The fourth round brought Town a tie with reigning County Amateur champions Salts, but a hat-trick from Thompson saw a similar 4-0 scoreline for the new force in local football. Pudsey Amateurs put up a much stronger fight the following round. The Leeds side led 2-0 after only 18 minutes play and it was a hard route back for the locals. Derek Hobson pulled a goal back, before being sent off, and it took two late strikes from Dembickjy to see the locals through to the last eight. The quarter final draw brought Town in opposition with Eccleshill United. Following a 3-0 league victory over their rivals, a much closer cup game followed with Keith Lowe scoring the all important goal two minutes from time, setting up a crunch semi final with holders Armthorpe Welfare, who had swept all before them in the Doncaster Senior League since their reformation. Although Town failed to match the exploits of Keighley Central some fifteen years earlier, going down 0-3 in the tie at Ossett Town F.C, they were hardly disgraced against a side preparing for life in the Northern Counties East League (a league into which Eccleshill United followed them soon afterwards).

Chasing Glory

Despite going out of the County Cup, Keighley Town were still in with a chance of lifting the County Amateur League title. The side went top of the table late in December when Rawdon Old Boys were defeated 5-0, but unbeaten Dudley Hill were still proving difficult to overcome, coming back from two goals down late in the game to force a draw in a league game at Utley and then beating Town by a single goal in a league cup tie. (Prior to these two games Town had met – and lost 0-5 – in a return match under lights at Mossley.) However, the Bradford side's bubble burst and a league encounter between the leaders at East Bierley proved to be the title decider. With Athletic needing a win, they pressed hard in the early stages, kept out by a resolute Town defence. The deadlock was broken in the final ten minutes when the Keighley side scored twice, through a hotly disputed Isherwood penalty and Dembickjy clincher to take the premier title at the first attempt. It was no more than Keighley Town deserved, in a season that also saw them record a third successive District Cup final victory over Shamrocks. A torrential downpour actually caused the abandonment of the initial tie which was deadlocked at 1-1 following strikes from Bob Wellwood (Shamrocks) and Jeff Cummins (Town), the latter a diving header from Dembickjy's cross. The 'replay' ran to form as Shamrocks, who had finished just above half way in the County Amateur first division, went down to a double from Andy Isherwood, as they had done 12 months earlier.

THE GOAL THAT NEVER WAS !

Jeff Cummins equalises with a diving header for Keighley Town in the 1982-83 District Cup final at Marley against Shamrocks. Unfortunately the tie was later abandoned due to a torrential downpour and therefore Jeff's great finish did not count !

Hockey's Dream - Keighley Town '79

Not to be outdone, Keighley Town reserves also had a fine season, lifting the reserve division title for the first – and only – time, as well as their league cup for the second time in three seasons (they would lift the cup again the following year). The final could not have been closer, as following two goalless draws Town needed penalties to see off Crag Road United. The Keighley Supplementary Cup also found itself in the Town trophy cabinet during this time, Steeton reserves thrashed 8-1 in 1983 (Mitchell, 3) and then 4-2 a year later. The reserve side not only contained 'new blood' but many of the names associated with successful past Keighley sides.

The end of the 1982-83 season saw another charity match involving the top names in Keighley football. Leeds United All Stars – John Charles included – returned to Marley to defeat a Keighley select 5-4. The locals were represented by, among others, Bob Lee, Pete Turbitt, Trevor Storton, Alan Hockey, Mike and John Hellawell, John Fay, Bobby Ham and Stuart Woolley. The St.James' Kidney Machine Appeal was £700 richer for the players' efforts.

Keighley Town were certainly on a roll, but despite their reserve division league cup success at the end of the 1983-84 season no more silverware other than the District cup would come their way. Despite securing the use of Marley's centre field for home fixtures, the reserves staying at Utley, Trevor Hockey's 'dream' would gradually fade over the next few years. It did look as though the side would regain their County Amateur crown during the '83-84 campaign however as they led the table for the majority of the season, at one point six points clear of the chasing pack. Unfortunately Dudley Hill reversed their previous season's fortunes and ended the season with a great run that took them past both Town and Cleckheaton-based Littletown. Once again the end of season game between Town and Dudley Hill would prove the title decider, this time at Marley, although on an outside pitch due to the centre pitch being unavailable. In a bad tempered game on a field that was in severe need of mowing, Dudley Hill emerged victorious by 2 goals to 1 to leave the locals third in the table. To make matters worse, Dudley Hill took the league and cup double, Town defeated 4-2 in their first and only premier division cup final. Andy Isherwood scored the lone Town goal in the league defeat, Keith Lowe and Jimmy Bland in the cup final.

Confident of another good County Cup run, Keighley Town faced Leeds Red Triangle side Huddersfield Arms (nowadays known as Pudsey Liberals in the County Amateur League) in the second round of the 1983-84 competition. Unfortunately the underdogs had not read the script and produced the shock result of the round to win 1-0 and put an end to local hopes of success in the competition.

Chasing Glory

The Keighley & District Cup almost provided a shock when Paul Brearley scored twice to give Craven League Oxenhope a 2-1 lead on their sloping village rec pitch against Keighley Town. Town recovered to win 3-2 to face a semi final tie with Silsden. The new look Cobbydalers had returned to the County Amateur set up from the Craven League, and they too led 2-1 at one stage thanks to a double from Andy Geary. However, Jimmy Bland responded with two goals in five minutes to set up a fourth Town v Shamrocks final. The final itself was nowhere as close as the previous three, or as close as Town's previous two battles in that year's competition, as Shamrocks were easily beaten 4-0. Ironically, within a few years both sides would be out of Saturday football and in Town's case out of competitive football altogether.

The 1984-85 season saw Keighley Town joined by not only Silsden and Shamrocks, but also initially by Cyprane in the County Amateur League. Despite rising quickly through the Craven League's divisions, the newcomers failed to take their place in division 1A and disbanded without kicking a ball in their new surroundings. An indication of the falling interest at Town was the disbanding of the successful reserve side before the season began, although there were still high hopes among Hockeys men that the league championship could be regained. Unfortunately Dudley Hill were far and away the top team in the division, winning 2-0 at Marley early in September before Town held them to a goal-less draw late in the season. Although Town finished well up the premier division table, a major loss that season was their grip on the Keighley & District Cup. Perennial bridesmaids Shamrocks had already gone out to Craven League Oxenhope, when despite leading 2-1 at the interval they went down to second half goals from Barton and Dyson. Silsden were conquerors of Town. Riding high in the first division the Cobbydalers won with goals from Fretwell (back from a spell at Thackley) and Colin Guest (2, who would later join his brother Ernie at Launceston Juventus in Tasmania). Although Malcolm Hagyard converted a penalty for Town, it meant that they would fail to lift the cup for the first time since their reformation. Despite going a goal down just after half time, Silsden went on to beat Cross Hills by a similar 3-1 margin in the final with Houldsworth joining Fretwell and Guest on the scoresheet.

Although Silsden had by now become the first side to win both District Saturday and Sunday competitions in the same season (1-0 versus Magnet in the Sunday cup), promotion to the premier division of the County Amateur was denied them for just a little longer following their final position of third. This was in contrast to Shamrocks who struggled all season towards the foot of the table and subsequently resigned from the league, this time without revival. It was to be ten years before the name would again grace the County Amateur League, although the Shamrocks Sunday side, run separately from the town's Shamrocks Athletic

Hockey's Dream - Keighley Town '79

Association continued in the Keighley Alliance (The Athletic Association had run the Shamrocks Saturday side until the 'go-it-alone' by the players a couple of years previously), and a Highfield Shamrocks operated from the Burgess Field ground at Highfield in the West Yorkshire League during the 1986-87 season.

The 1985-86 season saw Keighley Town regain the District Cup, although they made no impression on the leaders of the County Amateur League. Reverting to the sky blue colours associated with Manchester City they went out of the County Cup to the relatively unknown Wakefield side Cricketers, but gained revenge on Silsden with a 1-0 victory in the semi final of the Keighley Cup courtesy of a Russ Newton strike. A resurgent Haworth were Town's opponents in the final, fresh from their victory over County Amateur newcomers Steeton in their semi, and it was they who took the lead when Gillson got on the end of a free kick from former Town player Keith Lowe. Jimmy Bland replied soon afterwards, before Jeff Cummins and future Guiseley boss Gordon Raynor sealed a 3-1 victory in extra time.

Silsden had Barrett, Geary and Guest in top form as they gained promotion from the County Amateur League's first division. They finished one better than the previous season, as runner-up to Junction (now better known as Wibsey) whose Horsfall Stadium centre pitch was deemed unacceptable for the premier division. Steeton, skippered by Mark Houfe, narrowly missed out on promotion from division 1A, finishing in third place behind future premier division champions V.A.W. Low Moor and Farsley Celtic's reserve side.

The 1986-87 season was the last in the premier division for Keighley Town, and also the last time two Keighley sides appeared in the top division of the league. Despite a relatively sound defensive record, Town lacked the scoring prowess that had brought them success years earlier, and finished at the foot of the twelve team division. The side began their campaign at the old Keighlians rugby ground at Thwaites, unable to use Lawkholme Lane as promised by that ground's impending sale, before a ground was railed off for them on one of Marley's outside pitches. Silsden meanwhile consolidated in mid table in their first season back in the top flight, while Steeton were joined in a renamed division 2 by Haworth. The newcomers made a bright start, thrashing Bowling Celtic 7-1 in September, but despite a late season 7-0 success against Steeton, who were struggling at the foot of the table, they missed out on promotion. While Silsden spent much of the season just behind the premier division leaders, Keighley Town spent their campaign anchored to the bottom. A frustrated Trevor Hockey claimed in the local press, "If business had backed me...I think Keighley could have had that (Northern) premier league side. It's still possible, all we need is financial support".

Chasing Glory

Things got worse, not only for Town but for everyone associated with football in Keighley, when in April 1987 Hockey died suddenly while training at Oakbank sports centre. It was a devastating blow for those connected with him, not least his wife and grown-up daughter. Hockey certainly had his friends and supporters and it was announced almost immediately that his dream of a top class side in Keighley would not die. Led by Geoff Busfield, plans were made to form a new club in town, based at the recently reprieved Lawkholme Lane ground of Keighley Rugby League club. Known as Keighley Borough, the new club's aim was to reach Northern Counties East League standard within five years. Despite being turned down by the West Yorkshire League, they were accepted by the County Amateur League and placed in division three.

At the end of the season a Keighley & District XI, consisting of players originally selected by Hockey to play a Halifax Town side earlier in the season (KO'd when safety officers gave it the thumbs down), played a Keighley Sunday Alliance XI to raise funds for the new Keighley Borough.

Unfortunately things turned sour. The new side disbanded on the eve of the new season due to a lack of support on and off the field, Busfield understandably aggrieved at the situation. It was left to the town's existing sides to lead the way, yet within eighteen months both Town and Silsden would be missing from the County Amateur ranks.

Silsden (District Cup runners up two years in succession to Cross Hills in 1987 & 88) finished the 1987-88 season second from bottom of the premier division, and losing Andy Geary for part of the season as he joined the Guest brothers in Tasmania. What was amazing was that they actually managed to avoid the wooden spoon, as their first league victory did not come until the end of April when Fields were thrashed 5-0. Keighley Town also struggled at the wrong end of the first division table, despite reporting a much stronger line up at the start of the season. Goals from Wellwood, Burrows, Smith and Dlambulo were enough to give them a seasons best 4-0 victory over Wrenthorpe but there was to be no respite for the club, which was now in terminal decline. The only highlight of the season as far as Keighley sides were concerned was the success of Steeton reserves, who won the reserve division title.

Keighley Town disbanded during the summer of 1988. In less than a decade they had scaled the heights of the County Amateur League and then fallen back to earth with a bump. The main problem had been a lack of younger talent coming through to support the ever enthusiastic aging players. The name of Keighley Town lived on a little longer though, with junior sides still operating in the local youth leagues.

Silsden's Saturday side did not last much longer. By Christmas 1988 they too had resigned from the County Amateur League. Anchored firmly at the foot of the premier division table they had already pulled their reserves out of their division, claiming also that a lack of youngsters coming through was the main cause of their demise. The club continued to operate their Sunday side, but it would be a few seasons before Silsden would re-emerge in Saturday football.

The 1988-89 season was not a complete disaster for local clubs as Steeton clinched promotion from the second division with a league and cup double. Both they and Haworth had run premier division sides Crag Road and Halifax Irish close in the County Cup, following excellent victories in the previous round. Haworth had won 1-0 thanks to a Richard Clarkson goal at Yeadon/Ventus, runners-up in the competition the previous season, while Steeton had come from 1-3 down to defeat Great Preston 6-3 after extra time. Following a close battle with Campion Tyke and Ardsley Celtic, Steeton went to the top of the league with a 1-0 victory over Green Lane in March, sealing the title with a 5-2 victory over the same opposition a month later. To cap a great season, the side went on to beat Campion in the league cup final. The first game finished goalless, but in the replay George Heggarty popped up in the first and last minutes to see Steeton emerge victorious by 2 goals to 1. Holders Cross Hills were also accounted for in the District Cup final thanks to another Heggarty goal, this time five minutes from the end. It was the first time in their long history that Steeton had ever won the Keighley & District Cup.

Steeton and Haworth continued to be Keighley's sole representatives for two more seasons in the County Amateur league, Steeton starting the 1989-90 season a section higher in division 1, where for a few seasons they more than held their own. The side finished well up the table in the final season of the decade, benefitting from the goalscoring talents of Dale Hoyle. Haworth made all the local headlines that season though, defeating Cross Hills to win the District Cup, thanks to a Richard Clarkson winner at Lawkholme Lane, and reaching their league cup final, divisional champions Campion proving far too strong to win 5-1. Steeton's strong second string had the consloation of a Keighley Supplementary Cup win, defeating Haworth 3-1 in the final.

Very soon though, the league would see a new force emerge from Keighley, a side that had spent it's early years competing in local youth and Sunday leagues.

Chasing Glory

KEIGHLEY TOWN '79

An early Town side pictured before a game at Shamrocks' Burgess Field ground at Highfield. The side featured many familiar names from past Silsden/D.S.G/ Central/Shamrocks sides - including Trevor & Alan Hockey, Pete Turbitt, Jeff Cummins, Ian Greenwood, Barney Maude & Jimmy Bland.

(14)
INTO THE 80's – Saturday & Sunday highlights

With Trevor Hockey igniting the spark that would revive interest in the game in the town in the early 1980's, Keighley's soccer teams saw a little more success than had been obtained the previous decade in the Craven League, the Sunday Alliance was able to stabilise and Keighley's young talent would again rise to the fore. Unfortunately it would not see an end to the discipline problems associated with the game locally as another club was to hit the headlines for the wrong reasons.

The 1980's began with at last a revival of the Keighley Charity Cup. Attempts had been made by the local F.A. to revive the oldest football competition in Keighley towards the end of the 1970's, but poor weather prevented the competition from going ahead during the 1978-79 season. The famous trophy had originally been competed for under Rugby rules until revived as a soccer competition in 1904 (a full history of this competition is covered in Chasing Glory, volume 1). Following the second world war, it had become a local dominoes trophy and had then been passed on to the Craven Cricket League, who awarded it to the league championship runners up, at that time Pendle Forest C.C. Led by President Jack Fortune, the local F.A. had the trophy returned to them, although missing was the footballer statuette from the top. This was found early in 1980 in a pile of dominoes trophies, slightly damaged but nevertheless able to be reunited with the rest of the Charity Cup!

Ten sides, from both the Saturday and Sunday game, were invited to take part in the revived competition at the start of the 1979-80 campaign, Sunday side Silsden making light work of defeating Craven League United Lifts, thanks mainly to a hat-trick from Andy Isherwood, and Skipton Town defeating Steeton in a much closer game by a single goal. Other sides taking part were; Lifts 'B', Keighley News, Skipton B.R, Skipton Bulldogs, Salts, Magnet and Shamrocks. However, due to problems in arranging fixtures the competition was temporarily halted until the end of the season, and during the intervening period Tommy Holmes scrap metal merchants stepped in to sponsor the competition. Once fixtures had resumed it was Magnet and Shamrocks who made their way to the final, the Sunday side emerging victorious at Lawkholme Lane by 3 goals to 1. In front of a crowd of around 300 (pre war finals attracted a gate ten times bigger!), Lupton, Newton and Hobson struck for Magnet, with a long range effort from Jimmy Caulfield in reply. The competition raised £250 for the Airedale Hospital Body Scanner Appeal.

Magnet, with several new faces in their line up, had a poor first season by their standards in the Wharfedale Sunday League. Their season opened with Dickie Lupton on the mark in a 1-0 success against Silsden, the losers having two goals from Whittaker and Barrett disallowed, and top place being achieved in the league. Silsden gained revenge though with a 3-1 league cup success, followed by a 2-1 victory in the league, Andy Isherwood doing the damage in both games. Pudsey side Railway Athletic put Magnet out of the County Cup and no progress at all was made in the English Sunday Cup. This was because the competition had new rules which prevented council pitches, such as the Marley centre pitch, being used. This meant that there was now no suitable ground on which to play matches in this competition! Despite being beaten by Magnet early in December it was fellow newcomers Woodend Rangers from Shipley who took the Wharfedale title, four points ahead of the Keighley side (Woodend did a 'Silsden' at the presentation evening and got themselves thrown out of the league!). Magnet were left with only the Keighley Sunday Cup to add to their Charity Cup success, defeating Angel 2-0 in the final, although it had taken a Derek Hobson header in extra time to dispose of fellow Wharfedale Premier side Volts in the semi final.

1980 saw the arrival of new Magnet boss Tommy Lyness. Tommy had been manager of Keighley All-Stars, who in the late 70's and early 80's had played friendly fixtures around the country as well as locally. Losing only twice in five seasons (including once to Steeton), the side's most emphatic victory was a 16-0 rout of Beach Bar (Blackpool). Included in their line up was Stuart Woolley, who was still regularly bagging the goals.

The 1980-81 season saw Magnet again runners up in the Wharfedale League, this time on goal difference behind Ventus United, who also defeated them 4-1 in the league cup final. The side were incensed at losing the title in such manner as they had three matches, against struggling Westbrook (twice) and Skipton B.R. postponed, and although awarded the points missed the opportunity to improve their goal difference. As consolation, the Keighley Sunday Cup was won for the ninth time when fellow Wharfedale premier side Silsden were defeated in a replay, but undoubtably Magnet's greatest achievement of the season was their record breaking third appearance in the County Sunday Cup final. Following easy victories over Owlet Hall and Allerton in early rounds, a strong Elland Athletic were defeated in a second replay in round 4, this followed by a narrow 1-0 success against Bolton Woods (third round conquerors of Silsden White Star). A 2-1 victory over Huddersfield Sunday League side Junction then set up a semi final against Leeds side Corpus Christie, which

Into The 80's

was again won, this time much more easily by 5 goals to one. Magnet unfortunately lost the final 0-2 to another Leeds side, Aireville, but the Keighley side had proved that they were still as strong as ever despite failing to capture a league title for the past two seasons.

The following season at last saw the Wharfedale League title lifted. Despite an early setback against Ventus, Magnet not only finished eight points clear of the chasing pack but defeated Silsden White Star in the finals of both Wharfedale League cup and Keighley Sunday Cup competitions. The latter competition saw White Star lead for all of 15 seconds until a double strike from Derek Hobson ensured that the trophy would remain firmly in the hands of the Marley based side. It would be eight years before Magnet would win the Keighley Sunday Cup again following their 2-1 success on this occasion, and was White Star's last before their demise just a year later.

White Star had made a miserable start to the season, losing their first four league games. The tide was turned when the previous season's leading scorer Graeme Fretwell re-signed for the club, along with Andy Isherwood who had played just four games for Magnet.

Magnet's 1982-83 Wharfedale campaign brought another league and cup double, although the championship was a closely run thing with the ever improving Bolton Woods. Woods defeated Magnet 4-1 early in the season but the champions bounced back to win 2-0 at the end of January, before clinching the title with a 6-0 thrashing of White Star. White Star again made it to the league cup final, but this time Baildon Athletic deprived them of success with a 3-1 victory. The real shock of the season however was Magnet's shock defeat to the other Silsden side, Silsden F.C, in the final of the Keighley Sunday Cup. Following a hard fought victory over the emerging Bradleys, the Crossflatts based side that had chosen to affiliate with the Keighley F.A. and who had several Keighley faces in their side, in the semi final. Magnet were expected to have few problems with a side that had finished perilously close to the bottom of Wharfedale's premier division for the past three seasons. Despite an early strike from Hockey, a missed penalty saw Silsden gain the initiative in the game and they hit back with goals from Mark Whittaker and Colin Gust, the second just three minutes from time. For the first time, Magnet had failed to lift the Keighley Sunday Cup.

Supremo Tommy Lyness was also frustrated in his attempts to see Magnet win the County Sunday cup again. Glasshoughton defeated the locals 2-0 in the 1981-82 season, Leeds based Corpus Christi winning by the same score a year later, following Magnet victories over top Bradford sides Allerton and East Bowling Unity.

In Magnet's absence, the 1979-80 Keighley Sunday Alliance season was a race to the wire, with Keighley Grinders, New Grapes (formerly

Burlington) and Timothy Taylors (returning from the Wharfedale League) pulling away from the rest early on. Grapes were the only unbeaten side by December, and with Wellwood and Semenec regularly on target looked slight favourites. By the end of the season though, Grinders pipped their rivals to take their second championship in three seasons, with Taylors dropping off after Christmas to take third place. Grinders also took the league cup with a 4-1 defeat of improving Settle United in the final, but the Ribblesdale side returned to defeat Volts 3-1 in the Jeff Hall Trophy final.

Despite the temporary absence of a Saturday side in the village, Silsden could at one time boast SIX Sunday sides. Silsden and Silsden White Star each operated three sides during the 1979-80 season, including one each in the Keighley Alliance. White Star were on a roll, finishing runners-up in the Wharfedale second division following their fourth division success the previous year. They also ran Silsden close in a Keighley Cup tie, going down 4-3 in a cracking game. The only blot on what was a fine season for football in the village was a fire in the pavilion at Silsden playing fields, used by White Star and the Silsden Rugby League club. Ironically, Marley's cricket pavilion, latterly used by Brontë Ladies, was completely destroyed by fire earlier in the season. One year later White Star took the league's first division and thus completed a remarkable rise through the Wharfedale League through to the premier division.

The 1980-81 Keighley Alliance season saw Bradford side Robin Hood take the championship following a close battle with Grapes. They also won the Jeff Hall Trophy with a 1-0 defeat of Timothy Taylors in the final, although it was Taylors who took the league cup when, following victory over the new champions they defeated former champs Grinders 2-1 in the deciding game. Grinders had a poor season overall and finished well down the table, although they experienced far better fortunes than new club Pak Kashmir. The predominantly Asian side were on the end of some real hammerings during the season, not least 0-23 and 0-31 thrashings by Robin Hood and Grapes, yet still managed to finish just above Wells United at the foot of the table.

Robin Hood, who had entered the Keighley Alliance following their failure to register with the Bradford Sunday League on time in 1980, moved back to their intended league for the 1981-82 campaign. Among new faces in the alliance were Phoenix, formerly known as Greenhead Youth Centre, who would enjoy a great deal of success throughout the years, and re-entrants Juventus. The Italian side, who originally played as A.C.Alassio – reflecting the name of the coffee bar they used as headquarters – were late replacements for Grapes, who had originally changed their name to Commercial but had subsequently disbanded.

There was no stopping Timothy Taylors this season. With the likes of Jeff Cummins, Andy Gaughan and Richard Snowden in their ranks the

Into The 80's

side won the title with ease, dropping not a single point in their eighteen league fixtures. There were some high scoring victories along the way, 12-0 against Juventus and 11-0 against Keighley News among those. Jimmy Bland and Roger Nelson both hit hat-tricks in a 7-1 defeat of News in the league cup final, although league runners up Skipton B.R, who had switched from the Wharfedale League, surprised them with a 2-1 victory in the Jeff Hall Trophy. The same side almost knocked Taylors out of the league cup, leading their semi final with only seconds remaining before going down 2-3 in extra time. The final of the Jeff Hall Trophy matched Keighley News with Phoenix, who had started the season at the foot of the ten team league but who had since made great strides. Phoenix surprisingly took the trophy in their first season, and would become only the third side behind D.S&G and Magnet to win the competition three times in succession over the next two seasons. Magnet themselves had proved who was still the top Sunday team in Keighley when they defeated Taylors 4-2 in a Keighley Cup tie.

What was encouraging to see during the 1981-82 Alliance season was that, in response to the league's new fair play trophy, only three of the ten member clubs had players sent off, while four clubs had not so much as a booking marked against them. Another fine record was that of league president Jack Holmes, who was granted life membership of the Alliance at the end of the season in recognition of his fifteen years tireless and devoted service. The league's fair play trophy was actually named "The Jack Holmes Fair Play Trophy' in honour of one of Keighley's finest servants to the game.

The 1982-83 season saw Timothy Taylors successfully defend their title, although several of their top stars had moved on and they did it without a 100% record. The top four positions in the first division were in fact identical to the previous year – Skipton B.R. runners up, Keighley West Yorkshire 3rd and Keighley News 4th. For the first time in eight years the league were able to operate two divisions, with Shoulder, thanks to the continued goalscoring exploits of Stuart Woolley, taking the second division championship ahead of Juventus and Parkwood United (formerly Broom). Shoulder were actually assured of promotion by the end of January, Woolley hitting no less than ten of their goals in a 24-0 rout of Victoria Hotel!

On their way to a second Jeff Hall Trophy success, Phoenix surprised Taylors with a 2-1 victory. Malcolm Cobb scored a late winner for the improving side, and it was the same player who scored the only goal of the final against Cullingworth Sports.

While the East Lancashire domination continued in the Craven League, Cross Hills retained the Keighley & District Cup at the end of the 1979-80 season with a 2-0 defeat of County Amateur side Shamrocks. Cowling made the headlines for the first time in several seasons when, during a Craven league cup tie at Mansfield, a Dale Tyson shot was cleared off the line by a spectator!

Twelve months later, Cononley Sports came within a whisker of their first Craven title when they forced a play off with Trawden for the premier division championship. The sides were neck and neck at the top of the table for most of the season, the Lancashire side winning the deciding game before moving into the new East Lancashire League, which had been in the pipeline for a number of years. For Cononley it was a second successive runners up spot; they had finished three points behind Trawden the previous season. Cross Hills meanwhile reached the last 32 of the County Cup for the first time, before going down 1-4 to Pudsey Amateurs, Dave French scoring their consolation. Spare a thought for Cononley's young Craven Minor team though. They struggled all year and suffered several heavy defeats, not least 0-25 & 0-24 drubbings to Barrowford and Bingley Juniors respectively.

Sunday sides Reservoir Sports and Green Gables applied unsuccessfully to join the Craven League for the 1981-82 season. It was argued that their presence could lead to established clubs such as Lothersdale and Haworth losing their grounds at Marley to the new sides, a lack of suitable grounds in these villages as well as the limit to the number of teams that could play at Marley being the key argument. Cononley were again to the fore this season, along with Steeton and Silsden, but again the local sides were deprived at the death, this time by Barrowford United, who pipped the Cobbydalers on goal difference for the title. Steeton finished a further two points behind in third place. Silsden did have the consolation of lifting the Craven League cup, defeating Oxenhope 3-0 in a replay with goals from Mick Tillotson (2) and Dale Tyson. It was hard luck on the losers, who had led the original tie 2-1 before a last gasp Silsden equaliser.

Silsden lost a number of their players to Steeton during the summer of 1982, and not surprisingly it was the Summerhill Lane side's turn to finish as runners up in the league at the end of the 82-83 season. In Barrowford's absence, a resurgent Gargrave took the honours, dropping only three points all season (a feat they would repeat the following season). Despite the continued lack of success in the league's premier division, Keighley sides were making progress in the lower divisions. Cyprane took the 1982-83 first division title only a year after winning the second division, while improving Haworth took the second division title themselves in 1983.

Success continued for Brontë Ladies, winning the 7-a-side ARCO cup competition at Hull during the 1979-80 season. Three times Lancashire champions St.Helens were defeated 2-1 in the final, Pauline King and Lorraine Kelly each hitting four of the 14 they scored during the

Into The 80's

competition. Later in the season there were four Brontë players in the North West/Lancashire representative side against the North East, while Eileen Lillyman became the side's first ever international, selected for the England Women's team against Holland. Brontë's first and second teams then finished as runners up in their respective Lancashire League divisions during the 1980-81 season.

The following season saw the North West Ladies league cup won by Brontë, when Clare Taylor hit a hat-trick in a 3-1 victory over their great rivals Preston North End in the final. Even their goalkeeper Debbie Smith made the scoresheet this season, during a 7-1 success against Ingol Belles. Two years after winning an invitation tournament in Benidorm, the side returned to Spain towards the end of the 1981-82 season, defeating top Majorcan sides Atletico Vivero 6-0 and Santa Maria 4-0. Julie Lister led the Brontë scorers with a brace in each game.

Keighley had six boys in the West Yorkshire schools team that defeated Derby 3-0 in the 1979-80 season, including goalkeeper Andy Beer, who for a while was on the books of Leeds United. The same year saw the under 15's side go down to Rotherham in the South Yorkshire Shield final. South Craven meanwhile became the first local school to enjoy a run in the English schools under 19's cup, drawing 1-1 with Roundhay in the final of the West Yorkshire regional competition. Other youngsters were also doing well, 18 year old Ernie Guest of Steeton playing for Launceston F.C. in Tasmania, (his brothers Steve and Colin also spent time with Bury) while Keith Bailey, also 18, who had been released by Bradford City and spent time in the reserve and 'A' sides at Oldham Athletic and Halifax Town, was suddenly thrust in front of 55,000 crowds playing for Tampa Bay Rowdies in the North American League.

In addition, young goalkeeper Sean McNulty, a regular at Trevor Hockey's soccer camp, had trials with Wolves, featuring in a Midland Intermediate League match against West Bromwich Albion during the 1980-81 season.

Unfortunately Keighley Minors could not add to their success of 1980 during this time. The Keighley Minor League itself was having problems attracting clubs and by the 1982-83 season had merged with the Craven Minor League before going into hibernation. A relatively new junior club, Sutton Rovers, meanwhile, had attracted some useful players – not least one Lee Duxbury, who was regularly on the scoresheet, including six in one game against Embsay.

Chasing Glory

One of the first ever Greenhead Youth Club sides, photographed in May 1976. At that time they played in the junior section of the Wharfedale Sunday League.

THE KEIGHLEY CHARITY CUP (Below)
The famous old trophy, first competed for under rugby rules at the end of the 1800's and subsequently played as a soccer competition until the second world war, was again competed for during the early 1980's.

GREENHEAD YOUTH CLUB 1981
Winners of the N.A.Y.C. North Eastern Regional 5-a-side championships at Cleckheaton.
BACK: Philip Wood, Dale Parnham, Mike Breeze, John Nixon,
FRONT: Darren Whitaker, Paul Smith & Dale Scott.

(15)
THE MID AND LATE 80's –
Saturday & Sunday Highlights

The 1983-84 season was marred by the last minute withdrawals of several Keighley sides from their respective leagues. Keighley Lifts surprisingly pulled out of the Craven League at the eleventh hour, Mick Holmes unable to run the club single handedly (although they would return to the league by the end of the decade). In the Sunday game, Silentnight were unable to attract sufficient players to take their place in the Keighley Alliance second division, those that were on their books joining Shoulder in the first division. But by far the biggest shock was the disbanding of Silsden White Star. Secretary David Hird made the sad decision to withdraw his Wharfedale premier division side from the league with "great, great regret and disappointment", citing financial problems for their demise and having had to dig into his own pocket, as many club officials seem to be forced to do to keep their sides afloat, once too many times. White Star's reserve team, run separately from a Silsden pub, did continue in the Wharfedale Triangle although they changed their name the following summer.

    Once the season was underway, the Keighley Sunday Alliance was rocked by the resignation of newcomers Rodney, the pub side that had just entered two teams in the league. Trevor Hockey had recently been installed as licensee there, only yards from the Keighley Town offices near Church Green, and had persuaded Otley Town (& ex -Daleside) boss Brett Farraday to run the Rodney sides. In exchange Hockey agreed to spend one evening a week coaching at Otley, who were then in the premier division of the West Yorkshire League. For whatever reason this obviously did not work out because by Christmas 1983 Rodney had resigned from both divisions, despite their first team being championship contenders, Hockey claiming that he had no-one to run the sides. There was to be no reprieve for sides, particularly as Hockey soon left his job at the pub.

    Those sides that did complete the Alliance season saw Skipton British Rail take the title, following two successive runner-up positions behind Timothy Taylors since switching from the Wharfedale League. Juventus were also in contention early in the season. They were benefiting from the occasional presence of Andy Gaughan and Keith Lowe in their side, the players turning out for Keighley Town on a Saturday, Magnet on a Sunday morning, and whenever possible Juventus the same afternoon –

Lowe scoring four times for Juventus in a dramatic 6-5 victory over the eventual champions before Christmas!

The Skipton side also won their league cup competition, defeating Keighley News (who actually beat them twice in the league) 4-3 in the final. They were denied a treble when a double strike from Ian Brett gave Phoenix a treble of their own – a third successive Jeff Hall final victory.

The 1984-85 Keighley Alliance season was again closely contested by the leading clubs, with Highfield (formerly Timothy Taylors) winning the title for the third time in four years. Following a 2-1 victory over holders Skipton B.R. in December the side never looked back and sealed the championship when they came from behind to defeat runners up Keighley News 4-1 in the closing weeks of the season, thanks to goals from Milner (2), Rickaby and Done. Brontë Lifts put their troubles behind them to finish a fine fourth in the first division. Previously known as Snooker Centre, their existence was put in doubt when the sports club closed down, until they were able to find a new firm to back them. Incidentally, the name of Keighley Lifts was revived for this season in division two, the same division seeing a new Timothy Taylors (run from the pub of the same name) in operation.

The first division league cup meanwhile was won by Keighley News, who defeated Highfield 2-1 in the final, while second division runners up Green Gables lifted the Jeff Hall trophy, defeating News by the same score.

By now there were two local sides in the Wharfedale Triangle. Alongside Airedale Hospital, who had switched from the Wharfedale League, were Silsden Town – in effect the renamed White Star reserve side. This side were to take off in a big way very soon.

In a season when Keighley F.A. officials Jack Holmes and Jack Fortune were again honoured for their long service (Fortune being honoured by the national F.A. a year later for 50 years' hard work!), the 20 or so soccer and amateur rugby league clubs that regularly used Marley were devastated when the wooden changing pavilion was completely gutted by fire. Although plans were by now well underway to remove Marley's famous centre pitch and surrounding running track to make way for the much delayed and revised new trunk road, the changing rooms were to be left as they were and therefore had to be rebuilt quickly by Bradford Council. In the meantime, the clubs were forced to make alternative arrangements for changing and showering.

Highfield again swept to the 1985-86 title. As they had done the previous season they lost once, early in the season (to Keighley News), before an unbeaten sequence assured them of top spot again. They also won the first division cup, while Keighley News at last won a trophy when second division champions Campion Bell Dean were thrashed 6-2

The Mid And Late 80's

in the Jeff Hall final. I.S.Calder enjoyed an improved season following their merger with Raiseprint, who had originally intended fielding their own side under the new banner of Kings Arms.

Back in the Wharfedale League, Magnet failed to recapture the 1983-84 title despite coming from a goal down to defeat eventual champions Bolton Woods 5-1 in March. Bland, twice, and Isherwood were on the mark as Ilkley Dynamo were defeated 3-0 in the league cup final. Silsden were beaten 1-0 in the semi final, but it was the Silsden side who ended Magnet's title aspirations with a 2-1 success late in the season. The same week saw Bradley's end their jinx by defeating Magnet 2-0 in the semi final of the Keighley Sunday Cup, the Crossflatts side having lost at the same stage to the same opponents for the previous three seasons. They went on to win the final with a 3-1 victory over Silsden thanks to goals from Micky Collins (2) and Mick Starr.

Although Magnet failed to recapture the County Sunday Cup again, going out to Leeds based Spring Close, they achieved one of their biggest ever victories in an earlier round when a poor Adelphi side from Bradford were routed 21-2! Nine players got on the scoresheet, including Keith Lowe who grabbed five and Andy Gaughan with four. During the season, foreman Bob Taylor was honoured by the club for his tireless work over the past 20 years with Magnet, Silsden and Keighley Town.

The 1984-85 season saw Magnet complete their fixtures without a trophy, something that had not happened before. They were pipped by Baildon Athletic for the league title on goal difference, although the new champions did have several Keighley based players, such as Ian Greenwood, in their line up. Magnet, who fielded Stan Natynczyk who was back following several years playing semi professional football in New Zealand, and ex Blackburn Rovers centre half Andrew Lodge during the season, also lost out in the Keighley Sunday Cup final to a single goal from Silsden's Andy Geary, Silsden themselves enjoying their best season for many years in the Wharfedale League. There was an unlucky K.O. in the County Sunday Cup for Magnet when they fielded a player who, unknown to them, was still under county suspension for failing to pay a fine accrued with another club.

The 1985-86 season proved much more successful for Magnet as they enjoyed a league and cup double as well as a good run in the County Cup. They stood only fourth in the league table by Christmas, but with games in hand were able to rise to the top ahead of Bolton Woods. Baildon Athletic were defeated 2-1 in the league cup final at Otley, Bland and Kilner scoring the decisive goals, while the last quarter final stage of the County Cup was reached following victories over Craven Heifer, 5-0 (0-0 at half time), and New Pellon (Halifax) 1-0. Eventual winners, Hunslet's Goodman Tavern, proved too strong in the last eight, winning 2-1 despite a Jeff

Cummins strike for the locals. Magnet failed to land the Keighley Sunday Cup when Alliance champions Highfield surprised them with a 3-1 victory, Bradleys eventually winning the competition for a second and final time with goals from Wood (3) and Conroy (2) in a 5 goal rout of Silsden Town in the final. Magnet's fellow Keighley sides in the Wharfedale premier division fared badly, Silsden unable to capitalise on a fine season the year before suffered relegation, while newcomers Royal themselves just escaped the drop.

Keighley Alliance champions Highfield, along with Druids, joined the Wharfedale League for the 1986-87 season, but were placed only in division three of their new league. It was obvious from the start they were misplaced as the sides battled it out for the divisional title between themselves way ahead of the chasing pack. From their 20 league fixtures, Druids led the way, winning nineteen and drawing one, with Highfield runners up just five points behind – fifteen ahead of third placed Busfeild Arms, the Morton side themselves enjoying one of their best seasons. A sign of Druid's strength was their 6-4 replay defeat of holders Bradleys in that seasons Keighley Sunday Cup. Bradleys had all sorts of problems by then and resigned from the league later in the season, less than a year after their finest season. Highfield and Druids earned themselves a 'double' promotion for their efforts, but neither side was able to make inroads on the leaders in the first division the following year.

In Highfield's absence, the Keighley Alliance was no longer dominated by one club. Keighley News were unbeaten champions by the end of the 1986-87 season ahead of a new Green Gables (the new name for Shoulder, the 'old' Gables disbanding). News defeated Gables 3-0 in a key game at the end of November through goals from Gaines, Ross and Ettenfield, but their opponents gained revenge in the league cup final when they won with a brace of goals from Richard Huck. The same season saw an Alliance representative side, the first since the 1970's, defeat their Harrogate counterparts, Huck again on the scoresheet with the only goal of the game. Cullingworth were champions the following season after a late run took them clear of the previous season's champions, with Green Gables coming from behind to defeat improving Shamrocks 2-1 in the Jeff Hall Trophy final.

Beeches took the 1988-89 Alliance title after Parkwood United had looked home and dry. United had an eleven point lead at the top of the table before losing two key games at the death, allowing their opponents to win their games in hand and claim the title. Beeches also had a side in the Wharfedale Sunday League at that time, but despite a moderately successful 1987-88 campaign they languished at the foot of the first division the following year, obviously fielding their better side in the Keighley League, which by now had recovered from its dark days of the late 70's

The Mid And Late 80's

and early 80's. With Paul Ettenfield, Roy Mason and Steve Kernan regularly on the scoresheet, Beeches richly deserved their title success, although they failed to lift the Jeff Hall Trophy, Shamrocks gaining a revenge victory over Green Gables in this year's final.

Red Pig, containing many familiar Gables faces, took the 1989-90 Alliance championship, just ahead of Beeches and Shamrocks, Beeches defeating Sandy Lane 3-2 in the Jeff Hall final as consolation for losing their title. The title was not decided until the final stages of the season, Red Pig defeating Beeches 1-0 in a key game before wrapping things up with a 7-0 defeat of Sandy Lane. The first point Red Pig dropped was in a delayed game against Knowle Arms in February. The match was held up for fifteen minutes when the match referee was inadvertently locked in the changing room!

Despite the increased status among local sides of the Keighley Sunday Alliance, the top sides in the area still preferred the Wharfedale League. Not since the 1978-79 season, when Magnet defeated Silsden, had an Alliance side won the Keighley Sunday Cup, every one of the competition's finals since then featuring Wharfedale League sides – with one exception. That exception was Silsden Town, who were to become only the second side after Magnet to win the competition three years in a row. As the strength of the Wharfedale Triangle grew, so did the reputation of Town, who featured the evergreen Andy Isherwood in attack. Having been soundly thrashed by Bradleys the year before, the Silsden side (who after sharing players with neighbouring Silsden F.C.) were far tighter in defence for the 1986-87 final against Magnet. They had enjoyed a memorable season in the Wharfedale Triangle while Magnet had become the first side to reach four County Sunday Cup finals. It was Andy Geary who was the difference between the sides, scoring twice in a 2-1 victory for the new holders of the trophy. Magnet also lost their league cup final, 0-3 to champions Bolton Woods, but their highlight was that County Cup run. The locals reached the last 16 stage with a 3-0 victory over Wibsey United in a delayed fourth round tie, before overcoming the cup favourites Torre Social 2-1, with goals from Jimmy Bland and Darren Whittaker. Spring Close were Magnet's quarter final opponents, but their was to be no repeat of the previous result between these sides as the Keighley side emerged victorious with another Whittaker goal, in extra time. Huddersfield side Junction were Magnet's victims in the semi final, edging the tie 2-1, but the competition had re-established Magnet among the best in the county again.

Silsden Town retained the Keighley Sunday Cup in the 1987-88 season when Black Horse went down to a late Kevin Whittaker penalty, the final score 2-1. Town had needed extra time to defeat Beeches in the semi final, and were again pushed all the way by Black Horse in the final.

Chasing Glory

The beaten finalists had changed their name from Royal at the start of the previous season and had actually just been pipped by Bolton Woods for the Wharfedale title on goal difference, despite defeating the Bradford side 3-1 in their final game and despite, officially, going through the season unbeaten. (Their one defeat at the hands of Baildon Town being annulled). Woods defeated Beeches in the league cup final, while Horse had the consolation of lifting the league's Vera Cookson trophy when they beat Stanley Road 1-0 in the final, Eddie Dlambulo scoring the decisive goal. Magnet, the only other side to defeat Bolton Woods in the league that season, had actually led the table early in the season. Now known as Airedale Magnet, reflecting the dual sponsorship of Magnet and the Airedale Shopping Centre, they were also involved in several close games with Black Horse during the season. Horse won a league encounter 1-0, Magnet gained revenge with a 1-0 league cup victory, before Horse again won 1-0 in the Keighley Cup thanks to a strike from Wellwood two minutes from time.

    The 1988-89 season saw a repeat final in the Keighley Sunday Cup between Silsden Town and Black Horse. Town won again, 2-0, against a side that had failed to scale the heights of their previous campaign. A Lund penalty and Tyson screamer at Lawkholme lane were enough to bring Town their third and final success in the competition. Magnet too endured a poor season by their standards, they never looked like living with the league leaders and lost 1-5 to Black Horse early in the season. Torre Social put paid to their County Cup hopes too. Although Horse won the league's Russell Stone Merchants cup final against Baildon Athletic, the tie proved to be the last for both sides in the Wharfedale League. They left under a cloud following a bad tempered final which was at one point delayed for 25 minutes following a poor 'tackle' that hospitalised Black Horse's Andy Gaughan. With the sponsors threatening to withdraw their backing of the league, both sides moved on to the Wharfedale Triangle, in the case of the Keighley side under a new name, that of Keighley Star.

    The 1989-90 season saw Magnet's name back on the Keighley Sunday Cup. They defeated Silsden Town 5-1 in the semi final (Geary 3) before an equally impressive 4-1 victory over Keighley Star in the final. Grapes and Silsden enjoyed fine seasons in the Wharfedale League, although Magnet were in mid table for most of the campaign with matches in hand due to their cup committments. As they caught up on their matches it looked as if the league title would again be won, until things went wrong in the final weeks of the season. Stanley Road defeated the side 2-1 in the Russell Stone final, and then when Magnet needed only a draw to win the championship the same team defeated them again to win it themselves!

    Another good County Sunday Cup run was enjoyed by Magnet. A strong Sun Inn from Lightcliffe were defeated 3-1 in an early round before

The Mid And Late 80's

Beechwood Santos, who had none other than Terry Yorath on their books, were defeated 2-1 in extra time courtesy of a Kev Bailey goal. Unfortunately Castleford side Prince of Wales put paid to local hopes in the quarter final with a converted penalty winner in extra time. The season did see a return to the national Sunday cup for Magnet, although a first round defeat to Liverpool side Nicosia meant that no progress was made. Due to the lack of a suitable ground in Keighley, a situation made worse by the digging up of the Marley centre pitch, home games in this competition for Magnet would in future have to take place at over ten miles away at Gargrave.

On the Saturday scene, Gargrave again ran away with the Craven title in the 1983-84 season, again leaving Steeton, who also lost the league cup final, as runners-up. Haworth meanwhile continued their resurgence by emulating Cyprane's record of successive titles in divisions 1 and 2. It looked as if Haworth, under the management of Paul McLoughlin, would actually win their third successive title when they led the Craven premier division going into the final weeks of the 1984-85 campaign. They needed only one win in their final three games to finish ahead of Gargrave and Barnoldswick United but could only manage a solitary draw. It was Cononley who spoiled the Haworth club's dreams in the final match of the season. Still smarting from a league cup final defeat against the title hopefuls only four days earlier, the mid table side won 3-1 to leave Barnoldswick champions and Haworth in third place.

Local sides were at least finding Craven League silverware a little easier to come by following several lean years, even if the premier division title still proved elusive. Steeton defeated Cross Hills in the final of the the new T.A.P. trophy before moving on to the County Amateur League, while Airedale Heifer (formerly Great Northern & Three Horses) saw their first and second team win both division 2 and 3 titles in the same season, despite the reserves later being axed due to a shortage of players. Newcomers Grafton Garage, formed by those involved with Wharfedale Sunday side Royal (later Black Horse/Keighley Star) who wanted to play together on a Saturday, took the first division title – but they were attracting attention for all the wrong reasons. They went through the season with an appalling record of indiscipline, including a bad tempered league cup final against Bingley Juniors and were described as 'animals' by their opponents Rolls Royce following a bruising early season encounter. Things were to get worse in the next twelve months as the side attempted to establish themselves in the league's premier division. Despite finishing well up the table in the 1985-86 season the league were rapidly losing patience with them, and following disgraceful scenes at the end of their T.A.P trophy final with Skipton Town, a game they lost after giving away a two goal lead, when they begrudgingly accepted their medals, the league and its member clubs took action. In what was an unprecedented move by the

Chasing Glory

Craven League, Grafton were expelled following a vote by its membership. Over 85% of those clubs that voted said that they did not want Grafton in their league. Dave Trolley's men now had to find somewhere else to play football.

On a much brighter note, despite Colne United pipping Haworth for the Craven title and some clubs having to endure a 13 week break due to the poor winter weather, Cross Hills won the league cup with an emphatic 5-1 victory over Cowling, who despite finishing well down the league accounted for Haworth and Grafton in earlier rounds. Reape, Isherwood (2 each) and Booth sealed victory for the side that was on the verge of becoming the major force in the Craven League.

Another local side during the mid 1980's were Grapes, who competed briefly in the Bradford Red Triangle. Their debut in the 1985-86 season saw them finish as champions, just ahead of Holme Wood in division two. The side enjoyed several fine victories – the pick of the bunch being against Southfield 10-2 (Dale Seddon, 4), Black Dyke Stags 10-0 (Seddon another 4) and Thornaby 10-0 (Steve Duff 5). The following season saw Grapes joined by Grafton in the Red Triangle, with Highfield Shamrocks spending their one and only season in division four of the West Yorkshire League alongside several of the reserve sides of well established clubs.

As the 1987-88 season opened, only Grafton remained of the three. They changed their name to Eastwood Sports during the summer, Trevor Hockey intending to introduce a side to their Eastwood Tavern base himself before his untimely death. The Eastwood side, with a much changed line-up from that which had caused so much controversy, made a name for themselves for their standard of football during the 1988-89 season, finishing as runners up in the Red Triangle's top division behind Pile Bar. They were narrowly defeated by a single Cross Hills goal in the semi final of the Keighley & District Cup, but later went on to win their league's supplementary cup competition with a fine 3-2 victory over Druids (Bradford), Steve Duff netting the winner with just seven minutes remaining. By now the side was based at the Volunteers Arms, and intended changing their name to Keighley Volunteers Sports the following season. As it happened, they re-emerged as Rodney (no connection with Trevor Hockey's former team) for the 1989-90 campaign, enjoying another successful season in runners-up position behind Shipley Rangers.

Back in the Craven League, Cross Hills at last ended the jinx preventing local sides from winning the Craven League title. Fourteen years had passed since Cross Hills themselves had become the last local side to win the title, this time they made sure that their name would not be forgotten as they embarked on a run that would bring them five league titles in six seasons before embarking on pastures new in the 1990's.

The Mid And Late 80's

The first of Cross Hills' title successes came during the 1986-87 season. They and a rejuvenated Cowling were first to show alongside champions Colne United (Cowling's reserve side made the headlines when they demolished Grassington reserves 19-0, 13 coming in the second half, with Nigel Sellars leading the way with 6). By April, however, the champions elect had a ten point lead at the top of the table, Colne needing to win their games in hand to seriously challenge for the title. Relegated Cononley Sports again put paid to the hopes of title aspirants, holding Colne to a 2-2 draw late in the season to ensure that the championship went to Cross Hills. Andy Isherwood, as he was for Silsden Town on a Sunday, was a key factor in his side's success, and it was he who scored the winner with a neat lob in their first Keighley Cup final success for seven years, when Silsden were defeated 2-1. Silsden had led the tie through a Duncan Bairstow goal at half time, only for Richie McPike to score an equaliser and Isherwood to hit the winner in extra time.

The champions proved even more impressive the following season when Silsden were again defeated in the Keighley & District Cup final. Once again Silsden took the lead through Reape, only for Cross Hills to equalise through Feather before winning in extra time. This time Isherwood scored twice in the extra period to see his side win 3-1. The winners had needed a replay to see off County Amateur side Steeton earlier in the competition, the first game between the sides being delayed at one point when an irate driver, wrongly thinking that a footballer had blocked his driveway, drove onto the field and parked in one of the goalmouths! Cross Hills also won the league's T.A.P. trophy that season, coming from behind to defeat Trawden 2-1, but they lost out in the league cup when Skipton Town, the only side to beat them in the league that year, did the same in that competition. Despite being in third place at Christmas, the league title was retained with relative ease as the champions maintained a 100% league record from January through to the end of the season.

The side certainly weren't finished yet and sped to a remarkable third successive title in the 1988-89 season, this time unbeaten in their 24 league fixtures and dropping only three points, all before Christmas, in the process. The championship was sealed when struggling West Bradford were thrashed 5-2, although third placed Settle United accounted for the side in both league cup and T.A.P. competitions, the North Craven side winning the former with victory over Oxenhope in the final. The Oxenhope club actually lost three finals in a short space of time, their reserves also losing their league cup final, while Cowling defeated them on penalties at the end of a drawn T.A.P. final.

Cross Hills couldn't quite match their three league titles with a third District Cup final success as they came up against a much improved Steeton in the final and lost to a late winner. As consolation, their reserves thrashed Steeton 5-1 in the Keighley Supplementary Cup final.

A measure of the new found standing of the Cross Hills side was their progress in the County Cup competition. The 1987-88 season saw the Sutton Fields side reach the last 16 for the first time following a 4-2 victory over County Amateur premier side Trinity Athletic. Extra time goals from Isherwood and Thompson were enough to see the Baildon side off following two Dave French goals in normal time. Despite losing to Aberford Albion later on, Hills had certainly laid claim to being equal to many of the region's County Amateur sides. The following season another of those sides, Altofts, were defeated 2-0 thanks to a double strike from Mark Robinson. Unfortunately a strong Huddersfield League side in Black Stars United halted further progress in the third round with a 2-1 victory in a game where Kevin Whittaker suffered a broken leg.

The final season of the decade saw Cross Hills lose their grip on the title – albeit temporarily – when Colne based Rock Rovers won a tight contest. It was not their year, with Haworth defeating them in the Keighley Cup final, following victories over Steeton (in extra time) and Rodney. Another good County Cup run though saw the side again reach the last 16. There were two outstanding victories along the way, with County Amateur sides T.S. Harrison and Fields, 1-0 and 4-0 respectively, losing out to the locals. Unfortunately V.A.W. Low Moor, who had emerged as a major force in the County Amateur set up spoilt the party with a 3-1 victory despite a strong second half fightback by Cross Hills.

Oxenhope Rec finished off the decade with Craven silverware when they defeated Barnoldswick United 3-1 in the league cup final, but were prevented from a cup double when promoted Earby side Band Club Rangers thrashed them 6-1 in the T.A.P. final. Lower down the league, Cross Roads, in their second season, took the second division title, denied a double when Intake defeated them in their league cup final, while Keighley Lifts made their return to Saturday football in the same division.

The biggest success to come Keighley's way at this time was a second County Minor Cup success for the town. Exactly ten years after they had first lifted the trophy, another strong under 17 Keighley F.A. side remained unbeaten in the tournament in the 1989-90 season, which now had a revised format of two group competitions, with the winners of each playing in the final – as opposed to the old knockout system. Keighley topped their group following victories over Goole (1-0), Bradford (4-1) and Leeds (4-3). The latter game, at Silsden, saw Mark Price hit a thunderous winner near the end, leaving the locals needing only a draw in their final group game with Harrogate in order to qualify for the final. In a tight game a late Ian Shoesmith goal earned a 1-1 draw, to see Keighley through to play Heavy Woollen at Thackley. Managed by Paul Nevison, and coached by Bryan Pamment and Andy Brook, Keighley put up a great performance in the final. Their opponents were defeated 3-1 thanks mainly to a great hat-trick from Owen Malcolm and an outstanding performance from Paul Smith.

The Keighley Minor squad for the final was:
C.Wilson, M.Vickers, P.Smith, C.Brown, J.Knowles, M.Ross, M.Ferguson, A.Howard, S.Clarkson, O.Malcolm, M.Price, I.Shoesmith, J.Dyminski, S.Lilley, J.Smith & S.Pamment.

In 1986 James Murray, who had played most of his football with Keighley Cental Youth Club, becoming later a referee at local and county level, and later still an official with both Keighley Sunday Alliance and Minor leagues, was killed in a road accident whilst on work in London. His employers (Laing Construction) and Timothy Taylors F.C. (of which he was a founder member), provided a trophy in his memory. His widow, Nancy, gave this to the Keighley & District F.A to present annually to the outstanding youth player in the district. The first winner, in 1987, was Ian Singleton, followed by Steven Lister, then of Cowling – both of whom are still playing locally.

A number of individuals made their mark elsewhere during the mid to late 80's. Colin Guest joined his brother Ernie at Launceston Juventus in Tasmania during the 1986-87 season, finding his feet in no time. They were later joined by Silsden's Andy Geary. While Keighlians Geoff Busfield and Phil Cole, who refereed mostly in the Northern Counties League, were on either side of the line during a first division match between giants Newcastle United and Chelsea. Lee Duxbury was meanwhile on his way into the big time. He signed a two year contract with Bradford City during the 1987-88 season following his two year spell as a Y.T.S. apprentice, during which time he had become established in City's reserve team. Unfortunately Keighley lost Brontë Ladies. As the women's game became better organised, the side needed a suitable home ground. As Keighley was without a football ground of sufficient quality, the move out of the town was inevitable, a permanent base for the club being set up at Salts F.C. in Shipley.

Chasing Glory

LEE DUXBURY

A product of the successful Keighley Minor side in the 1980's, Lee has gone on to star for Bradford City and Huddersfield Town among others.

The Mid And Late 80's

GRAFTON GARAGE
The first side ever to be thrown out of the Craven League.

OXENHOPE RECREATION 1985-86
Proudly displaying their new kit, courtesy of Norman Bairstow Sports, are:
BACK: A.Bentham, P.Brearey, R.Nelson, D.Maddocks, G.Sheffield, R.Yeadon, A.Snaith
FRONT: G.Bairstow, D.Scott, K.Yates, P.Turbitt, A.Bevan, P.Ousey.

Chasing Glory

SILSDEN TOWN 1986-87

The side that won the Keighley Sunday Cup three years in succession during the 1980's. Town were originally Silsden White Star's second string until their sudden demise.

BLACK HORSE 1988-89

The club began as Volunteers in the Keighley Alliance, becoming Royal and moving onto the Wharfedale Sunday League. Changing their name to Black Horse in 1996 the side were unbeaten in the league throughout the 1987-88 season, yet lost the championship on goal difference ! They later achieved success as Keighley Star

The Mid And Late 80's

CONONLEY SPORTS 1988-89
BACK: S.Hardacre, W.Naylor, A.Bell, D.Tuttle, M.Steventon, B.Johnson, A.Clark, M.Watson,
FRONT: D.Holdsworth, D.Mason, R.Mason, J.Naylor, C.Naylor, N.Alverson.

CROSS HILLS
The side dominated the Craven League in the late 80's/early 90's.

Chasing Glory

CROSS ROADS
During their four years in the Craven League between 1988-92, the side rose from the second division through to the premier division.

HAWORTH 1989-90
The side are featured following their Keighley & District Cup final victory over Cross Hills. Matchwinner Richard Clarkson is in the centre of the back row.

The Mid And Late 80's

KEIGHLEY F.A. MINORS - COUNTY CHAMPIONS 1989-90

KEIGHLEY F.A OFFICIALS 1990

Photographed with the County Minor Cup are, from left; Mike Breeze, Bill Hook, John Nevison, Jack Holmes, Tony Atherton, Bryan Pamment, Andy Brook Dennis Coburn & Peter Pamment.

Chasing Glory

KEIGHLEY F.A. MINORS - COUNTY CHAMPIONS 1994-95

PHOENIX F.C.
KEIGHLEY'S TOP SIDE IN THE 1990'S

(16)
THE 1990's – Cross Hills & the Craven League

The 1990's began in the same way that the eighties ended – Cross Hills dominating the Craven League. They won the league championship for the first two seasons of the decade, making that five titles in six seasons, before inevitably moving on to pastures new.

Oxenhope Recreation and Settle United pushed the champions hard in both championship seasons. In fact, Oxenhope probably created the bigger headlines during the 1990-91 season for their exploits in cup competitions. A third successive T.A.P. Trophy final was achieved, but the side's greatest moments were reserved for the County Cup. There was a fair measure of success for local sides this season against higher rated opposition, Haworth defeating Otley Town 4-1, Cross Hills getting the better of former Yorkshire League side Thorne Colliery 3-0 and Oxenhope themselves thumping Morley Miners 4-0. Goals from Burrows and Higgins then swept them into the last 16 with a 2-0 defeat of Salts, the end coming with a 2-3 reversal to Tyersal, but Oxenhope had proved that Cross Hills were not the only local Craven League side who could make a name for themselves in the County Cup.

Cross Hills themselves reversed the previous season's Keighley & District Cup final result when they secured a 3-1 victory over Haworth, Haworth's reserves doing the same to beat Steeton in the Supplementary Cup. Cross Hills' reserve side were actually strong enough to take the Craven League's first division title, denied promotion to the premier division because their first team already played there.

The 1991-92 season was to be the last for Cross Hills' first team in the Craven League. On their way to that fifth title in six years, Andy Isherwood's men enjoyed several high scoring victories, not least a 14-0 rout of Barnoldswick United, when future Phoenix manager Paul Ettenfield scored five. Rather than opting for the West Riding County Amateur League, they applied successfully to the East Lancashire League, which is more geographically suited to them, and as a result joined up with many of the top sides that had been 'creamed' from the Craven League over the past ten years. Their debut season in the league brought third place in the second division, not enough for promotion but nevertheless a bright start. The side won their league cup competition but went down to Steeton in the 1992-93 Keighley Cup final, despite dominating the game for long periods. The following season did see the side promoted to the league's

Chasing Glory

top flight as second division champions, Oswaldtwistle Town defeated 3-1 in a crunch fixture late in the season, Snowden, Whittaker and Newton on target for the locals.

Although the next few seasons in the first division of the East Lancashire League were spent consolidating their position, Keighley & District's Cup success continued. The holders Phoenix were defeated 3-1 in the 1994-95 final, in front of the largest District Cup final for many years. Whitaker, Snowden and Gilbert surprised the County Amateur side, who had taken an early lead, to see their team become the first winners of the new 'Peter Pamment Trophy', named after Keighley's long-serving F.A. official. Hills' reserve side made it a double that season by collecting the Supplementary Cup with a 2-0 defeat of Keighley Lifts in the final. The District Cup was retained twelve months later when Haworth were defeated 2-1 in the final.

Cross Hills surprised many when they took the East Lancashire League title at the end of the 1997-98 season. They finished three points ahead of reigning champions Oswaldtwistle after having been in contention from the start of the campaign, underlining just how much this friendly club has progressed in recent years.

Since Cross Hills left the Craven League, local sides have again failed to win the Craven League's premier division championship. Gargrave took two successive titles before returning to the East Lancashire League, while Skipton Bulldogs have returned to the top flight to dominate proceedings in recent years. Keighley Lifts have since risen again to the premier division, following successive lower division championships in 1992-93 and 1993-94 (when they also won their league cup competition and reached the Northern Plant Hire Trophy final), and have recently renamed themselves Keighley F.C, while Oxenhope have finished as runners up for no less than five of the last eight seasons. They lost only once during the 1993-94 season, losing out by a single point to Gargrave after having led the table for so long – a 4-4 draw between the sides in September being one of the highlights of the season. Cross Hills reserves pushed Bulldogs the hardest the following season, although Oxenhope defeated the same Cross Hills side 2-0 to win the league cup final – Haworth defeating Barnoldswick Park Rovers in the final of the division one competition to add to the league title.

The 1995-96 season saw Keighley Lifts beat Bulldogs in the Northern Plant Hire Trophy final. Steve Smith gave the side a surprise lead before Bulldogs came back to force extra time, but a David Hannam strike in the extra half hour was enough to see the unbeaten champions defeated. Oxenhope again won the league cup, this time defeating Embsay 2-0 in the final with goals from Higgins and Bailey. Three new sides to enter the Craven League during this era have been Brontë Wanderers,

Eastburn Rangers (switching from the Keighley Sunday Alliance) and Sutton, the latter two playing home fixtures at South Craven School, on the site of the former Sutton United base on Holme Lane. Sutton had a highly successful 1997-98 campaign, with a fourth division league and cup double (5-0 v Grassington in the league cup final).

A new Silsden reappeared in the Craven League for the 1996-97 season. They were basically the successful Silsden under 17 team from the previous season, and although playing at Keighley Road were unrelated to past Saturday sides in the village. In their first season they finished second to St.Pauls (Colne) in the second division, and surprisingly won the Northern Plant Hire Trophy with a win over Haworth in the final. A year later they gained promotion to the premier division, again as runners up in the first division, Ryan Hook and the experienced Andy Geary netting over 50 goals between them to help the side along. Oxenhope won the premier division league cup again this 97-98 season, defeating a tired Bulldogs side 2-0, second half goals from Stephen Murray, from an inch perfect Steve Potts cross, and a late David Collier penalty.

Cononley Sports, who have enticed Jeff Cummins and Dean Woolley out of retirement in recent seasons, have come close to cup success, losing a premier division league cup final to Embsay in 1997 (the same year their reserves also lost their league cup final to Hellifield Sports) and a year later going down 1-2 to Rimington in the Northern Plant Hire Challenge Cup final.

One side who surprised everyone with their cup success in 1997 were Cowling, who won the Keighley & District Cup for the first time since the 1927-28 season (when they defeated Haworth Wesleyans 7-2 in the final). After being early pacesetters they finished a fine third in the Craven League behind Bulldogs and Oxenhope, defeating the latter 3-2 in a thrilling cup final tie, Spellman, Smith and Ayrton, in the last minute of the game, sealing victory in a match that could have swung either way.

The rise of Phoenix & the County Amateur League

It was a pretty uneventful County Amateur League season for Haworth and Steeton during the 1990-91 season, both sides leading their respective divisions early in the season before dropping back. In fact Haworth failed to win a league game from the end of September until mid January.

A new side to Saturday football at this time were Welcome Inn, comprising mainly of players from the Braithwaite and Guardhouse area. They chose to play in the Bradford Grattan League, in the absence of Rodney (ex Grafton & Eastwood) who had failed to reappear in that league.

Chasing Glory

They joined the Craven League for the 1993-94 season but failed to complete their fixtures, despite being comfortably in mid table at the time of their resignation.

Another side to emerge in Saturday football were Phoenix. Mike Breeze's young side made the brave decision to step up to the County Amateur League from the Keighley Sunday Alliance and what a successful move that has proved to be! With several of the successful Keighley Minor team playing for the side from 1990, Phoenix left a side in the local Sunday League, but were able to call on the services of other rising stars such as Roy Mason, Steven Lister, Gareth Turbitt and Richard Clarkson. A measure of the continuity at the club, which has no doubt been one of the keys to their success, is that several of the players that signed up with Phoenix for the 1991-92 season are still with the club. Gareth Turbitt currently manages their successful reserve side, his dad Pete, himself a famous face from Keighley's footballing past, managing the team in their first season in Saturday football.

Based at Beckfoot School, and then from 1993 at the the old Keighley Town ground at Utley, the side made their County Amateur third division debut with a 2-1 win against against Crag Road reserves, Mason and Paul Frazer scoring their first competitive goals. The following week saw Mason hit a hat-trick in a resounding 7-0 success against Saville Arms, but the side were brought down to earth with a bump as Brighouse Town's reserve string saw them defeated for the first time, 4-0. Phoenix eventually settled for a mid table place in the league, with early exits being made in the County Cup (to Halifax side Boothtown) and Keighley Cup competitions. The later competition saw Steeton illustrate the difference between the County Amateur first and third divisions with a 3-0 success against Phoenix, although following victory over Haworth, who had themselves K.O'd Cross Hills from the competition, Steeton went down in the final to Denholme United, who thus became the first and only Halifax League side to win the Keighley & District Cup.

Haworth had a mixed season, withdrawing their first team from the County Amateur League on the eve of the season due to a shortage of players. Their Craven League side were then thumped 1-6 by Cross Hills in their opening fixture, before recovering to finish fourth in the league, successfully reapplying to the County Amateur League for the following season.

The 1992-93 season saw Steeton trounce Denholme United 5-0 in the semi final of the Keighley Cup following an epic dual with Phoenix, who had taken them to a second replay in an earlier round. A crowd of 500 at Lawkholme Lane saw Stephen Gray score the only goal of the game in the final against Cross Hills. Their reserves meanwhile went down 2-3 to Haworth in the Supplementary Cup, Haworth's first team finishing at

The 1990's

the foot of the County Amateur third division at the end of the season, returning again to the Craven League.

In their second season, Phoenix made no mistake in gaining promotion. Richard Clarkson grabbed five of his side's 13 against Old Modernians early in the season, Paul Ettenfield scoring another five in the league cup as Littletown reserves were thrashed 15-1 weeks later. Other high scoring victories included a 10-1 defeat of Eccleshill United reserves, an 8-1 success against Crag Road reserves and a 6-0 defeat of Pudsey Liberals in a league cup semi final. It was no surprise therefore to see the side achieve a league and cup double, Allerton pipped for the division three title – both sides scoring over a century of goals and losing only once all season – and Salthorn defeated in the league cup final, a late Paul Smith goal levelling scores at 1-1 before a four goal burst (3 from Ettenfield) in extra time saw the Keighley side winners by 5 goals to 1.

In the County Cup, County Amateur premier division side Gascoigne United were defeated before another premier side, Salts, knocked Phoenix out in a replay, Steeton also enjoying a fairly successful run in the competition.

The 1993-94 season went very much the same way for Phoenix as they shot straight to the top of their league's second division. A second successive promotion was never in doubt as they sped to the title, on goal difference from Ardsley Celtic. A useful County Cup run saw Bradford Grattan League side Holme Wood Athletic thrashed 6-0 in the first round, before a great 3-0 defeat of premier division Campion in a second round replay. Phoenix had let a two goal lead slip in the first game but they made no mistake in the second, with Mark Atkins scoring twice, along with a single strike from Pete Darroch, who was soon to fracture his leg in a league game with Allerton. Crag Road proved too strong in the third round, edging a close game 3-2 to end local hopes in the competition.

Phoenix clinched promotion with a 3-1 success against Littletown, who had fallen on hard times since their heady days of the 1980's when they enjoyed an intense rivalry with Keighley Town. Weeks later the same opponents were defeated 3-0 to clinch the championship. To add to this, Phoenix reserves, who had just moved into the league from the Grattan League, won the division 4B title, and to cap things the Keighley & District Cup was won for the first time when holders Steeton were defeated by two more Mark Atkins goals.

Steeton themselves had more then held their own a division above Phoenix. They enjoyed a long unbeaten run, but were never really in with a chance of promotion. The District Cup was not the only final they lost that season, losing out to Golcar United in the division one league cup final too.

131

Chasing Glory

The following three seasons in the County Amateur first division proved extremely frustrating for Phoenix. In each season they looked good bets for promotion before losing out to well established sides at the death. The 1994-95 campaign opened with a double over Steeton, 4-0 and then 3-2, when they had to come from two goals down to win. Phoenix were at the top of the league at Christmas and seemingly heading for their third successive promotion when rivals Farnley WMC were defeated 3-2, thanks to goals from Knowles, Bryceland and Clarkson. Unfortunately the bubble burst and the side lost several key fixtures late in the season, eventually finishing in fifth place in the table – Farnley and Golcar earning promotion to the premier division. The side did reach their league cup final, losing out to Aberford, also losing the Keighley Cup final 1-3 to Cross Hills. Steeton had a poor season, finishing adrift at the foot of the table, and being relegated to the second division. The same season, however, saw the return of Keighley Shamrocks to Saturday football. Moving back into the County Amateur League from the Wharfedale Sunday League, they made a sound start to life in division three with two victories in the opening month. Unfortunately another league match was not won until February, during which time they had dropped perilously close to the foot of the table. The wooden spoon position was avoided, as they prepared for the following season with the acquisition of several faces from Keighley Juniors' successful Sunday side.

The 1995-96 season saw Guiseley F.C. considering the option of moving to Lawkholme Lane (now Cougar Park) due to the shortcomings of their own facilities, which were unable to be upgraded sufficiently to see them promoted to the Vauxhall Conference if they were to win their league title. It also saw the County Amateur league's first division strengthened considerably by the presence of Storthes Hall of Huddersfield and Hemsworth Miners Welfare. It was obvious that promotion from this division would be far harder than in past years, yet Phoenix once again started like a steam train. Early season form was terrific as Yeadon/Ventus were defeated 3-0, followed by a 4-1 thrashing of the much revered Hemsworth side, Danny Spencer (2), Richard Clarkson and Jimmy Spencer on the mark for the locals. The side won nine of their first ten league fixtures – their only defeat in October when Hemsworth gained revenge, the 4-1 scoreline this time in their favour. Another useful County Cup run was put together – neighbours Cross Hills defeated 3-1 in the first round, when young 'keeper Paul Linyard, who had at one time had a spell at Hartlepool United, was outstanding. Two great strikes from Jimmy Spencer and Paul Ettenfield were enough to see off Sowerby Bridge 2-1 in the second round after extra time, before eventual division one champions Storthes Hall spoilt the party with their own extra time victory in round three. Paul Linyard made the headlines again later in the season when he scored one

The 1990's

of his side's four goals against Brighouse Town reserves direct from a long kick from his own area. This wasn't enough for promotion however, key games were lost to Dudley Hill Athletic and Storthes Hall late in the season to see these rivals promoted and Phoenix left ruing their luck in fourth place, level on points with third placed Hemsworth and only one behind runners-up Dudley Hill. Phoenix reserves meanwhile ended their season in division 4 with a league cup victory.

It looked like a second successive relegation for Steeton as they started the 1995-96 season at the foot of division two, before a great surge saw them safely in mid season by the season's end. They also had a good run in the league cup, losing to Overthorpe in the final. What a difference a season made for Keighley Shamrock, as they marched to the County Amateur third division title. George Heggarty and ex Phoenix player Martin Ross were among those that inspired the side to a much improved season.

Phoenix improved their division one position to third the following season, again narrowly missing out on promotion. Again the side were in contention until the greater consistency of Hemsworth and Aberford Albion saw these sides promoted instead. Steeton consolidated in mid table in the second division, while Shamrocks narrowly avoided relegation, performing a remarkable Houdini act in the final weeks of the season to rescue what seemed an impossible situation. They also reached the semi final of the Keighley & District Cup following a 4-2 defeat of the holders, Cross Hills, Heggarty, Finn and Spurr (2) sending them through to meet Oxenhope, who defeated them in extra time. The real success in the league this season were Phoenix reserves, with the first of two successive promotions. They won 21 of their 24 fourth division fixtures, remaining unbeaten in league fixtures and scoring an average of over four per game.

The 1997-98 season at last saw Phoenix gain promotion to the premier division of the County Amateur League. As usual they went to the top of the table early in the season, but this time maintained their form and had a comfortable margin between themselves and runners-up Pontefract Borough, whom they defeated 5-2 to seal promotion. They also regained the Keighley & District Cup – defeating Sandy Lane 1-0 after a Ross goal in extra time in the final. Sandy Lane, based at Haworth Road in Bradford, but also using the old Parkwood ground for reserve team Sunday league games, were in their first season of Saturday football. Interestingly they had won the first division title in the West Yorkshire League, so a cup final between the division one champions of parallel leagues was eagerly anticipated, and not surprisingly closely contested. It had been a hard passage to the final for Phoenix, needing extra time to account for Silsden and a replay to see off East Lancashire champions-elect Cross Hills.

Chasing Glory

Another hard passage was in store for Phoenix in the County Cup, with West Yorkshire premier division sides lying in wait in both the second and the third rounds. Two Jimmy Spencer goals helped the locals to a 2-1 success against Bramley, and this was followed by an even more encouraging 3-0 victory over Knaresborough Town, before Marsden, who were on the verge of the County Amateur League title, ended the Keighley side's hopes with a single goal victory in the fourth round. Nevertheless, Phoenix had proved beyond doubt that they were now ready to compete at the top amateur level in the county.

Phoenix reserves took the league's third division title in the 1997-98 season to earn themselves derby games with Steeton and Shamrocks for the coming campaign. They also took the Keighley Supplementary Cup for the third successive year with a 3-0 defeat of Cowling in the final. Shamrocks made a great start in division two, but as Phoenix had done in the past, they faded late in the season and could only finish in mid table. Steeton started moderately well until a disastrous sequence of defeats left them one off the foot of the table until the final week of the season when they managed to sneak above Bradford side Dynamoes F.C.

Sunday Soccer

The 1990's have seen the emergence of a new force in Sunday football too. St.Annes Celtic joined the Keighley Alliance for the 1989-90 season, and despite taking a season or two to establish themselves, they have come close to emulating the feats of Dean Smith & Grace and Magnet in the County Sunday Cup. Local sides have also come to completely dominate the premier division of the Wharfedale Sunday League in recent years, while the Keighley Alliance, now well over its problem years, has at last seen success in the Keighley Sunday Cup.

Keighley Shamrocks took the Keighley Alliance title for the 1990-91 season, as previous champions Red Pig moved on to the Wharfedale League. They were pushed all the way by Druids Arms and Phoenix though, before opting also to join the Wharfedale League the following season. Shamrocks actually achieved a glorious 'treble' in their final season in the league, defeating Phoenix 1-0 in the league cup final and Sutton 6-2 in the Jeff Hall final. Druids meanwhile became the first Keighley Alliance side to progress to the Keighley Sunday Cup final for twelve years, when they were narrowly defeated by the holders Airedale Magnet. They actually led through a Buckley goal at half time, the striker being a valuable asset during the season, scoring well over fifty goals for them. However, Magnet came back strongly in the second half and forced an 88th minute equaliser before Andy Geary popped up with a dramatic winner a minute later. Although it was not known at the time, it was to be the final time that

The 1990's

Magnet would win the trophy they once completely dominated. The main talking point of the Keighley Sunday Cup competition that year was the abandoned quarter final tie between Shamrocks and Druids, which prompted a local F.A. enquiry. With only two minutes remaining, Shamrocks were reduced to seven men, which lead to the halting of proceedings. Druids, themselves with only ten men on the field, had come from 0-3 down to lead 4-3, going on to defeat Keighley Star after extra time in rather less controversial circumstances.

The 1990-91 Wharfedale title went to Star Athletic, a 3-2 victory over Magnet at the end of February proving crucial. The locals gained revenge with a 1-0 victory in a league cup semi final before defeating Stanley Road 2-1 in the final. Kevin Bailey became the new Magnet manager during the season, only two weeks after initially leaving the club for Stanley Road. Unfortunately he could not prevent the side from going out of the County Cup at the first hurdle, but he was able to see them progress to the second round of the national competition with a 2-0 success against Ironbridge (Liverpool). Keeper Sean McNulty was in fine form as goals from Feather and Packer set up a second round meeting with Queens Arms (Cleator Moor). Unfortunately the Whitehaven side put paid to any further progress with a 3-2 victory.

During the summer of 1991, the top three Wharfedale League clubs all left for pastures new. Stanley Road joined the Bradford Sunday Alliance, while Star Athletic (who moved from their Crossflatts base to the new ground on the site of the old Beckside/Parkwood Stadium) and Airedale Magnet linked up with the rival Wharfedale Triangle, joining Silsden Town and Keighley Star in the premier division.

Silsden and Druids Arms took advantage of those resignations in the Wharfedale League to begin their great rivalry that would continue to the present day. Bradford side Wrose Albion chased them home in both the 91-92 & 92-93 seasons as the two local sides fought it out for the honours. With Roy Mason in top form, Druids led the 91-92 campaign for much of the season, a double strike from Hird seeing off Silsden in January. However, the tide turned and in their return meeting at the end of March Silsden turned in an incredible performance to win 7-2, Grey helping himself to a hat-trick. The Keighley Road side went on to win the title on goal difference with a 3-1 victory over fourth placed Shamrocks. .

Meanwhile Magnet won the Triangle title at the first attempt, finishing eight points ahead of Star Athletic. They defeated the runners up 2-1 on the opening day of the season, although Star gained revenge with victory in a league cup semi final after extra time and followed this up with a resounding 5-1 success in the return league fixture towards the end of the season. Magnet actually recorded a 17-2 success against Old Ball in an earlier league cup round, Dale Hoyle scoring no less than ten times himself. They also produced a thrilling performance in their County Cup third round tie with Baildon Athletic, by now playing in the Bradford Sunday Alliance. They won the game 3-2, with Ian Singleton, a Keighley F.A. 'young player of the year', becoming villain then hero – first missing a penalty in extra time before moments later scoring a dramatic late winner. Unfortunately there was to be no further progress in this competition for the local side.

Star Athletic went on to defeat Keighley Shamrocks 3-2 in the 1991-92 Keighley Sunday Cup final. Shamrocks had knocked out both Wharfedale champions-elect, Silsden and Magnet, in earlier rounds, but they did earn some silverware when Wrose Albion were defeated 1-0 in the Russell Stone Cup final. Knowle Arms won the Keighley Alliance title this season, followed closely by Market Arms and Cullingworth, who met in a bruising Jeff Hall Trophy final. Although Market Arms won by three goals to one, three players were ordered off and one player finished up in hospital. Cullingworth's consolation for defeat in the tie was a league cup final success against Great Northern. Market Arms did not slip up in their chase for the title the following year, winning for the first time under their new name of Cavendish Arms, following a late run at the end of the season.

Long time leaders, and Jeff Hall Trophy winners, Knowle Arms were defeated 2-1 in a key game in April, when Andy Gaughan and former Knowle player Nicky Carr scored the vital goals. In second place were the emerging St.Annes Celtic, who were about to embark on their long run of success. Between 1991-93 there was actually a 'rival' Sunday league in Keighley. The 'Keighley & District League' was more of a friendly, informal league, although clubs were affiliated to the County F.A.. The 1992-93 season saw Albert, Schindler, Black Cat, Goats Head, White Bear, New Inn and Harrison & Clough competing in the league, the latter four all competing in the Keighley Alliance the following year.

The 1992-93 Wharfedale Triangle season saw Keighley Star finish within a point of joint champions Star Athletic and Regent Victoria, and lose their third successive league cup final. Druids and Silsden meanwhile renewed their rivalry at the top of Wharfedale's other Sunday league, Silsden preserving a 100% league record until the end of February. Despite three defeats late in the season it was the Keighley Road side who retained the title, although runners-up Druids had the consolation of a Keighley Cup final against the holders Star Athletic. Unfortunately, despite Tim Hird and 'keeper Heath Maddocks having outstanding games, Star were victorious by 2 goals to nil. Keighley Shamrocks grabbed some silverware with a 3-0 defeat of Sandy Lane in the Russell Stone Cup final, while emerging Keighley Juniors won the Ingham Sports Cup to add to their third division title the previous season.

The 1990's

The 1993-94 season opened without one of Keighley's biggest names – that of Magnet. They had lost their grip on the Wharfedale Triangle title in the 1992-93 campaign due mainly to poor end of season form, and during the summer had seen an exodus of players, who, according to Tommy Lyness, had "...just deserted the club". It was intended to resurrect the side the following year but this never happened, and so the famous old name of Magnet, who along with Dean Smith & Grace had brought so much success to the town, was sadly confined to history.

In the absence of Magnet, and Star Athletic who had merged with Pile Bar of the Bradford Sunday Alliance, Keighley Star took over as the top Sunday side in the town with two glorious and highly successful seasons. In the first they achieved a league and cup double, an 8-1 defeat of Caroline Street Social sealing their first title during which Gilbert, Cottam and Wellwood were regularly on the scoresheet, and Wrose Bull defeated by a Martin Ross goal in the league cup final. They then lifted the Keighley Sunday Cup for the first time with a 2-0 defeat of Keighley Shamrocks in the final to once and for all lose their 'bridesmaids' tag. Amazingly the following season proved even more spectacular as a great County Cup run was added to their long line of success. The league championship was again won, this time on goal difference, another league cup final, Silsden defeated in the Keighley Sunday Cup final, and a place in the semi final of the cup that only two Keighley sides had ever lifted.

It was the amazing goalscoring talents of Dale Hoyle who set Star's County Sunday Cup campaign alight. He scored four times as Swillington Miners Welfare were brushed aside in an earlier round, repeating that number as Birkenshaw were defeated 6-1 in the fourth round. The following game against Brighouse Star was won 5-3 – Hoyle yet again scoring four (by this time he had scored nearly 70 goals in less than 20 games!). The quarter final of the competition paired Keighley Star with former winners Ventus United, but again the locals won through, this time thanks to Nick Gilbert who scored two cracking goals in a 3-1 victory. The run was ended when Castleford's Prince of Wales won their semi final tie, before they themselves were defeated in the final.

Keighley Star moved back into the Wharfedale League for the 1995-96 season, but within weeks of what had been a fine start they were no more, their final match a Keighley Cup tie when they fell to an embarrassing 3-7 defeat after extra time to Keighley Alliance strugglers Cullingworth.

Meanwhile things continued the same way as the Wharfedale League's premier division looked more and more like a premier Keighley League. Silsden secured their third successive title at the end of 1993-94 despite a poor start to the season, Keighley sides again monopolising the various league cup competitions, and then a year later Keighley Juniors joined the elite in the absence of Shamrocks, who had moved back into the County Amateur League. The three Keighley sides took the top three positions, ahead of Sandy Lane, the Bradford side who at least played Wharfedale fixtures in Keighley. Keighley Juniors, with Mostyn Hockey (junior) in their ranks, actually led the table early in the season, their first defeat coming at the hands of Silsden, who had again made a poor start. Richard Snowden scored twice in a close game that the Cobbydalers eventually won 4-3.

To say that the three Keighley sides were evenly matched this season is an understatement, Druids and Keighley Juniors drew three times during the campaign before Druids won a close Keighley Cup tie in extra time. The Druids team also needed a last gasp Colin Buckley goal to force a 3-3 draw with Silsden in mid April to keep their title hopes intact. Following this, a last gasp winner against Sandy Lane and a 3-1 defeat of Thackley Shoulder meant that they were at last Wharfedale champions in what had been one of the league's closest races for the title. Steve Kernan and Paul Ettenfield then gave Druids a fine double as Sandy Lane were defeated 2-0 in the senior league cup final.

It was Keighley Juniors' turn to lift the championship at the end of the 1995-96 season. Lee Whittaker hit four as Silsden were defeated 6-4 early in the season, but following the withdrawal of Keighley Star, Juniors' main rivals turned out to be Bay Horse from Baildon. However, by winning their final two games of the season they ensured the premier division trophy remained in Keighley, Silsden defeating the Baildon side 4-1 in the league cup final with goals from Fenton, Clapham, Carling and Gray. Silsden enjoyed a 17 match winning run during the season, ended by Druids late in the season, as they marched to a second cup success that season – the Keighley Sunday Cup, which was won at the expense of the emerging St.Annes Celtic. Keighley Juniors in fact were Silsden's victims in both league cup and Keighley Cup competitions. During the season, several players from the Keighley clubs in the Wharfedale League were selected to play for the league's representative side against the Bradford Sunday Alliance to aid Thackley F.C's new stand appeal, the previous one having recently burned down.

St.Annes Celtic became only the third side behind Dean Smith & Grace and Magnet to win the Keighley Alliance title three times in succession during the 90's. The 1993-94 saw the side remain unbeaten in their league fixtures, although they were knocked out of both league and Jeff Hall cup competitions by Cullingworth. A new Timothy Taylors line up won the latter competition, defeating St.Annes' second string in the final, and after having put twenty past Girlington in an earlier round (Taylors were known as Reservoir the following year).

The 1990's

Knowle Arms won the 1993-94 league cup but were unlucky not to depose St.Annes as league champions the following season. They defeated the champions 1-0 in the Jeff Hall final and would have won the league title had St.Annes not been favoured with points adjustments. St.Annes were clear league champions in their final Alliance season as they finished eight points clear of Knowle Arms and Boltmakers. They defeated Knowle 3-2 after extra time in the league cup, although Knowle themselves held on to the Jeff Hall Trophy when Phoenix's Sunday side were defeated in a replay.

This was also Boltmakers' final season in the Alliance as, along with St.Annes, they turned to the Wharfedale League for the 1996-97 season. The club made the headlines at the beginning of their final Alliance campaign when Yorkshire Television cameras were present to see their opening league game at Gargrave against Old Swan Clarets. The club had as their sponsors Oasis, due to Roger Nowell's involvement with the band, and this attracted nationwide interest.

Three Horses took the Keighley Alliance title in the 1996-97 season, overhauling Skipton (formerly Rose & Crown) at the death. They also took the league cup, defeating Stanbury in the final, while Cross Hills based Craven Athletic took the first of their two successive Jeff Hall final wins. Golden Fleece, with Darren Golding in fine form, were the first to show in the single division league, scoring 26 times in their first three fixtures, but by the season's end they were placed well down the table. Phoenix's Sunday side had a good season, all of the players who started their league game against Silsden Bridge Inn getting on the scoresheet (including Paul Linyard, his side's first choice goalkeeper, who scored a hat-trick!) in a 25-0 victory.

There were five local sides in the Wharfedale premier division for the 1996-97 season, St.Annes coming straight into the top division from the Keighley Alliance, and Silsden Kings Arms, with some of the old Silsden Town faces, earning promotion. Keighley Juniors completed a clean sweep of the available trophies in the league, as they not only won the championship, but beat Bay Horse in the Phoenix Trophies Senior Cup final and St.Annes in a penalty shoot out in the Cookson Cup. Silsden Kings Arms were the early leaders of the division, Andy Isherwood again in fine form, and they were the first side to defeat St.Annes in what turned out to be a great season for the newcomers. Juniors boasted a 100% league record by the turn of the new year though, and they were not to be caught.

It was St.Annes who made all the headlines though, when they not only won the Keighley Sunday Cup, defeating Boltmakers by a single goal in the final, but became only the third Keighley side to reach the final of the County Sunday Cup in a run that saw them go 21 league and cup matches unbeaten.

Chasing Glory

Fancied Bradford Moor were the Keighley side's first round opponents in the County Cup, going down 2-1, before fellow locals Silsden Kings Arms were disposed of in the following round. Rob Horton, Gareth Turbitt, Paul Driver and Jimmy Spencer were all on the mark in a 4-2 victory. The third stage saw Ventus United, the previous season's beaten finalists, again lose to a Keighley side as St.Annes won easily, 4-0. John Mitchell's first half goal was added to by Rob Henson (twice) and Wayne Raistrick in the second, to see the locals into the last 16 of the competition.

Plumbers Arms were clear favourites to take the side's fourth round tie, but a dramatic winner in the last minute of extra time from Spencer saw St.Annes win 3-2. John Durkin had given them the lead a minute into the second half, but the Leeds side had come back to lead 2-1 until Driver equalised late in the game with his first touch to force extra time. By now the Keighley side were still in four cup competitions, and were in with a chance of the league title, but this did nothing to dent their fine County Cup form. Their quarter and semi final ties in the competition proved to be incredibly close affairs, the key to St.Annes victories in both being a solid defence which at times was forced to sustain long periods of intense pressure. The holders, Hounds F.C. from Selby, were quarter final opponents, a single strike from Joe Bryceland proving the only goal despite a Hounds onslaught on the St.Annes goal, Mark Atkins the pick of the locals who kept them out. The semi final, played at the new County F.A. ground at Fleet Lane, Woodlesford, saw another clean sheet for 'keeper Robert Yaxley as again a first half goal, this time from Mark Knowles, proved decisive. Over 200 supporters of the side had travelled to South Leeds to see the game, and they were to return weeks later for the final against Bolton Woods. Since leaving the Wharfedale League at the end of the 1980's Woods had risen to the top of the Bradford Sunday Alliance, and it was they who spoilt the Keighley side's party with an emphatic 7-0 victory. It was one of those days when nothing went right for St.Annes, but they could take credit from a fantastic run that had seen them overcome the strongest of opposition.

St.Annes recovered sufficiently to win the Wharfedale title at the end of the 1997-98 campaign, despite losing Jimmy Spencer with a broken leg part way through the season. In a year when three premier division sides – including Silsden Rangers (formerly Kings Arms) – withdrew during the season, St.Annes were always on top. Five of the seven teams that finished the season were Keighley sides, Druids, Silsden and Keighley Juniors again in contention, along with promoted Boltmakers who struggled in their new surroundings. Keighley Juniors, despite a shock Keighley Cup final defeat, won the league's senior cup, defeating St.Annes in a penalty shoot out for the second successive season, this despite a heavy session at Beverley races the day before! Druids meanwhile finished as runners up to Pudsey's Royal Hotel in an Inter-league competition between the Wharfedale premier division and division 1A of the Bradford Sunday Alliance, both of whose teams were struggling for fixtures following the withdrawals of other clubs.

The 1997-98 Keighley Alliance campaign was a close one, Craven Athletic coming from behind to take the title from the grasp of Phoenix and Skipton at the death. It was left to the final game of the season, when Craven defeated Phoenix to decide the destination of the premier division trophy. Division One champions Crown were defeated 5-3 in the Jeff Hall Trophy final, while Skipton were defeated 3-1 in the premier division league cup final to seal a remarkable treble for the side that struggled at the foot of division one just two years earlier. Craven also had a good run in the County Sunday Trophy, going out to Miners Welfare (Castleford) in the fifth round. This was the first season of the County Saturday and Sunday 'trophy' competitions, intended for sides of a lower standard than those in the County Cup competitions. The biggest surprise was yet to come though as Craven became the first Alliance side for 19 years to lift the Keighley Sunday Cup, coming from behind to defeat the hot favourites Keighley Juniors in extra time.

Young Talent and Silsden Ladies

Keighley's young footballers have continued to impress in recent years. With several young stars again attracting the eyes of Football League and Premiership clubs there is no shortage of young talent in the town. Eddie Presland's 'Friendly' Youth league, backed by Norman Bairstow, who has done so much to help local soccer over the years, has gone from strength to strength in recent years with now over 70 teams taking part from under 7's to under 11's, Eddie one of a number of hard working coaches helping Keighley's youngsters on their way.

Keighley's Minor side won their third County Minor Cup during the 1994-95 season, adding to their previous victories in 1980 and 1990. Daniel Gaudosi scored both goals in their semi final tie with Craven at Steeton, to set up a final against Leeds. The first tie at Guiseley was drawn, before a 2-0 replay victory for the locals when James Smith (10 minutes) and Michael Morrell (70 minutes) were on the mark.

The winning squad on this occasion was:
M.Foulger, D.Wilkinson, M.Watson, R.Holmes, A.Suttlewood, N.Wojtas, D.Gaudosi, R.Pearson, J.Smith, M.Morrell, A.Ree, D.Watson, G.Florence, J.Anderson & G.McLafferty.

Meanwhile Steeton's under 16 side emulated the former Shamrocks Juniors in reaching the final of the West Riding Junior cup, when they defeated Farsley Celtic 3-0 in a replayed semi final. Unfortunately Kippax beat the locals with a controversial second half goal, although Airdrie and Horton both came close for Steeton, for whom Sean Kennedy was outstanding.

There was international success for Greenhead youngster Graeme Tomlinson, who made the England Schoolboys team during the 1990-91 season. He was proving a success at Bradford City, having scored 23 goals in 16 games for them at the time of his call up. By the end of the 1993-94 season he had been snapped up by Manchester United, impressing the Old Trafford club with his performance in City's F.A. Youth Cup victory over them.

With the demise of Brontë Ladies in the 1990's, a new ladies side has been established at Silsden. Multi-talented sportswoman Sara Raine, a former Brontë player herself, helped to set up Silsden Ladies, who played several friendlies during the 1997-98 season and were sponsored by Yorkshire Cable. Their first game saw a 1-4 defeat to Roger Ingham's newly formed Skipton Ladies, for whom junior cricket international Claire Atkinson, from Riddlesden, kept goal. Silsden gained a revenge win over Skipton later in the season, and have now moved on to compete in the Yorkshire & Humberside Women's League for the 1998-99 campaign. The new side have certainly been in the headlines since their formation – teenager Louise Hall became a millionaire when she won the national lottery, and then the club won a nationwide competition sponsored by Vauxhall Motors to 'win a manager for the day'. The prize – attracting the expected local television coverage – was a coaching session with none other than Ron Atkinson, who was left highly impressed by the commitment shown by the girls.

(17)
...AND INTO THE FUTURE

As we reach the millennium, Keighley remains the largest town in Britain never to have had a top class soccer team. For there not to be a side of at least Northern Counties East League standard in the district indicates just how much Keighley has missed the boat, and to see places the size of Ossett, or Guiseley, or even Emley, supporting semi professional sides makes us realise just how far behind other towns we are in terms of being able to progress into the pyramid of non-league football.

There have been numerous attempts to form a truly successful side in the town over the years. The early years of the round ball game saw the top local sides flounder when faced with opposition from Leeds and Bradford, yet since the second world war Keighley has possessed sides that have been able to compete successfully against some of the best sides in the county. Unfortunately all of these sides have been held back in their attempts to make it further up the ladder.

The post war Keighley Town possessed a suitable ground, but not the support of the people of the town, who were unwilling to pay to watch a struggling Yorkshire League side; Keighley Central certainly had a strong enough squad, but were frustrated by their lack of facilities at Marley; the Silsden of the 70's may have made it into the Yorkshire League & the later Northern Counties East League, but they were victims of their own indiscipline; while Trevor Hockey fired the imagination of the Keighley public with his reformed Keighley Town, but again found facilities and a lack of support from local business blocking his way.

In an age where money and ground facilities are of increasing importance, the town is desperately in need of a means to acquire those vital ingredients that, when put together, can lead to a successful side that can compete at the highest level. Phoenix have made a remarkable rise through the lower divisions of the West Riding County Amateur League in recent years, and with a predominantly youthful side have the capacity to compete with the best in the premier division. But where would a successful side turn next?

One thing that will always remain in Keighley though is a genuine passion for the game that is loved around the world. Although Marley no longer has its famous centre pitch, the playing fields there, and in the surrounding villages, are witness to the trials and tribulations of the game at the local level, played by those who love the game and supported by those tireless club and local F.A. officials without whom there would be no organised football in the town.

KEIGHLEY'S SOCCER LEGENDS

Every town and village has had its own footballing legends over the years; some have been stars on the world stage, some have excelled in the Football League, while others have made their mark in the local game or at senior 'non-league' level. Keighley is no different. It would be impossible in the pages of this volume to list all of the famous names from every club in the Keighley district, so a small selection of those names, the 'best' known are featured in brief below.

Jeff Hall

Although Jeff hailed from Scunthorpe and lived just outside Keighley, in Wilsden, his links with the town are such that a history of Soccer in Keighley could not possibly be complete without reference to the former England international.

In his early years, Jeff played for his village team, as well as two seasons with the Keighley St.Annes side, before signing for Bradford Park Avenue as an amateur at the age of 18. He was spotted by scouts from Birmingham City whilst playing in an army match during National Service, making his debut at the age of 20 against Bury on January 20th 1951, and he was soon a regular in the first team. Such was Jeff's popularity in Wilsden that it was not uncommon for coachloads of villagers to travel to St.Andrews to see their hero play. Making 254 appearances for Birmingham City in the old first and second divisions, he also played in the 1956 F.A. Cup Final against Manchester City. In all, Jeff made 17 appearances for England, and featured in England's first ever international against Brazil in 1956.

Jeff was cruelly struck down with polio in 1959, only months after marrying, but his name lives on today in the form of the 'Jeff Hall Memorial Trophy', competed for by member clubs of the Keighley Sunday Alliance. The trophy was donated by his father, and one of the league's founder members, Percy Hall.

Jeff Hall: International record:

		date	venue	result
v	Denmark	02.10.55	Copenhagen	W 5-1
v	Wales	22.10.55	Cardiff	D 1-1
v	Northern Ireland	02.11.55	Wembley	W 3-0
v	Spain	30.11.55	Wembley	W 4-1

Keighley's Soccer Legends

JEFF HALL

v	Scotland	14.04.56	Glasgow	D 1-1
v	Brazil	09.05.56	Wembley	W 4-2
v	Sweden	16.05.56	Stockholm	D 0-0
v	Finland	20.05.56	Helsinki	W 5-1
v	West Germany	26.05.56	Berlin	W 3-1
v	Northern Ireland	06.10.56	Belfast	D 1-1
v	Wales	14.11.56	Wembley	W 3-1
v	Yugoslavia	28.11.56	Wembley	W 3-0
v	Denmark	05.12.56	Wolverhampton	W 5-2
v	Scotland	06.04.57	Wembley	W 2-1
v	Rep. Ireland	08.05.57	Wembley	W 5-1
v	Denmark	15.05.57	Copenhagen	W 4-1
v	Rep. Ireland	19.05.57	Dublin	D 1-1

Mike Hellawell

Mike was a sporting all rounder. His success was not limited to soccer, being a Yorkshire County Cricket Second team and Colts representative. His main sport brought him two full England caps in 1962 and was thus the first Keighley born player to play for England.

Mike's early years were spent at County Amateur outfit Salts. Selected for the West Riding under 18 side in the 1950's and turning professional in August 1955, he made his full league debut for Queens Park Rangers as an outside left on 25th February 1956 in their Third Division (South) fixture against Exeter City. He later went on to play for Birmingham City, Sunderland, Huddersfield Town, Peterborough United and non-league Bromsgrove Rovers, making his England appearances, under Walter Winterbottom, as an outside right, and gaining experience of European club competition whilst with Birmingham.

Before hanging up his boots, Mike took on the role of player-coach at Cross Hills for a period during the 1970's, when they were a major force in the Craven & District League. He then turned to refereeing the game in the Keighley area.

Mike also played for Keighley Cricket Club, captaining them during the 1972-73 season. Whilst at Birmingham City he also spent two years with Warwickshire County Cricket Club (1962 & 63) and played as a professional at Walsall in the established Birmingham Cricket League.

Mike Hellawell : International record:

		date	venue	result
v	France	03.10.62	Hillsborough	D 1-1
v	Northern Ireland	20.10.62	Belfast	W 3-1

John Hellawell, Mike's younger brother, also made it to the professional ranks, making 48 appearances and scoring 13 goals for Bradford City between 1961 and 1963. He later moved to Rotherham United before returning to Bradford to play for Park Avenue. Before hanging up his boots, John also had a spell at Bromsgrove and featured in the Keighley Central line up prior to their demise in 1973.

Trevor Hockey

One of the games most enigmatic individuals, Trevor made his Football League debut for Bradford City at the age of 16 during the 1959-60 season as a left flanker. Following his 5 goals in 53 appearances for the Valley Parade club he went on to play for Nottingham Forest, Newcastle United, Birmingham City (where he had his own fan club!), Sheffield United and Aston Villa, before returning to Bradford City for two seasons during the mid 70's, following his nine Welsh caps. Trevor also sampled the game in the North American football league, and it is claimed, once played a pink piano in a pop group!

Trevor made a major impact on the local football scene in the early 1980's, when, following a successful stint at Silsden alongside coach Ian Patrickson in the mid 1970's, he declared that the town was easily big enough to support a Northern Premier League side. He set about achieving that aim with the formation of a new Keighley Town that at one point looked as it if might just fulfil his ambitions, and also a popular soccer camp for youngsters. Towards the end of his career, Trevor regularly turned out for Town and Sunday League giants Magnet. Unfortunately his sudden death in 1987 coincided with the end of the Keighley Town dream, but he will be long remembered as one of the town's most enigmatic footballing heroes.

Trevor Hockey : International record:

		date	venue	result
v	Finland	13.10.71	Swansea	W 3-0
v	Romania	24.11.71	Bucharest	L 0-2
v	England	15.11.72	Cardiff	L 0-1
v	England	24.01.73	Wembley	D 1-1
v	Poland	28.03.73	Cardiff	W 2-0
v	Scotland	12.05.73	Wrexham	L 0-2
v	England	15.05.73	Wembley	L 0-3
v	Northern Ireland	19.05.73	Liverpool	L 0-1
v	Poland	26.09.73	Chorzow	L 0-3

TREVOR HOCKEY

The Welsh international is pictured here with members of his highly successful 'soccer camp' in the early 1980's.

Trevor's brother, Alan Hockey, has also made a considerable mark on the local footballing scene. Although not making the professional ranks, Alan turned out for every one of Keighley's top sides during the 1960's, 70's & early 80's – assuming the role of captain for the majority of the time.

Geoff Smith

Of those Keighlians who went on to play for Football League clubs, few have managed to set unbeaten records for their club. Goalkeeper Geoff Smith did just that while playing for Bradford City. In the 1957-58 season, he established a club record of 18 clean sheets, helping the club to third place in the Third Division (North).

Discovered by City while playing for the successful Central Youth Club side in 1948, he was initially released by the club before being invited back for a trial following a spell playing in the Lancashire Combination. His Football League debut was on 17th January 1953, and despite conceding four goals retained his place in the side. Later that year he became a part time professional at the club before turning fully professional two seasons later. Geoff played in 200 consecutive games for Bradford City between 28th April 1954 & 11th October 1958, a run of four seasons ever present.

The Stortons

Keighley's footballing history would not be complete without more than a passing mention of this famous family of soccer players. Whereas Messrs. Hall, Hellawell and Hockey all had links with Birmingham City at one time in their careers, Trevor, Stan and Neil Storton all had spells with Tranmere Rovers on Merseyside.

Stan Storton first made his name with the Central Youth Club side in the late 1950's before going on to play at left back for Bradford City. After making 110 appearances for the club, scoring five times, he moved on to Tranmere in 1963. In 1985 Stan made a name for himself when, as manager of non-league Telford United, his side dumped Bradford City – then top of the old Third division – out of the F.A. Cup.

Trevor Storton also had a spell at Tranmere before going on to play for Liverpool, where he spent most of the time in the reserves. In his later playing career he played for Telford, under the guidance of his older brother, and has also established himself as a top manager in senior non league football. He is currently manager of Bradford Park Avenue in the N.P.L.

Neil Storton, said by many to be the most talented of all the Stortons, first made a mark in the Keighley & District League for Parkwood Amateurs. In the 1958-59 season he scored 49 times in only 16 league fixtures, helping the side to an easy title success. He also featured in the line up of the famous Dean Smith's Sunday side at the height of their success and also had a spell at Tranmere as an apprentice.

Peter Jackson

First making his name as captain of a strong Keighley schoolboys team in the 1970's, Peter first signed schoolboy terms with Burnley. Released by the Turf Moor outfit, and following a three month trial at Valley Parade, he was offered an apprenticeship with Bradford City in July 1977.

Jackson made his league debut on 1st April 1979 against Torquay United, and was later signed as a full time professional. He was made captain of the Bantams for the 1984-85 season. After 328 league and cup appearances for City, Peter signed for Newcastle United in October 1986 for what equalled the Magpies record transfer payment, £250,000. He was an instant success and was voted player of the year in his first season there. After 60 games with Newcastle, Jackson returned to Bradford City, playing another 55 times for the club before his departure to Huddersfield Town.

Peter began the 1997-98 season playing in the Vauxhall Conference with a resurgent Halifax Town – however he jumped at the opportunity

Chasing Glory

Bradford School's champions Greenhead had Peter Jackson (bottom, third from right) starring for them in the late 1970's.

of taking his first manager's role, back at Leeds Road, and successfully guided struggling Huddersfield clear of relegation from the First Division.

There have, of course, been many other Keighley footballers who have made the professional ranks, among them **Tom Hindle, Maurice Lindley, Pete Turbitt** and more recently **Lee Duxbury**, a member of the town's successful Minor side in the 1980's.

Maurice Lindley

Maurice was another of Keighley's sons to sample life in the football league. Born in the Ingrow area, he initially played two games for Bradford City's A-team before signing for Everton in 1936 and played as wing half or centre half for them. He stayed at Goodison Park until 1953, then he left to become manager at Swindon Town. Two years were spent at the Wiltshire club before a brief spell in charge at Barry Town and two years at Crewe before joining Leeds United as coach.

It was at Elland Road as Don Revie's right hand man that Lindley become best known, bringing in young stars and talented youngsters such as Billy Bremner, Peter Lorimer and Terry Yorath and Eddie and Frank Gray. Lindley also spent several brief periods as caretaker manager there.

Keighley's Soccer Legends

Unfortunately a club rule stated that employees had to leave Leeds United at 65 years of age and so his highly successful Elland Road era came to a close.

It was then, in 1982, that Roy McFarlane, the then Bradford City manager, called Maurice to Valley Parade where he featured as their chief scout for several years. In 1991 he was rewarded with a testimonial match when Bradford City and Leeds United met at Valley Parade in a curtain raiser for the 1991-92 season.

Best in the field for ALL sports!

LITESOME Sportswear

The latest 'LITESOME' Range of Clothing for Soccer—for Players, Linesmen, Referees, etc., is quite exceptional in modern design and cut, in quality and value.
Your Sports Dealer will give you details of the 'Spanish-Style' and Continental Jerseys; four types of Shorts; 'Plus-Four' Stockings; Bri-Nylon hose and the famous 'LITESOME' Tracksuits.
And, of course, a must for every Player is the 'LITESOME' SUPPORTER —worn the world over by active Sportsmen.

FRED HURTLEY & SON LTD KEIGHLEY · YORKSHIRE

KEIGHLEY CENTRAL A.F.C.

Season 1964-65

Official Programme 2ᴰ

Phone 3623	Telephone: 7233
HARRY FEARNSIDE	**DENNIS SWALLOW, R.P.**
CONTRACTOR, JOINER, PATTERN MAKER AND FUNERAL DIRECTOR	Plumbing, Heating & Sanitary Engineer
Green Gate Sawmills, Parker Street, Keighley and 8 Hospital Road, Riddlesden, Keighley	2 COLES WAY RIDDLESDEN, KEIGHLEY
For First Class GENTLEMEN'S HAIRDRESSING **NORTH STREET HAIRDRESSERS** Central Chambers North Street, Keighley	Telephone: Haworth 3120 **BRONTE TOURS LTD.** SUN STREET HAWORTH, KEIGHLEY *We serve the Club—Let us serve you*

KEIGHLEY CENTRAL PROGRAMME 1964-65

This side issued a four pager for home games in the West Yorkshire League during this season.

Tables

WARTIME KEIGHLEY CUP COMPETITIONS

1943-44
KEIGHLEY & DISTRICT CUP FINAL
Keighley Lifts...6 Dean Smith & Grace...1 (after 4-4 draw)

KEIGHLEY CHARITY CUP FINAL
Prince Smith & Stells...4 Dan Mitchells...1

1944-45
KEIGHLEY & DISTRICT CUP FINAL
Prince Smith & Stells...7 John Lunds...2 (replay)

KEIGHLEY CHARITY CUP
Winners: Prince Smith & Stells

FINAL WARTIME BRADFORD AMATEUR LEAGUE TABLES

1940-41

	P	W	L	D	Pts
KEIGHLEY TOWN	26	23	3	0	46
Slackside	26	21	4	1	43
Idle Celtic	26	18	5	3	39
Salem Athletic	26	16	6	4	36
Bingley Amateurs	26	14	6	6	34
Wilsden Rovers	26	13	8	5	31
Calverley	26	11	11	4	26
Moorside Amateurs	26	11	13	2	24
Thornton Amateurs	26	11	13	2	24
Woodlands	26	10	13	3	23
Army XI	26	7	14	5	19
Thackley Amateurs	26	3	20	3	9
Prospect Works	26	2	22	2	6
Victoria Road OB	26	2	24	0	4

1941-42

	P	W	L	D	Pts
KEIGHLEY TOWN	20	16	2	2	34
Army XI (2)	20	14	1	5	33
Army XI (1)	20	12	5	3	27
Thornton Amateurs	20	12	5	3	27
English Electric	20	9	10	1	19
Moorside Amateurs	20	8	9	3	19
Army XI (4)	20	5	10	5	15
Butterfields SC	20	6	12	2	14
Idle Celtic	20	5	14	1	11
Crompark	20	3	12	5	11
Salem Athletic	20	4	16	0	8
Park Rangers w/d	Army XI (3) w/d				

153

Chasing Glory

1942-43

	P	W	L	D	Pts
Army XI (5)	24	19	4	1	39
KEIGHLEY TOWN	24	18	5	1	37
Army XI (2)	24	15	5	4	34
Army XI (4)	24	15	6	3	33
English Electric	24	13	8	3	29
Butterfields SC	24	12	8	4	28
C.A.I.L.	24	12	10	2	26
Army XI (1)	24	10	11	3	23
Bfd NSF (C div)	24	8	12	4	20
Ingleby Magnets	24	8	15	1	17
Park View	24	3	17	4	10
Hollybrook SC	24	3	17	4	10
Bradford TTS	24	3	19	2	8
Army XI (3)	w/d				

1943-44

	P	W	L	D	Pts
Butterfields SC	26	24	2	0	48
KEIGHLEY TOWN	26	21	3	2	44
English Electric	26	18	4	4	40
Army XI (4)	26	15	5	6	36
Army XI (2)	26	15	9	2	32
Hardacres SC	26	11	13	2	24
Park View	26	10	13	3	23
Low Moor Hotspurs	26	9	15	2	20
C.A.I.L.	26	9	16	1	19
Ingleby Magnets	26	9	17	0	18
Canal Ironworks	26	7	16	3	17*
Low Moor Alloys	26	5	15	6	16
Y.E.W. Co	26	6	18	2	14
Hollybrook SC	26	4	21	1	9

* Canal Ironworks took over fixtures of Swifts FC

1944-45

	P	W	L	D	Pts
G.S.C & T.C.	30	27	1	2	56
English Electric	30	22	5	3	47
Butterfields SC	30	23	6	1	47
Hepworth & Gr	30	18	7	5	41
KEIGHLEY TOWN	30	18	8	4	40
Park View	30	16	10	4	36
R.A.P.C.	30	14	11	5	33
Low Moor Alloys	30	12	11	7	31
Low Moor Hotspurs	30	13	15	2	28
East Bierley (Res)	30	11	17	2	24
Hardacres SC	30	9	17	4	22
Martins SC	30	7	21	2	16
Canal Ironworks	30	6	21	3	15
Low Moor & Wyke	30	7	22	1	15
L.M.S. Rangers	30	6	22	2	14
P.A.M.	30	4	23	3	11

1945-46

Fourteen teams including KEIGHLEY TOWN (champions) & PRINCE SMITH & STELLS. No table available

1946-47

YORKSHIRE LEAGUE

	P	W	L	D	Pts
Thorne Colliery	38	25	7	6	56
Bradford United	38	25	8	5	55
Huddersfield Tn 'A'	38	21	10	7	49
York City 'A'	38	22	11	5	49
Ossett Town	38	20	9	9	49
Selby Town	38	20	12	6	46
Halifax Town 'A'	38	18	11	9	45
Wombwell Athletic	38	20	14	4	44
Scunthorpe U (Res)	38	20	15	3	43
Chesterfield 'A'	38	15	14	9	39
Goole Town	38	16	17	5	37
Harworth Colliery	38	14	16	8	36
Sheffield Wed 'A'	38	14	17	7	35
South Kirkby Coll	38	13	17	8	34
Leeds United 'A'	38	15	19	4	34
Yorkshire Amateurs	38	16	20	2	34
Gainsboro' Tr (Res)	38	9	20	9	27
KEIGHLEY TOWN	38	9	24	3	23
Hull Amateurs	38	6	26	6	18
Upton Colliery	38	2	33	3	7

BRADFORD AMATEUR LEAGUE

Senior Division	P	W	L	D	Pts
Wyke Old Boys	26	23	2	1	47
Tyersal	26	20	4	2	42
Scholes	26	17	7	2	36
Wilsden	26	16	7	3	35
U.S.M.P. Co	26	16	8	2	34
Dawson P&E	26	16	10	0	32
Swain House	26	13	8	5	31
Sedbergh Old Boys	26	13	13	0	26
Low Moor Hotspurs	26	9	10	7	25
English Electric	26	8	15	3	19
PRINCE SMITH & S	26	7	15	4	18
Ex Services	26	3	20	3	9
KEIGHLEY TN (Res)	26	3	21	2	8
Salts Ltd.	26	4	22	0	8

KEIGHLEY & DISTRICT LEAGUE

Haworth (champions), Cullingworth, Crossflatts, Denholme, Denholme (reserves), Steeton (reserves), Keighley Lifts, Oxenhope Rec, Trico S.C., St. Annes
Victory Shield Final: Cullingworth 4 Oxenhope Rec. 2

KEIGHLEY & DISTRICT CUP FINAL:

Sutton United 2 Silsden 0

CRAVEN & DISTRICT LEAGUE

local sides: Sutton United (+ reserves) champions (after 0-0 draw), Silsden (+ reserves) Steeton Lothersdale Athletic

Chasing Glory

1947-48

YORKSHIRE LEAGUE

	P	W	L	D	Pts
Goole Town	38	29	4	5	63
Gainsboro' Tr (Res)	38	24	11	3	51
Selby Town	38	20	8	10	50
Harworth Colliery	38	22	12	4	48
Bradford United	38	20	12	6	46
Ossett Town	38	17	10	11	45
Barnsley 'A'	38	18	12	8	44
Thorne Colliery	38	19	17	2	40
Scunthorpe U (Res)	38	15	14	9	39
Wombwell Athletic	38	17	17	4	38
Chesterfield 'A'	38	15	18	5	35
Halifax Town 'A'	38	13	16	9	35
Sheffield Wed 'A'	38	15	18	5	35
South Kirkby Coll	38	14	18	6	34
Yorkshire Amateurs	38	15	21	2	32
Leeds United 'A'	38	12	18	8	32
Sheffield United 'A'	38	11	20	7	29
Brodsworth Main	38	11	22	5	27
Huddersfield Tn 'A'	38	6	25	7	19
KEIGHLEY TOWN	38	6	26	6	18

BRADFORD AMATEUR LEAGUE

Premier Division	P	W	L	D	Pts
SUTTON UNITED	26	23	2	1	47
HAWORTH	26	19	6	1	39
Manningham Mills	26	15	7	4	34
Swain House	26	14	10	2	30
Wyke Old Boys	25	14	9	2	30
Wilsden	26	9	11	6	24
SILSDEN	26	11	13	2	24
Greengates	26	10	13	3	23
St.Josephs O.B.	26	10	13	3	23
Scholes	26	10	14	2	22
Dudley Hill & Tong	26	8	15	3	19
Salem Athletic	26	8	16	2	18
Crofts	26	8	16	2	18
Sunfield Rovers	25	3	19	3	9

CRAVEN & DISTRICT LEAGUE

Division 1	P	W	L	D	Pts
Gargrave	14	10	4	0	20
Cononley	14	9	3	2	20
Settle United	14	8	4	2	18
Skipton Bulldogs	14	8	4	2	18
Hellifield	14	7	6	1	15
Earby Victoria	14	6	6	2	14
Langcliffe Wndrs	14	2	12	0	4
Barnoldswick (Res)	14	1	12	1	3

Division 2 local sides: Lothersdale Athletic, Oakworth Albion (res), Bradley United, Cononley (res)

Tables

KEIGHLEY & DISTRICT LEAGUE

Guardhouse (champions), Trico S.C., Crossflatts, Oxenhope Rec, Oakworth Albion, Steeton, Harden, Cullingworth, YMCA, Denholme United, Wilsden (res), Haworth (res), Sutton United (res), Silsden (res) St.Annes w/d

Victory Shield Final: Guardhouse 1 Haworth (res) 1
(Guardhouse awarded cup when Haworth failed to appear for replay)

KEIGHLEY & DISTRICT CUP FINAL

Sutton United 2 Guardhouse 0

1948-49

BRADFORD AMATEUR LEAGUE

Premier Division	P	W	L	D	Pts
U.S.M.P. Co	26	21	5	0	42
Wyke Old Boys	24	16	6	2	34
Wilsden	26	15	7	4	34
Manningham Mills	26	15	8	3	33
HAWORTH	26	13	8	5	31
St. Josephs O.B.	26	12	10	4	28
SUTTON UNITED	26	11	10	5	27
Lightcliffe	22	12	8	2	26
SILSDEN	23	10	10	3	23
Dudley Hill & Tong	24	10	12	2	22
Tyersal	24	8	10	6	22
Scholes	26	7	17	2	16
Greengates	26	3	21	2	8
Swain House	26	2	23	1	5

Division 1: Ingrow United, Prince Smith & Stells **Division 4:** Haworth (reserves)

KEIGHLEY & DISTRICT CUP FINAL

Sutton United 3 Worth Village Albion 2 (after 3-3 draw)

CRAVEN & DISTRICT LEAGUE

Division 1	P	W	L	D	Pts
Settle United	20	17	1	2	36
Cononley	20	14	1	5	33
Bradley United	20	13	6	1	27
Silsden (Res)	20	11	6	3	25
Cowling	20	9	6	5	23
Skipton Bulldogs	20	9	9	2	20
Langcliffe Wdrs	20	7	12	1	15
Skipton L.M.S.	20	6	13	1	13
Hellifield	20	4	12	4	12
Sutton United (Res)	20	3	14	3	9
Carleton	20	3	16	1	7

Division 2: Lothersdale Athletic, reserve sides of Cononley, Bradley United & Cowling

KEIGHLEY & DISTRICT LEAGUE

Guardhouse (champions), Harden, Morton, Oxenhope Rec, Trico S.C., Ingrow United (reserves), Worth Village Albion, St.Annes, Steeton, Dean Smith & Grace, Oakworth Albion. Howden Sports w/d.

Victory Shield Final:
Guardhouse 4 Oxenhope Rec 1

Chasing Glory

1949-50

BRADFORD AMATEUR LEAGUE

Premier Division	P	W	L	D	Pts
SUTTON UNITED	26	21	3	2	44
U.S.M.P. Co	26	16	5	5	37
Swain House	26	16	7	3	35
HAWORTH	26	13	8	5	31
Bradford Electric	26	12	11	3	27
SILSDEN	26	11	11	4	26
Tyersal	26	12	12	2	26
Bingley Town	26	7	9	10	24
Frizinghall Rovers	26	9	14	3	21
Wilsden	25	9	13	3	21
Wyke Old Boys	24	9	12	3	21
St. Josephs O.B.	25	8	13	4	20
Thackley (Res)	25	7	13	5	19
O.D.R.A.	24	2	19	5	7

Division 1: Ingrow United   **Division 3:** Haworth (reserves)

KEIGHLEY & DISTRICT LEAGUE

	P	W	L	D	Pts
St. Annes	34	32	2	0	64
Guardhouse	33	29	3	1	59
Worth Village Alb	33	24	9	0	48
Addingham	30	21	5	4	46

Bingley Town (res), Steeton, Morton, Bingley St.Josephs, Oxenhope Rec, Silsden (reserves), Oakworth Albion, Riddlesden, Ingrow United (reserves), Harden, Sutton United (reserves), Oakworth Albion (reserves), Guardhouse (reserves)
Dean Smith & Grace w/d, Keighley Labour Youth w/d pre season

Victory Shield Final: Guardhouse   5   Addingham   2

KEIGHLEY & DISTRICT CUP FINAL

Guardhouse   2   St.Annes   2
(after abandoned game - trophy shared)

CRAVEN & DISTRICT LEAGUE

local sides: Cowling (+ reserves), Cononley (+ reserves), Bradley United (+ reserves), Lothersdale Athletic, Prince Smith & Stells, Cross Hills Y.C.

1950-51

BRADFORD AMATEUR LEAGUE

Premier Division	P	W	L	D	Pts
Swain House	26	22	1	3	47
U.S.M.P. Co	26	19	3	4	42
Birkenshaw Rovers	26	16	6	4	36
Wyke Old Boys	26	13	7	6	32
Bradford Electric	26	13	9	4	30
St.Josephs O.B.	26	13	10	3	29
East Ward L.C.	26	9	7	10	28
HAWORTH	26	11	10	5	27
SILSDEN	26	11	12	3	25
Bingley Town	26	10	13	3	23

INGROW UNITED	26	7	17	2	16
Crossflatts	26	5	17	4	14
Tyersal	26	5	19	2	12
Frizinghall Rovers	26	1	23	2	4

KEIGHLEY & DISTRICT CUP FINAL
Haworth 5 Eldwick 2

KEIGHLEY & DISTRICT LEAGUE
Guardhouse (champions), Guardhouse (res), St.Josephs, Oxenhope Rec, Morton, Prince Smith & Stells, Silsden (res), Haworth (res), Ingrow United (res) Steeton, w/d, St.Annes w/d pre-season
Victory Shield Final:
St.Josephs 1 Guardhouse 0

WEST RIDING COUNTY AMATEUR LEAGUE
Sutton United

CRAVEN & DISTRICT LEAGUE
local sides: Cowling (+ reserves), Cononley (+ reserves), Lothersdale Athletic, Cross Hills Y.C. (+ reserves), Sutton United (reserves), Bradley United

1951-52

BRADFORD AMATEUR LEAGUE

Premier Division	P	W	L	D	Pts
Swain House	18	10	1	7	27
Birkenshaw Rovers	18	11	4	3	25
GUARDHOUSE	18	9	4	5	23
Wyke Old Boys	18	8	4	6	22
U.S.M.P.Co	18	9	6	3	21
Hepolite	18	7	9	2	16
East Ward L.C.	18	5	9	4	14
HAWORTH	17	6	9	2	14
Bingley Town	17	2	11	4	8
Dick Lane United	18	3	13	2	8

Division 4 - Haworth (res)

KEIGHLEY & DISTRICT CUP FINAL
Silsden 1 Sutton United 0 (after 0-0 draw)

WHARFEDALE LEAGUE
Division 1: Silsden   **Division 2:** Silsden (reserves)

CRAVEN & DISTRICT LEAGUE

Division One Section 1	P	W	L	D	Pts
Gargrave	22	16	3	3	35
Cowling	22	14	2	6	34
Sutton United	22	15	5	2	32
Rolls Royce	22	11	9	2	24
Grassington United	22	9	9	4	22
Cononley	22	7	11	4	18
Langcliffe Wdrs	22	5	13	4	14
Section 2	P	W	L	D	Pts
Skipton Bulldogs	22	12	4	6	30

Chasing Glory

	P	W	L	D	Pts
Cross Hills Y.C.	22	7	12	3	17
Skipton L.M.S.	22	6	13	3	15
Lothersdale Ath	22	6	14	2	14
Carleton	22	4	15	3	11

Division 2 local sides
Bradley United, Cowling (reserves), Sutton United (reserves), Cross Hills Y.C. (res), Cononley (res)

BRADFORD RED TRIANGLE

Morton

KEIGHLEY & DISTRICT LEAGUE

	P	W	L	D	Pts	W	L	D	Pts
Oakworth Albion	20	6	2	2	14	7	0	3	17
Prince Smith & S	20	5	4	1	11	5	1	4	13
Harden	20	5	3	2	12	3	4	3	9
Oxenhope Rec	18	5	4	0	10	4	2	3	11
Steeton	20	3	6	1	7	4	6	0	8
Ingrow United	18	1	6	2	4	0	9	0	0

Oakworth Albion won both 'halves' of the season to win the championship.
St.Josephs w/d
Victory Shield Final: Oakworth Albion   3   Oxenhope Rec   1 (aet)

1952-53

BRADFORD AMATEUR LEAGUE

Division 1	P	W	L	D	Pts
Swain House	26	23	2	1	47
U.S.M.P. Co	26	17	3	6	40
Eldwick	26	15	8	3	33
Bowling Dyeworks	26	13	9	4	30
Wilsden	26	13	9	4	30
HAWORTH	26	14	11	1	29
Crofts United	26	12	10	4	28
Birkenshaw Rovers	26	12	11	3	27
Low Moor Celtic	26	8	13	5	21
Hepolite	26	8	13	5	21
East Ward L.C.	26	7	16	3	17
Bradford Electric	26	7	16	3	17
N.E.G.B.	26	8	17	1	17
Tyersal	26	2	21	3	7

Division 5 - Haworth (reserves)

KEIGHLEY & DISTRICT CUP FINAL

Worth Village   4   Silsden   1

WHARFEDALE LEAGUE

Division 1: Silsden   **Division 2:** Silsden (reserves)

CRAVEN & DISTRICT LEAGUE

local sides: Worth Village (champions), Sutton United (+ reserves), Oxenhope Rec, Cowling (+ reserves), Cononley (+ reserves), Prince Smith & Stells, Cross Hills Y.C. (+ reserves), Lothersdale Athletic, Bradley United

BRADFORD RED TRIANGLE

Morton   Keighley Trico S.C.

1953-54
BRADFORD AMATEUR LEAGUE

Division 1	P	W	L	D	Pts
Thackley (Res)	23	16	4	3	35
Girlington Y.C.O.B.	23	14	4	5	33
East Ward L.C.	22	14	7	1	29
Bfd Telephones	22	12	7	3	27
Birkenshaw Rovers	22	12	8	2	26
U.S.M.P. Co	22	11	7	4	26
Wilsden	22	9	10	3	21
Crofts United	22	8	10	4	20
Thornton United	22	6	11	5	17
HAWORTH	22	5	14	3	13
Eldwick	22	4	16	2	10
N.E.G.B.	22	2	16	3	9

Sutton United w/d
Division 2: Worth Village, Oakworth Albion

KEIGHLEY & DISTRICT CUP FINAL
Wilsden 2   Cross Hills Y.C. 1

KEIGHLEY & DISTRICT LEAGUE

	P	W	L	D	F	A	Pts
Grippon Sports	16	12	3	1	79	34	25
Morton Sports	16	11	4	1	61	37	23
Haworth (Res)	16	10	4	2	69	33	22
Central Y.C.	16	9	6	1	69	31	19
Oakworth Albion	16	7	7	2	53	60	14
Worth Village	16	6	9	1	36	55	13
Steeton	16	6	10	0	40	79	12
Sutton United	16	3	10	3	32	59	9
Silsden 'A'	16	2	13	1	28	84	5

Airedale S.C. w/d
Victory Shield Final:
Central Y.C. 4   Worth Village 1

WHARFEDALE LEAGUE
Division 1: Silsden   **Division 2:** Silsden (reserves)

BRADFORD RED TRIANGLE
Keighley Trico S.C.   Newtown Boys w/d

CRAVEN & DISTRICT LEAGUE
local sides: Oxenhope Rec, Cowling (+ reserves), Prince Smith & Stells (+ reserves), Cross Hills Y.C. (+ reserves), Cononley (+ reserves), Lothersdale Athletic, Bradley United

1954-55
KEIGHLEY & DISTRICT CUP FINAL
Wilsden 4   Cross Hills Y.C. 1

WHARFEDALE LEAGUE
Silsden (champions)

Chasing Glory

KEIGHLEY & DISTRICT LEAGUE

Steeton (champions), Grippon Sports, Silsden (reserves), Dean Smith & Grace, Oakworth Albion, Trico S.C., Worth Village, Prince Smith & Stells (reserves), Sutton Textiles
Victory Shield Final: Silsden   4   Steeton   2

CRAVEN & DISTRICT LEAGUE

local sides: Prince Smith & Stells, Oxenhope Rec, Cross Hills Y.C. (+ reserves), Lothersdale Athletic, Cowling, Cononley, Bradley United

1955-56

KEIGHLEY & DISTRICT CUP FINAL

Silsden   5   Steeton   3

WHARFEDALE LEAGUE

Silsden (champions)

WEST YORKSHIRE LEAGUE

Prince Smith & Stells

CRAVEN & DISTRICT LEAGUE

local sides: Silsden (reserves), Oxenhope Rec, Cross Hills Y.C. (+ reserves), Lothersdale Athletic, Cowling (+ reserves), Cononley, Bradley United

KEIGHLEY & DISTRICT LEAGUE

Worth Village (champions), Central Y.C., Steeton, Oakworth Albion, Cullingworth, Sutton United, Prince Smith & Stells (reserves), Dean Smith & Grace, Oxenhope Rec, Morton Sports, Trico S.C.
Victory Shield Final:
Worth Village   6   Sutton Utd   2
Jubilee Trophy Final:
Central Y.C   6   Oakworth Alb   0

1956-57

KEIGHLEY & DISTRICT CUP FINAL

Cullingworth Rovers   3   Wilsden   0

KEIGHLEY & DISTRICT LEAGUE

	P	W	L	D	Pts
Kly Shamrocks	16	14	1	1	29
Steeton	16	13	2	0	26
Haworth Sports	16	12	2	2	26
Morton Sports	16	7	7	2	16
Central Y.C.	16	7	8	1	15
Silsden (Reserves)	16	5	9	2	12
Cullingworth	16	3	11	2	8
Harden	16	2	11	3	7
Dan Mitchells	16	1	14	1	3

Victory Shield Final: Keighley Shamrocks   2   Central Y.C.   0

WHARFEDALE LEAGUE

Keighley Central (champions)   Silsden

CRAVEN & DISTRICT LEAGUE
local sides: Oxenhope Rec, Lothersdale Athletic, Cross Hills Y.C. (+ reserves), Worth Village, Cononley, Cowling, Bradley United

1957-58

KEIGHLEY & DISTRICT CUP FINAL
Keighley Shamrocks   6   Parkwood Amateurs   2

WHARFEDALE LEAGUE
Keighley Central, Silsden

CRAVEN & DISTRICT LEAGUE
local sides: Oxenhope Rec (+ res) champions, Cowling, Cononley, Prince Smith & Stells, Cross Hills Y.C. (+ reserves), Bradley United, Lothersdale Athletic Haworth w/d

KEIGHLEY & DISTRICT LEAGUE
Keighley Shamrocks (champions), Parkwood Amateurs, Steeton, Harden, St.Josephs, Cullingworth, Morton Sports, Silsden (reserves), Haworth (reserves)
Victory Shield Final: Parkwood Ams beat Kly Shamrocks

1958-59

KEIGHLEY & DISTRICT CUP FINAL
Eldwick   4   Silsden   2

WHARFEDALE LEAGUE
Keighley Central, Silsden

KEIGHLEY & DISTRICT LEAGUE

	P	W	L	D	F	A	Pts
Parkwood Ams	16	16	0	0	139	18	32
Oakworth Albion	16	11	2	3	71	37	25
Morton Sports	16	7	5	4	63	62	18
K. Shamrocks (Res)	16	8	6	1	50	60	17
St.Josephs	16	5	6	4	39	47	16
Keighley Grinders	16	6	9	1	57	61	13
Bingley Central	16	6	10	0	53	74	12
Prince Smith & S	16	4	9	3	36	60	11
Prince Smith (Res)	16	0	16	0	15	105	0

Victory Shield Winners: Parkwood Amateurs
Jubilee Trophy Winners: Keighley Grinders

CRAVEN & DISTRICT LEAGUE

Division 1	P	W	L	D	Pts
Oxenhope Rec	14	12	2	0	24
Grassington United	14	11	2	1	23
Hellifield	14	8	5	1	17
Cross Hills Y.C.	14	7	6	1	15
Settle United	14	4	6	4	12
Gargrave	14	5	8	1	11
Skipton L.M.S.	14	3	9	2	8
B'lick & Earby	14	1	13	0	2

Division 2: Steeton, Lothersdale Ath, Bradley Utd. ,Silsden (res), Cononley & Cowling. **Division 3:** reserve sides of Cross Hills Y.C. & Oxenhope Rec.

Chasing Glory

BRADFORD AMATEUR LEAGUE

Division 2: Kly Shamrocks

1959-60

KEIGHLEY & DISTRICT CUP FINAL

Keighley Central   2   Oxenhope Rec   1

KEIGHLEY & DISTRICT LEAGUE

	P	W	L	D	F	A	Pts
Keighley Grinders	14	12	0	2	76	17	26
Parkwood Ams	14	12	1	1	66	19	25
Oakworth Albion	14	7	4	3	47	44	17
Ilkley	14	6	7	1	40	36	13
St. Josephs	14	6	7	1	35	41	13
Prince Smith & S	14	3	10	1	28	68	7
Morton Sports *	14	2	10	2	25	35	6
Steeton (Reserves)	14	0	9	5	37	79	5

Morton w/d late in season, opponents awarded points in unplayed games.
Victory Shield Final: Keighley Grinders 3   Parkwood Ams   2
Jubilee Trophy Final: Parkwood Ams.   3   Steeton (res)   2 (a.e.t.)

WHARFEDALE LEAGUE

Keighley Central (champions)

BRADFORD AMATEUR LEAGUE

Division 2: Keighley Shamrocks

CRAVEN & DISTRICT LEAGUE

Division 1

	P	W	L	D	F	A	Pts
Skipton L.M.S.	24	16	4	4	100	37	36
Hellifield Sports	24	16	5	3	115	58	35
Steeton	24	16	6	2	134	50	34
Grassington United	24	16	6	2	94	39	34
Skipton Town	24	16	6	2	86	58	34
Cross Hills Y.C.	24	15	7	2	112	50	32
Oxenhope Rec	24	16	8	0	94	46	32
Skipton Bulldogs	24	15	7	2	91	56	32
Lothersdale Athletic	24	12	7	5	85	57	29
Settle United	24	12	10	2	95	54	26
Cononley Sports	24	8	12	4	65	84	20
Gargrave	24	9	15	0	80	124	18
Cowling	24	5	15	4	54	106	14
Silsden	24	6	17	1	44	81	13
B'lick & Earby Utd	24	6	17	1	49	101	13
Horton	24	1	22	1	40	145	3
Bradley United	24	1	22	1	30	222	3

Top 4 teams played off for title : Steeton beat Grassington United 1-0 in the final to win the championship.

CRAVEN & DISTRICT LEAGUE

Division 2 local sides: Lothersdale Athletic (reserves), Silsden (reserves), Cross Hills Y.C. (reserves), Oxenhope Rec (reserves)

Tables

1960-61

KEIGHLEY & DISTRICT CUP FINAL

Eldwick   4   Keighley Shamrocks   0

KEIGHLEY & DISTRICT LEAGUE

	P	W	L	D	Pts
Parkwood Ams	14	13	1	1	25
Keighley Grinders	13	9	3	1	19
St.Josephs	14	8	4	2	18
Prince Smith & S	14	8	4	1	17
Carleton (Res)	14	6	6	2	14
Steeton (Reserves)	14	4	10	0	8
N.S.F. Rangers	14	3	11	0	6
Ilkley	14	1	12	1	3

Victory Shield Final: Carleton (res)   4   Parkwood Ams.   2

WHARFEDALE LEAGUE

Keighley Central

BRADFORD AMATEUR LEAGUE

Division 2: Keighley Shamrocks

CRAVEN & DISTRICT LEAGUE

Division 1	P	W	L	D	F	A	Pts
Oxenhope Rec	26	19	4	3	123	48	41
Barnoldswick P.R.	26	18	5	3	94	40	39
Skipton L.M.S.	26	16	5	5	90	48	37
Cononley Sports	26	15	6	5	107	67	35
Lothersdale Athletic	26	15	8	3	99	60	33
Steeton	26	14	10	2	91	73	30
Hellifield Sports	26	14	10	2	90	91	30
Cross Hills Y.C.	26	13	11	2	89	88	28
Silsden	26	12	10	4	79	78	28
Skipton Bulldogs	26	12	13	1	79	75	25
Skipton Town	26	8	11	7	59	58	23
Rolls Royce	26	7	14	5	68	109	19
Grassington United	26	8	15	3	70	77	19
Settle United	26	8	18	0	62	102	16
Oakworth Albion	26	2	21	3	45	135	7
Gargrave	26	2	22	2	44	140	6

Oxenhope beat Skipton L.M.S. 2-0 in the top 4 play off final to win the championship.
Division 2 local sides: Cowling, Bradley United, Oxenhope Rec (reserves), Cross Hills Y.C. (reserves), Silsden (reserves), Lothersdale Athletic (reserves)

1961-62

KEIGHLEY & DISTRICT CUP FINAL

Keighley Central   2   Keighley Shamrocks   1

KEIGHLEY & DISTRICT LEAGUE

	P	W	L	D	F	A	Pts
Keighley Grinders	14	11	1	2	77	32	24
N.S.F. Rangers	14	11	3	0	71	30	22
Carleton (Res)	14	7	5	2	51	40	16

165

Chasing Glory

Kly Central (Res)	14	8	6	0	50	39	16
Prince Smith & S	14	6	6	2	53	42	14
Parkwood Ams	14	5	7	2	35	37	12
Keighley Lifts	14	2	11	1	23	65	5
Ilkley	14	1	12	1	18	84	3

Victory Shield Final: Keighley Central (res) 3   Parkwood Ams   0

WHARFEDALE LEAGUE
Keighley Central

BRADFORD AMATEUR LEAGUE
Division 1: Keighley Shamrocks

CRAVEN & DISTRICT LEAGUE

Division 1	P	W	L	D	Pts
Oxenhope Rec	26	21	3	2	44
Grassington United	26	19	4	3	41
Cononley Sports	26	19	4	3	41
Skipton L.M.S.	26	18	5	3	39
Barnoldswick P.R.	26	18	7	1	37
Steeton	26	18	6	4	36
Silsden	26	15	7	4	34
Skipton Bulldogs	26	12	8	6	30
Cross Hills Y.C.	26	12	9	5	29
Hellifield Sports	26	12	11	3	27
Skipton Town	26	9	13	4	22
Lothersdale Athletic	26	9	13	4	22
Rolls Royce	26	8	15	3	19
Gargrave	26	7	16	3	17
Settle United	26	3	19	4	10
Haworth	26	3	19	4	10
Silentnight	26	3	21	2	8
Central Y.C.	26	1	25	0	2

Grassington United beat Skipton LMS 2-0 in the top 4 play off final to win the championship.
Division 2 local sides: Oakworth Albion, Bradley United, Cowling, Oxenhope Rec (reserves), Steeton (reserves), Cross Hills Y.C. (reserves), Silsden (reserves), Lothersdale Athletic (reserves)

KEIGHLEY SUNDAY ALLIANCE (first season)
Victoria Star (champions), Volts All Stars, Bradford Moor, Shoulder of Mutton, Skipton Town, Gargrave, Keighley West Yorkshire, Fountain, Wask United, Bingley Holy Trinity
Jeff Hall Trophy Final: Victoria Star   4   Shoulder of Mutton   3

1962-63

KEIGHLEY & DISTRICT CUP FINAL
Keighley Central   5   Denholme United   2

KEIGHLEY & DISTRICT LEAGUE
Parkwood Amateurs (champions), Parkwood Y.C., Central Y.C., Prince Smith & Stells, Prince Smith & Stells (Reserves)

BRADFORD AMATEUR LEAGUE
Division 1: Keighley Shamrocks

Tables

CRAVEN & DISTRICT LEAGUE

Division 1	P	W	L	D	Pts
Oxenhope Rec	20	17	2	1	35
Barnoldswick P.R.	20	15	1	4	34
Steeton	20	16	2	2	34
Silsden	20	14	5	1	29
Skipton L.M.S.	20	14	5	1	29
Settle United	20	13	4	2	28
Cononley Sports	20	12	4	4	28
Grassington United	20	10	6	4	24
Gargrave	20	9	9	2	20
Cross Hills Y.C	20	8	10	2	18
Skipton Bulldogs	19	8	11	0	16
Rolls Royce	20	6	12	2	14
Oakworth Albion	20	6	13	1	13
Skipton Town	18	5	12	1	11
Lothersdale Ath	20	4	14	2	10
Silentnight	20	2	16	2	6
Haworth	19	2	16	1	5
Hellifield Sports	20	0	18	2	2

Oxenhope beat Barnoldswick Park Rovers 3-2 in the top 4 play off final to win the title.
Division 2 local sides: Keighley Lifts, Cowling, Bradley United, Oxenhope Rec (reserves), Steeton (reserves), Silsden (reserves), Cross Hills Y.C. (reserves), Cononley Sports (reserves), Lothersdale Athletic (reserves)

WHARFEDALE LEAGUE – 1st 5

	P	W	L	D	F	A	Pts
KLY CENTRAL (RES)	23	19	1	3	109	25	41
Ives Sports	23	19	2	2	122	38	40
Baildon Rovers	23	17	5	1	122	40	35
Otley	23	15	6	2	105	53	32
KEIGHLEY N.S.F.	23	15	7	1	101	56	31

KEIGHLEY SUNDAY ALLIANCE

	P	W	L	D	F	A	Pts
Victoria Star	23	20	1	1	120	31	41
Silsden	23	18	2	2	121	27	38
Kly West Yorkshire	23	17	4	1	96	30	35
Bradford Moor	23	14	4	4	111	49	32
All Stars	23	11	9	2	75	36	24
Woodside Rangers	23	10	8	3	67	43	23
Gargrave	23	10	9	2	72	55	22
Bingley B.S.	23	10	11	0	55	62	20
Beaconsfield	23	8	12	2	61	59	18
Park Rangers	23	6	16	0	37	103	12
Vine Tavern	23	6	16	0	29	81	12
Bingley Wanderers	23	4	18	0	31	134	8
Bingley Holy Trin	23	0	22	0	16	169	0

Wask United w/d
Jeff Hall Trophy Final: Woodside Rovers 2 Beaconsfield 1

WEST YORKSHIRE LEAGUE

Division 2 South : Keighley Central

1963-64

KEIGHLEY & DISTRICT CUP FINAL
Keighley Central   2   Keighley N.S.F. 0

YORKSHIRE LEAGUE - Division 3

	P	W	D	L	Pts
KEIGHLEY CENTRAL	16	12	3	1	27
Farsley Celtic	16	10	4	2	24
Harrogate Town	16	8	5	3	21
Ossett Albion	16	8	1	7	17
Yorkshire Amateurs	16	6	2	8	14
Harrogate Railway	16	5	4	7	14
Salts	16	4	3	9	11
Ossett Town	16	4	2	10	10
Slazengers	16	2	2	12	6

WHARFEDALE LEAGUE
Keighley Shamrocks (champions), Keighley N.S.F. Rangers, Keighley Central (res)

KEIGHLEY SUNDAY ALLIANCE

Division 1	P	W	D	L	F	A	Pts
Bradford Moor	18	14	1	3	89	46	29
Kly West Yorkshire	18	13	1	4	103	48	27
Dean Smith & Grace	18	13	0	5	56	42	26
Bradford Gaelic	18	10	2	5	63	32	22
Crown Rangers	18	10	0	8	68	61	20
Silsden	18	8	2	8	62	47	16
Provincial B.S.	18	7	0	10	42	73	14
Woodside Rovers	18	7	0	11	45	52	14
Victoria Star	18	2	2	14	28	64	6
Bingley B.S.	18	0	2	16	17	117	2

Division 2: Bradford West Yorkshire, Kly West Yorks (reserves), Park Rangers, Silsden (reserves), Bradford Moor (reserves), Bingley Wanderers, Crossflatts, Y.E.B. (Keighley), Bingley Holy Trinity

Jeff Hall Trophy Final: Dean Smith & Grace 4 Woodside Rovers 2 (after 3-3 draw)

CRAVEN & DISTRICT LEAGUE

Division 1	P	W	D	L	Pts
Grassington United	26	22	1	3	45
Skipton Bulldogs	26	22	1	3	45
Silsden	26	19	3	4	41
Keighley Lifts	26	18	1	7	37
Oxenhope Rec	26	16	3	7	35
Skipton L.M.S.	26	15	3	8	33
Steeton	26	16	1	9	33
Lothersdale Ath	26	14	3	9	31
Settle United	26	13	3	10	29
Cross Hills Y.C.	26	8	7	11	23
Cononley Sports	26	7	4	15	18
Skipton Town	26	7	2	17	16
Prince Smith & S	26	3	4	19	10
Gargrave	26	2	3	21	7
Oakworth Albion	26	3	1	22	7
Keighley Grinders	26	2	2	22	6

Silsden beat Keighley Lifts 3-2 (a.e.t.) in the top 4 play off final to win the title.
Division 2 local sides: Cowling , Bradley United and reserve sides of Lothersdale Athletic, Steeton Oxenhope Rec, Cross Hills Y.C. & Silsden.

BRADFORD RED TRIANGLE
Division D: Haworth Y.C. & Prince Smith & Stells
Division E: Guardhouse & Haworth Y.C. (reserves)

1964-65

KEIGHLEY & DISTRICT CUP FINAL
Silsden   3   Keighley Central   1

WEST YORKSHIRE LEAGUE

Premier Division	P	W	D	L	F	A	Pts
Guiseley	20	15	2	3	73	22	32
Snydale Road Ath	20	14	4	2	52	19	32
Thackley	20	15	0	5	65	23	30
Micklefield	20	12	2	6	61	40	26
East End Park WMC	20	10	1	9	34	45	21
KEIGHLEY CENTRAL	20	6	3	12	33	53	15
Altofts	20	6	2	12	35	46	14
Monckton Colliery	20	6	2	12	29	48	14
Methley United	20	5	3	12	23	44	13
Britannia Works	20	5	2	13	36	71	12
D.P. & E. (Otley)	20	5	1	14	37	67	11

Division 3 North: Woodhouse Rovers

WEST RIDING COUNTY AMATEUR LEAGUE
Division A: Silsden   Division B: Keighley N.S.F. Rangers

BRADFORD RED TRIANGLE
Division 1: Haworth Y.C. **Division 3**: Guardhouse **Division 4**: Parkwood United, Haworth Y.C. (reserves) **Division 5**: Guardhouse (reserves)

KEIGHLEY SUNDAY ALLIANCE
Clifton Driving School (champions), Bradford West Yorkshire, Dean Smith & Grace, Bradford Moor (reserves), Park Rangers, Keighley West Yorkshire, Burley Trojans, Provincial Building Society, Fell Lane Dynamos, Bingley Wanderers, Parkwood United, Bingley Holy Trinity, Airedale Rovers, Crossflatts
Silsden w/d
Jeff Hall Trophy Final: Dean Smith & Grace   8   Parkwood United   1

CRAVEN & DISTRICT LEAGUE

Division 1	P	W	D	L	Pts
Skipton Bulldogs	30	25	3	2	53
Barnoldswick P.R.	30	23	3	4	49
Oxenhope Rec	30	20	4	6	44
Keighley Lifts	30	17	8	5	42
Grassington United	30	18	3	9	39
Cross Hills Y.C.	30	17	3	10	37
Rolls Royce	30	14	7	9	35
Lothersdale Ath	30	13	5	12	31
Settle United	30	13	4	13	30
Steeton	30	11	5	14	27
Prince Smith & S	30	11	4	15	26

	P	W	D	L	F	A	Pts
Skipton L.M.S.	30	7	7	16	21		
Cononley Sports	30	8	2	20	18		
Oakworth Albion	30	5	5	25	15		
Skipton Town	30	3	4	23	10		
Gargrave	30	3	2	25	8		

Division 2 local sides: Cowling, Bradley United, Steeton (res), Lothersdale Ath (res), Cross Hills Y.C. (res), Prince Smith & S (res), Oxenhope Rec (res)

WHARFEDALE LEAGUE

	P	W	D	L	F	A	Pts
Ives Sports	28	22	2	4	165	49	46
Baildon Rovers	28	22	2	4	124	43	46
KLY SHAMROCKS	28	20	3	5	115	32	43
Rawdon B.L.	28	19	2	7	95	55	40
Thackley (Res)	28	18	3	7	97	46	39
Taytors (Shipley)	28	17	5	6	127	63	39
Bingley Central	28	15	5	8	95	66	35
KLY CENTRAL (RES)	28	14	4	10	106	90	32
Shipley Town (Res)	28	14	2	12	86	70	30
Ilkley	28	12	4	12	83	92	28
Otley	28	13	1	14	82	85	27
SILSDEN (RES)	28	11	4	13	87	74	26
Wilsden	28	9	2	17	74	108	20
Westfield United	28	7	2	19	67	111	16
Esholt St. Pauls	28	7	0	21	47	140	14
Carleton (Res)	28	4	1	23	43	141	9
Menston St. Johns	28	2	3	23	41	152	7
Otley Council Spts	28	2	3	23	45	162	7

1965-66

KEIGHLEY & DISTRICT CUP FINAL

Oxenhope Rec   1   Keighley Central   .0

WEST YORKSHIRE LEAGUE

Premier Division	P	W	D	L	F	A	Pts
Thackley	20	17	2	1	78	23	36
Snydale Road Ath	20	17	1	2	65	21	35
Micklefield	20	13	2	5	60	31	28
KEIGHLEY CENTRAL	20	9	4	7	50	41	22
Guiseley	20	7	5	8	41	28	19
Salts	20	8	2	10	41	42	18
Altofts	20	5	5	10	39	60	15
East End Park WMC	20	5	3	12	34	73	13
D.P.& E. (Otley)	20	4	4	12	47	72	12
Methley United	20	4	4	12	32	56	12
Monckton Colliery	20	3	4	13	31	71	10

Division 1: Keighley Shamrocks
Division 3 North: Woodhouse Rovers, Keighley Central (res)

WEST RIDING COUNTY AMATEUR LEAGUE

Division A: Silsden (+ res, div C)   Division B: Keighley N.S.F. Rangers (+ res, div C)

BRADFORD RED TRIANGLE

Parkwood United   Keighley A.F.C.

Tables

KEIGHLEY SUNDAY ALLIANCE
Jeff Hall Trophy Final: Dean Smith & Grace 4 Fell Lane Dynamos 3

Division 1	P	W	D	L	Pts
Dean Smith & Grace	17	17	0	0	34
Park Rangers	18	12	2	4	26
Provident B.S.	16	10	3	3	23
Clifton Dr. School	14	9	1	4	19
Parkwood United	18	9	1	8	19
Fell Lane Dynamos	17	8	0	9	16
Shearbridge United	15	5	0	10	10
Airedale Rovers	17	4	1	12	9
Parkson United	17	2	1	14	5
Greenwoods	17	1	1	15	3

Division 2
Crossflatts, Bingley Road, Bingley Holy Trin., Tarn United, Keighiey W. Yorks, Bfd/Bingley B.S., Airedale Rov (Res), Cottingley Manor, Keighley G.P.O., Holcroft Y.C.

CRAVEN & DISTRICT LEAGUE
local sides Premier Division: Oxenhope Rec (+ res, div 2) (champions) Keighley Lifts, Cross Hills Y.C. (+ res, div 1), Lothersdale Ath (+ res, div 2), Steeton (+ res, div 2)
Division 1: Oakworth Albion, Haworth Y.C., Cowling, Cononley Sports (+ res, div 2), Prince Smith & S (+ res, div 2), Bradley United

1966-67

KEIGHLEY & DISTRICT CUP FINAL
Keighley Central   4   Cross Hills Y.C.   0

WEST YORKSHIRE LEAGUE

Premier Division	P	W	D	L	F	A	Pts
Thackley	22	16	4	2	63	19	36
Monckton Colliery	22	15	5	2	47	25	35
KEIGHLEY CENTRAL	22	12	4	6	64	38	28
Fryston Colliery	22	11	3	8	48	26	25
Snydale Road Ath	22	8	9	5	57	39	25
Salts	22	11	3	8	34	35	25
Guiseley	22	9	5	8	56	48	23
Methley United	22	8	4	10	41	49	20
Altofts	22	7	3	12	28	45	17
Rothwell Athletic	22	4	6	12	24	42	14
East End Park WMC	22	3	3	16	22	66	9
D.P. & E. (Otley)	22	3	1	18	27	79	7

Division 1: Keighley Shamrocks
Division 3 North: Woodhouse Rovers   Keighley Central (res)

KEIGHLEY SUNDAY ALLIANCE
Jeff Hall Trophy Final: Dean Smith & Grace   9   Shearbridge   1

Division 1	P	W	D	L	F	A	Pts
Dean Smith & Grace	20	20	0	0	119	13	40
Shearbridge United	21	17	1	3	84	35	35
Westfield Rovers	20	14	2	4	68	36	30
Morton	21	12	1	8	81	49	25
Ventus United (Res)	18	11	1	6	59	40	23
Crossflatts	21	10	2	9	83	67	22
Fell Lane Dynamos	20	7	3	10	65	57	17

171

Chasing Glory

Parkson United	21	6	1	14	47	78	13
Magnet	21	5	2	14	25	113	12
Parkwood United	22	3	2	17	53	90	8
Tarn United	20	1	1	18	26	97	3

Park Rangers w/d
Division 2
Holycroft Y.C., Bingley Road, Crossflatts (Res), Peter Blacks, Marshfields, Bingley Holy Trin., Keighley G.P.O, Bfd/Bingley B.S., Airedale Rovers, Silsden United, Shipley Con. Club, Cottingley Manor, Netherfield, Keighley W. Yorks

WEST RIDING COUNTY AMATEUR LEAGUE
Division A: Silsden (+ res, div C)

WHARFEDALE LEAGUE
Keighley Shamrocks (reserves)

CRAVEN & DISTRICT LEAGUE

Premier Division	P	W	D	L	Pts
Earby	22	15	4	3	34
Keighley Lifts	22	16	1	5	33
Haworth	22	12	7	3	31
Grassington United	22	13	5	4	31
Skipton Bulldogs	22	11	6	5	28
Cross Hills Y.C.	22	11	3	8	25
Barnoldswick P.R.	22	10	2	10	22
Oxenhope Rec	22	10	2	10	22
Rolls Royce	22	5	2	15	12
Settle United	22	5	2	15	12
Oakworth Albion	22	4	3	15	11
Lothersdale Ath	22	1	1	20	3

local sides Division 1: Prince Smith & Stells (+ res, div 2), Cononley Sports (+ res, div 2), Steeton (+ res, div 2), Bradley United, Cowling (+ res, div 2), Cross Hills Y.C. (reserves) **Division 2:** Haworth (reserves), Oxenhope Rec (reserves), Keighley Lifts (reserves), Lothersdale Ath (reserves) w/d

1967-68

KEIGHLEY & DISTRICT CUP FINAL
Keighley Central   3   Cross Hills Y.C.   1

WEST YORKSHIRE LEAGUE

Premier Division	P	W	D	L	F	A	Pts
Snydale Road Ath	22	17	3	2	55	27	37
Fryston Colliery	22	17	1	4	62	22	35
Methley United	22	16	2	4	42	19	34
Monckton Colliery	22	14	1	7	55	29	29
Guiseley	22	11	3	8	57	35	25
Salts	22	10	3	9	47	42	23
KEIGHLEY CENTRAL	22	9	4	9	37	44	22
Altofts	22	8	5	9	44	36	21
Rothwell Athletic	22	5	4	13	24	45	14
D.P. & E. (Otley)	22	3	3	16	32	64	9
East End Park WMC	22	2	4	16	16	60	8
Ardsley Celtic	22	2	3	17	26	74	7

Division 1: Keighley Shamracks **Division 3 North:** Woodhouse Rovers, Keighley Central (reserves), Keighley Shamrocks (reserves)

Tables

KEIGHLEY SUNDAY ALLIANCE

Division 1	P	W	D	L	Pts
Dean Smith & Grace	13	13	0	0	26
Westfield Rovers	14	10	0	4	20
Morton	14	9	1	4	19
Shearbridge United	13	7	0	6	14
Crossflatts	13	6	1	6	13
Ventus United (Res)	13	4	0	9	8
Holycroft Y.C.	14	2	2	10	6
Cottingley Dynamo	14	0	2	12	2

Division 2: Magnet, Bingley Holy Trinity, Keighley G.P.O., Marshfields, Peter Blacks, Crossflatts (res), Provincial B.Society, Tarn United. **Division 3:** Silsden, Silsden United, Heatons, Airedale Rovers, Bfd & Bly B. Society, Shipley Con Club, Great Northern, Cottingley Manor. **Division 4:** Addingham, Shipley Rovers, Netherfield, Kensington Club, Keighley West Yorkshire, High Royds, Broom United, N.S.F., Central Y.C., Stells United
Jeff Hall Trophy Final: Dean Smith & Grace 3 Westfield Rovers 1

CRAVEN & DISTRICT LEAGUE

PREMIER DIVISION	P	W	D	L	Pts
Keighley Lifts	26	18	3	5	39
Skipton Bulldogs	26	19	1	6	39
Haworth	26	18	2	6	38
Earby	26	15	5	6	35
Cononley Sports	26	15	3	8	33
Grassington	26	14	3	9	31
Cross Hills	26	12	5	9	29
Prince Smith and Stells	26	14	0	12	28
Settle	26	9	2	15	20
Oxenhope Rec	26	9	2	15	20
Rolls Royce	26	6	5	15	17
Barnoldswick Park Rovers	26	6	4	16	16
Carleton	26	4	4	18	12
Oakworth Albion	26	2	3	21	7

Division 1: Cowling, Prince Smith and Stells Res, Steeton, Lothersdale Athletic. **Division 2:** Keighley Lifts Res, Steeton Res, Cross Hills Res, Oxenhope Rec Res, Oakworth Albion Res, Haworth Res, Cowling Res, Cononley Res.

WEST RIDING COUNTY AMATEUR LEAGUE

Premier Division: Silsden (+ res div)

1969-70

KEIGHLEY & DISTRICT CUP FINAL

Keighley Central 1 Silsden 0

KEIGHLEY SUNDAY ALLIANCE

Jeff Hall Trophy Final: Westwood 4 Holycroft Y.C. 3 (a.e.t)
Division 1: Dean Smith & Grace (champions), Westfield Rovers, Morton, Ventus Utd, Westwood, Pile Bar, Alma, Victoria Utd, Wrose Rangers, Great Northern, Crag Road Utd. **Division 2:** Holycroft Y.C., Marshfields, Heatons, Prince Smith & Stells, Scalebor Park, Addingham, Shipley, Station United, Magnet, Knowle. **Division 3:** Silsden United, Ilkley Town, Kensington, Broom United, Kly W. Yorks, Moorhead Rvrs, Murgatroyds, Shire Rovers, Robin Mills, Ilkley Phoenix, Wask United. **Division 4:** Harden Pk Rgrs, Shipley

Chasing Glory

Con. Club, Airedale Rovers, , High Royds, Ilkley Rovers, Provincial B. Soc., Tong United, Kly Central Y.C, N.S.F.

CRAVEN & DISTRICT LEAGUE

Premier Division	P	W	D	L	Pts
Barnoldswick P.R.	30	29	0	1	58
Cross Hills Y.C.	30	24	2	4	50
Gisburn	30	20	4	6	44
Steeton	30	20	3	7	43
Earby	30	18	7	5	43
Cowling	30	14	5	11	33
Rolls Royce	30	15	2	13	32
Skipton Bulldogs	30	14	3	13	31
Grassington United	30	11	7	12	29
Oakworth Albion	30	12	3	15	27
Cononley Sports	30	8	6	16	22
Oxenhope Rec	30	9	1	20	19
Settle United	30	8	3	19	19
Skipton Town	30	6	3	21	15
Skipton L.M.S.	30	3	2	25	8
Haworth	30	2	3	25	7

other local sides: **Division 1:**
Lothersdale Ath, Prince Smith & Stells + reserve sides of Cross Hills & Silsden
Division 2: reserve sides of Steeton, Cowling, Prince Smith & Stells, Haworth Oxenhope Rec, Oakworth Albion, Cononley Sports & Lothersdale Athletic

WEST YORKSHIRE LEAGUE

Premier Division: Keighley Central (champions)

WEST RIDING COUNTY AMATEUR LEAGUE

Premier Division: Silsden   **Division 1:** Keighley Lifts

1970-71

KEIGHLEY & DISTRICT CUP FINAL

Silsden   2   Keighley Central   0

WEST YORKSHIRE LEAGUE

Premier Division: Keighley Central

WEST RIDING COUNTY AMATEUR LEAGUE

Premier Division: Silsden (+ reserves)

KEIGHLEY SUNDAY ALLIANCE

Jeff Hall Trophy Final: Dean Smith & Grace   4   Holycroft Y.C.   0
Division 1: Dean Smith & Grace (champions), Westfield Rovers, Westwood, Holycroft Y.C., Marshfields, Ventus United
Division 2: Odsal, Ilkley Town, Fieldhead Y.C., Scalebor Park, Skipton Town, Heatons, Cullingworth, Kensington, Wrose Rangers, Addingham, Magnet
Division 3: Keighley West Yorkshire, Shipley, Broom United, Murgatroyds, Harden Park Rangers, Moorhead, Shipley Con. Club, Silsden United, Knowle, Hattersleys
Division 4: Airedale Rovers, N.S.F., Tong United, Repton, Shire Rovers, High Royds, Ilkley Phoenix, Ilkley Rovers, Saltaire County, Slingsbys, Ryshworth Athletic, Silsden

Tables

CRAVEN & DISTRICT LEAGUE

Premier Division: Cross Hills Y.C. (+ res, div 1) champions, Steeton (+ res, div 1), Cowling (+ res, div 1), Oakworth Albion (+ res, div 2), Cononley Sports (+ res, div 2), Oxenhope Rec (+ res, div 2) **Division 1:** United Lifts, Lothersdale Ath (+ res, div 2), Prince Smith & S (+ res, div 2)

1971-72

KEIGHLEY & DISTRICT CUP FINAL

Silsden   4   Cowling   0

WEST YORKSHIRE LEAGUE

Premier Division: Keighley Central

WEST RIDING COUNTY AMATEUR LEAGUE

Premier Division: Silsden (+ reserves) champions

CRAVEN & DISTRICT LEAGUE

Premier Division	P	W	D	L	Pts
Colne B.L.	22	20	0	2	40
Gisburn	22	15	3	4	33
Cross Hills	22	14	4	4	32
Barnoldswick P.R.	22	14	2	6	30
Steeton	22	9	3	10	21
Cowling	22	10	1	11	21
Grassington United	22	9	2	11	20
Settle United	22	6	6	10	18
Carleton	22	6	3	13	15
Crossflatts	22	4	5	13	13
Skipton Bulldogs	22	3	5	14	11
Earby	22	2	6	14	10

other local sides Division 1: Prince Smith & S, Oxenhope Rec, Haworth, United Lifts, Cononley Sports, Lothersdale Ath, Oakworth Albion **Division 2** (all reserve sides): Cross Hills, Steeton, Oxenhope Rec and Cowling **Division 3** (all reserve sides): Haworth, Cononley Sports, Oakworth Albion and Lothersdale Athletic.

KEIGHLEY SUNDAY ALLIANCE

Division 1: Ventus United (champions), Cullingworth, Fieldhead Y.C., Scalebor Park, Westfield Rovers, Holycroft Y.C., Ilkley Town, Odsal, Shipley Con. Club, St.Annes Shamrocks **Division 2:** Magnet, Addingham, Young Christians, Britannia United, Broom United, Trinity Athletic, Harden Park Rangers, Keighley West Yorkshire, Wrose Rangers, Fleece **Division 3:** Tommy Holmes, Shire Rovers, Saltaire County, Moorhead Rovers, Worth Valley, Ilkley Phoenix, Silsden United, Shipley, N.S.F. Rangers, Tong United, Knowle, Hattersleys. **Division 4:** Long Lee, Turkey Rangers, Timothy Taylors, Oakworth Wanderers, Ryshworth Athletic, Slingsbys, Airedale Rovers, Ilkley Rovers, Craven Herald, Kings United, High Royds, Bradford & Bingley B. Society

Jeff Hall Trophy Final: Magnet   5   Fieldhead Y.C.   1

1972-73

KEIGHLEY & DISTRICT CUP FINAL

Westfield Rovers   2   Keighley Central   0

KEIGHLEY SUNDAY CUP FINAL

Magnet   6   Fleece (Haworth)   0

175

Chasing Glory

WEST YORKSHIRE LEAGUE
Premier Division: Keighley Central
WEST RIDING COUNTY AMATEUR LEAGUE
Premier Division: Silsden (+ reserves)
KEIGHLEY SUNDAY ALLIANCE
Jeff Hall Trophy Final: Ventus United beat Fleece (Haworth)
Division 1: Magnet (champions), Ventus United, Tommy Holmes, Ilkley Town, Cullingworth, Scalebor Park, Fieldhead Y.C.
Division 2: Shire Rovers, Keighley St.Annes, Fleece, Coustle Dynamos, Broom United, Royd Ings Rovers, Skipton L.M.S., I.W.S., Keighley West Yorkshire, Harden Park Rangers
Division 3: Saltaire County, Long Lee, Turkey Rovers, Timothy Taylors, Worth Valley, Slingsbys, Silsden, Addingham, Tong United, Y.C.W., Ilkley Phoenix, Moorhead Rovers. **Division 4:** Oakworth Wanderers, Ryshworth, Sandhill Rovers, Kings United, Hattersleys, Nunroyd Park, Ilkley Rovers, N.S.F. Rangers, Bradford & Bingley B.Society, Airedale Rovers, High Royds, Burtons. **Division 5:** Keighley Pakistanis, Monaco, G.P.O., Keighley Grinders, Silsden B.L., Horsfalls.

CRAVEN & DISTRICT LEAGUE
local sides: **Premier Division:** Cross Hills (+ res, div 2) champions, Oxenhope Rec (+ res, div 2), Prince Smith & Stells, Cowling (+ res, div 2), Steeton (+ res, div 2)
Division 1: Haworth (+ res, div 2), Cononley Sports (+ res, div 3), Lothersdale Ath (+ res, div 3) United Lifts, Oakworth Albion
Division 3: Bradley

1973-74

KEIGHLEY & DISTRICT CUP FINAL

Silsden	5	Westfield Rovers	2

KEIGHLEY SUNDAY CUP FINAL

Magnet	2	Keighley Grinders	0

WEST YORKSHIRE LEAGUE
Division 1: Silsden (+ reserves)

KEIGHLEY SUNDAY ALLIANCE

Jeff Hall Trophy Final: Magnet 4 Ventus United 0

Division 1	P	W	D	L	F	A	Pts
Magnet	14	12	2	0	47	9	26
Ventus United	14	8	4	2	45	25	20
Fieldhead Y.C.	14	8	2	4	44	32	18
Shire Rovers	14	6	4	4	35	25	16
Saltaire County	14	6	4	4	24	25	16
Scalebor Park	14	3	3	8	25	37	9
Skipton L.M.S.	14	2	0	12	23	29	4
Ilkley Town	14	0	1	13	16	43	1

Division 2: Yeadon, Long Lee, Broom United, Oakworth Wdrs, Fleece, St.Annes, Gargrave Celtic **Division 3:** Silsden United, Tong United, Keighley Grinders, Ilkley Phoenix, Harden Park Rngrs, Horsfalls, Timothy Taylors **Division 4:** Volts Villa, Addingham, Airedale Rovers, Northern, Airedale Hospital, High Royds, Burlington Arms, Hattersleys, Kings United.

CRAVEN & DISTRICT LEAGUE

local sides Premier Division: Cross Hills (+ res, div 2), Oxenhope Rec (+ res, div 2) Prince Smith & Stells, Cowling (+ res, div 2), Steeton (+ res, div 2)
Division 1: Haworth (+ res, div 2), Cononley Sports (+ res, div 3), Lothersdale Ath (+ res, div 3), United Lifts. **Division 2:** Oakworth Albion. **Division 3:** Bradley

1974-75

KEIGHLEY & DISTRICT CUP FINAL

Silsden	5	Westfield Rovers	0

KEIGHLEY SUNDAY CUP FINAL

Magnet	2	Cross Hills W.M.C.	0

WEST YORKSHIRE LEAGUE

Division 1: Silsden (+ reserves)

KEIGHLEY SUNDAY ALLIANCE

Jeff Hall Trophy Winners: Magnet
Town Division: Magnet (champions), Keighley Grinders, Cross Hills W.M.C., Broom United, Volts Villa, Burlington, St.Annes, Northern, Timothy Taylors (res), Ondura, Queens. **District Division:** Ventus United, Silsden United, Saltaire County, Tong United, Harden Park Rangers, Addingham, Airedale Rovers, Airedale Hospital, Timothy Taylors.

WHARFEDALE LEAGUE

Keighley Shamrocks

WHARFEDALE SUNDAY LEAGUE

local sides include: Silsden United, Grapes & Oakworth.

CRAVEN & DISTRICT LEAGUE

Premier Division	P	W	D	L	Pts
Colne B.L.	20	15	3	2	33
Trawden Celtic	20	12	5	3	29
Cross Hills	20	10	5	5	25
Skipton Bulldogs	20	10	4	6	24
Steeton	20	9	6	5	24
Barnoldswick P.R.	20	8	5	7	21
Rolls Royce	20	7	4	9	18
Settle United	20	5	6	9	16
Earby	20	4	4	12	12
Oxenhope Rec	20	4	2	14	10
Cowling	20	2	4	14	8

other local sides Division 1: United Lifts, Haworth, Cononley Sports, Lothersdale Ath
Division 2: Oakworth Albion + reserve sides of Cross Hills, Oxenhope Rec, Steeton, Cowling & Haworth
Division 3: Bradley & reserve sides of Cononley Sports & Lothersdale Athletic

1975-76

KEIGHLEY & DISTRICT CUP FINAL

Silsden	3	Bingley Juniors	0

KEIGHLEY SUNDAY CUP FINAL

Magnet beat Ryshworth

Chasing Glory

WEST YORKSHIRE LEAGUE
Premier Division: Silsden (+ reserves) champions

KEIGHLEY SUNDAY ALLIANCE
Jeff Hall Trophy Winners: Magnet
Magnet (champions), Cross Hills W.M.C., Keighley Grinders, Volts Villa, Broom United, Druids, Tong, Addingham, Burlington, St.Annes, Timothy Taylors, Ondura, New Steeton, Queens.

WHARFEDALE SUNDAY LEAGUE
local sides include: Silsden United (+ reserves), Airedale Hosp & Bracken Bank C.C.

CRAVEN & DISTRICT LEAGUE

PREMIER DIVISION	P	W	D	L	Pts
Trawden Celtic	22	18	2	2	38
Steeton	22	16	3	3	35
Cross Hills	22	12	7	3	31
Skipton Town	22	12	3	7	27
Skipton Bulldogs	22	10	6	6	26
Haworth	22	8	9	5	25
Cononley Sports	22	9	3	10	21
Oxenhope Rec	22	7	6	9	20
Settle United	22	5	4	13	14
Earby*	22	2	6	14	9
Rolls Royce	22	3	3	16	9
Cowling	22	3	2	17	8

*1 pt deducted - playing unregistered player.
Division 1: United Lifts, Oakwood Albion, Lothersdale Athletic.
Division 2: Steeton Res, Cononley Res, Cross Hill Res, Haworth Res, Oxenhope Res, Cowling Res. **Division 3:** United Lifts Res, Bradley.

1976-77

KEIGHLEY & DISTRICT CUP FINAL
Silsden beat Cross Hills

KEIGHLEY SUNDAY CUP FINAL
Magnet beat Saltaire County

WEST RIDING COUNTY AMATEUR LEAGUE

Division 1 (Top)	P	W	D	L	Pts
Phoenix Park	26	23	2	1	48
SILSDEN	26	23	1	2	47
Ventus United	26	14	3	9	31

Division 1A (Top)	P	W	D	L	Pts
Dudley Hill A (Res)	34	26	7	1	59
KLY SHAMROCKS	34	24	6	4	54

Reserve Division: Silsden (reserves)

KEIGHLEY SUNDAY ALLIANCE
Jeff Hall Trophy Winners: Magnet
Magnet (champions), Broom United, Black Bull, Keighley Grinders, Dog & Gun, Henry Boot, Trico, Landis Lund, Queens, A.C.Alassio.

Tables

WHARFEDALE SUNDAY LEAGUE
local sides include: Silsden United, Airedale Hosp, Timothy Taylors & Druids Arms.

CRAVEN & DISTRICT LEAGUE

Premier Division	P	W	D	L	Pts
Trawden Celtic	26	20	4	2	44
Skipton Bulldogs	26	16	3	7	35
Cononley Sports	26	14	6	6	34
Steeton	26	13	8	5	34
Skipton Town	26	14	6	6	34
Barrowford United	26	13	5	8	31
Ilkley	26	12	6	8	30
Pendle Forest	26	11	4	11	26
Oxenhope Rec	26	10	5	11	25
Cross Hills	26	9	5	12	23
Earby	26	5	5	16	15
Haworth	26	4	4	18	12
Settle United	26	2	7	17	11
Rolls Royce	26	3	3	20	9

other local sides Division 1: Cowling, Bradley & United Lifts **Division 2:** Lothersdale Athletic & reserve sides of Steeton, Cononley Sports, Cross Hills, Oxenhope Rec & Haworth **Division 3:** reserve sides of Bradley, Cowling & United Lifts.

1977-78

KEIGHLEY & DISTRICT CUP FINAL
Silsden 3 Steeton 0

KEIGHLEY SUNDAY CUP FINAL
Magnet 2 Silsden United 0

WEST RIDING COUNTY AMATEUR LEAGUE
Division 1: Silsden (+ reserves) Keighley Shamrocks

KEIGHLEY SUNDAY ALLIANCE
Jeff Hall Trophy Final: Magnet 5 Keighley Grinders 2
Keighley Grinders (champions), Magnet, Settle United, Masons Arms, Keighley West Yorkshire, Juventus, Great Northern, Bay Horse, Queens, Burlington Arms

WHARFEDALE SUNDAY LEAGUE
local sides include: Timothy Taylors, Druids Arms, Silsden United (+ reserves), Keighley Post Office, Silsden White Star, Haworth C.C, Busfeild Arms, Oxenhope, Dog & Gun and Airedale Hospital.

CRAVEN & DISTRICT LEAGUE

Premier Division	P	W	D	L	Pts
Trawden Celtic	26	20	3	3	43
Steeton	26	16	6	4	38
Skipton Town	26	16	6	4	38
Barrowford United	26	16	5	3	37
Skipton Bulldogs	26	13	7	6	33
Cononley Sports	26	12	6	8	30
Ilkley	26	11	3	12	25
Foulridge Corinth	26	9	6	11	24

Chasing Glory

Pendle Forest	26	10	2	13	22
Oxenhope Rec	26	9	2	15	20
Cross Hills	26	8	4	14	20
Bingley Juniors	26	5	5	16	15
Earby	26	4	3	19	11
Haworth	26	2	3	21	7

local sides Division 1: Morton Village, Bradley Cowling, United Lifts. **Division 2:** reserve sides of Cross Hills, Oxenhope Rec, Steeton, Haworth& Cononley Sports. **Division 3:** Lothersdale Athletic & reserve sides of Cowling, United Lifts & Bradley.

1978-79

KEIGHLEY & DISTRICT CUP FINAL
Cross Hills   2   Morton Village   0

KEIGHLEY SUNDAY CUP FINAL
Magnet   3   Silsden   0

WEST COUNTY AMATEUR LEAGUE
Division 1: Keighley Shamrocks

KEIGHLEY SUNDAY ALLIANCE
Jeff Hall Trophy Final: Magnet   6   Keighley Grinders 1
season unfinished - no official champions
Burlington Arms, Magnet, Keighley Grinders, Keighley West Yorkshire, Settle United, West Ward W.M.C., Broom United, Timothy Taylors, Keighley News, Juventus

WHARFEDALE SUNDAY LEAGUE
local sides include: Silsden, Timothy Taylors, Silsden White Star, Keighley Post Office, Haworth C.C & Airedale Hospital.

CRAVEN & DISTRICT LEAGUE

Premier Division	P	W	D	L	Pts
Barrowford United	26	21	4	1	46
Skipton Bulldogs	26	19	2	5	40
Ilkley	26	12	10	4	34
Steeton	26	10	11	5	31
Trawden Celtic	26	11	4	11	26
Mansfield	26	10	5	11	25
Cross Hills	26	10	4	12	24
Cononley Sports	26	8	7	11	23
Pendle Forest	26	8	6	12	22
Foulridge Corinth.	26	8	5	13	21
Skipton Town	26	6	9	11	21
United Lifts	26	7	7	12	21
Bingley Juniors	26	6	5	15	17
Oxenhope Rec	26	4	4	18	12

other local sides Division 1: Cowling, Bradley & Haworth **Division 2:** Morton Village & reserve sides of United Lifts, Cononley Sports, Cross Hills, Steeton, Haworth and Oxenhope Rec **Division 3:** Lothersdale Athletic & reserve sides of Cowling & Bradley.

1979-80

KEIGHLEY & DISTRICT CUP FINAL
Cross Hills   2   Keighley Shamrocks   0

Tables

KEIGHLEY SUNDAY CUP FINAL
Magnet 2 Angel 0

KEIGHLEY CHARITY CUP FINAL
Magnet 3 Keighley Shamrocks 1

WEST RIDING COUNTY AMATEUR LEAGUE
Division 1: Keighley Shamrocks

KEIGHLEY SUNDAY ALLIANCE
Jeff Hall Trophy Final: Settle United 3 Volunteers (reserves) 1

	P	W	D	L	Pts
Keighley Grinders	22	20	1	1	41
New Grapes	22	19	2	1	40
Timothy Taylors	22	14	2	6	30
Volunteers (Res)	22	14	1	7	29
North Bradford	22	9	4	9	22
Settle United	22	8	6	8	22
Broom United	22	9	1	12	19
Keighley W. Yorks	22	6	4	12	16
Silsden W.S. 'A'	22	6	3	13	15
Silsden 'A'	22	3	6	13	12
Keighley News	22	3	5	14	11
Wells United	22	3	1	18	7

WHARFEDALE SUNDAY LEAGUE

Premier Division	P	W	D	L	Pts
Woodend Rangers	20	18	1	1	37
MAGNET	20	16	1	3	33
Baildon Athletic	20	12	3	5	27
SILSDEN	20	12	1	7	25
Ventus United	20	11	2	7	24
VOLUNTEERS	20	10	1	9	21
Cullingworth	20	9	1	10	19
Old Otliensians	20	5	0	15	10
Cullingworth Spts	20	4	1	15	9
Bolton Woods	20	3	2	15	8
Shoulder of Mutton	20	3	1	16	7

other local sides include: Haworth Community Centre, A.E.F.C, Airedale Hosp, Silsden (res),Silsden White Star (+ res) and Low Mill Lane.

CRAVEN & DISTRICT LEAGUE

Premier Division	P	W	D	L	Pts
Trawden Celtic	26	22	2	2	46
Cononley Sports	26	18	7	1	43
Skipton Bulldogs	26	18	5	3	41
Barrowford United	26	15	4	7	34
Ilkley	26	14	4	8	32
Mansfield	26	10	6	10	26
Cross Hills	26	10	4	12	24
Pendle Forest	26	8	5	13	21
Skipton B.R.	26	7	4	15	18
Earby	26	7	3	16	17
Skipton Town	26	7	3	16	17
Cowling	26	5	6	15	16
United Lifts	26	6	3	17	15
Steeton	26	5	4	17	14

Chasing Glory

local sides Division 1: Oxenhope Recreation, Haworth & Bradley. **Division 2:** reserve sides of Cross Hills, Steeton, United Lifts, Cononley Sp & Oxenhope Rec. **Division 3:** Lothersdale Athletic and reserve sides of Cowling & Haworth.

1980-81

KEIGHLEY & DISTRICT CUP FINAL
Keighley Town   3   Keighley Shamrocks   1

KEIGHLEY SUNDAY CUP FINAL
Magnet   2   Silsden   0 (after 0-0 draw)

KEIGHLEY CHARITY CUP FINAL
Keighley Town   2   Silsden   0

WEST RIDING COUNTY AMATEUR LEAGUE
Division 1: Keighley Town (+ reserves) Keighley Shamrocks

CRAVEN & DISTRICT LEAGUE

PREMIER DIVISION	P	W	D	L	Pts
Trawden Celtic	30	26	2	2	54
Cononley Sports	30	27	0	3	54
Mansfield	30	19	5	6	43
Barrowford United	30	19	2	9	40
Skipton BR Sports	30	18	4	8	34*
Skipton Town	30	14	5	14	33
Cross Hills	30	12	3	15	27
Pendle Forest	30	11	5	14	27
Steeton	30	12	1	17	25
Cowling	30	10	4	16	24
Ilkley	30	10	4	16	24
Earby	30	9	4	17	22
Bingley Juniors	30	8	6	16	22
Oxenhope	30	9	3	18	21
Keighley Lifts	30	7	5	38	19
Skipton Bulldogs	30	2	1	27	5

* Six Points deducted
Division 1: Silsden, Bradley, Haworth. **Division 2:** Cononley Sports Res, Cross Hills Res, Keighley Lifts Res, Lothersdale Athletic, Oxenhope Res, Steeton Res, Cyprane, Three Horses FC

WHARFEDALE SUNDAY LEAGUE

Premier Division	P	W	D	L	F	A	Pts
Ventus United	18	13	3	2	56	19	29
MAGNET	18	12	5	1	33	14	29
Baildon Athletic	18	10	4	4	51	34	24
Culingworth	18	7	6	5	47	37	20
A.E.F.C. (KEIGHLEY)	18	7	3	8	30	49	17
Owlet Hall	18	6	4	8	34	51	16
SILSDEN	18	6	0	12	30	40	12
Westbrook Wdrs	18	5	2	11	30	41	12
Skipton B.R.	18	5	1	12	30	52	12
Old Otliensians	18	3	4	11	24	41	10

other local sides include: Silsden White Star (+ reserves), Silsden (res), Haworth C.C, Busfeild Arms, Airedale Hosp & Low Mill Lane * (+ res) * = Low Mill Lane changed their name to Green Gables during the season.

Tables

KEIGHLEY SUNDAY ALLIANCE
Jeff Hall Trophy Final: Robin Hood '80   1   Timothy Taylors   0
Robin Hood '80 (champions) New Grapes, Timothy Taylors, North Bradford, Royal Hotel, Broom United, Keighley West Yorkshire, Keighley Grinders, Keighley News, Wells United, Pak Kashmir. Settle United w/d pre-season

1981-82

KEIGHLEY & DISTRICT CUP FINAL
Keighley Town   2   Keighley Shamrocks   0

KEIGHLEY SUNDAY CUP FINAL
Magnet   2   Silsden White Star   1

WEST RIDING COUNTY AMATEUR LEAGUE
Division 1: Keighley Town (+ reserves) Keighley Shamrocks

KEIGHLEY SUNDAY ALLIANCE
Jeff Hall Trophy Final: Phoenix   3   Keighley News   1

	P	W	D	L	F	A	Pts
Timothy Taylors	18	18	0	0	98	13	36
Skipton B.R.	18	12	2	4	94	22	26
Kly West Yorks	18	11	3	4	58	32	25
Keighley News	18	9	4	5	42	54	22
Broom United	18	8	3	7	56	58	19
Juventus	18	8	1	9	36	43	17
Kly Grinders	18	7	1	10	61	48	15
Phoenix	18	4	2	12	39	68	10
Devonshire Park	18	3	1	14	17	79	7
Victoria Hotel	18	1	1	16	19	103	3

CRAVEN & DISTRICT LEAGUE

Premier Division	P	W	D	L	F	A	Pts
Barrowford Utd	28	18	8	2	86	39	44
Silsden	28	18	8	2	60	27	44
Steeton	28	19	4	5	87	37	42
Skipton Town	28	18	4	6	65	35	40
Skipton B.R.	28	16	5	7	79	47	37
Cross Hills	28	15	5	8	53	36	35
Cononley Sports	28	12	6	10	64	50	30
Cowling	28	11	5	12	48	57	27
Trawden C (Res)	28	11	5	12	64	49	27
Oxenhope Rec	28	9	4	15	58	71	22
Keighley Lifts	28	6	6	16	29	56	18
Mansfield (Res)	28	5	5	18	49	70	15
Ilkley	28	7	0	21	49	90	14
Earby	28	5	4	19	34	112	14
Bingley Juniors	28	3	5	20	38	87	11

other local sides Division 1: Cononley Sports (res) & Bradley.
Division 2: Cyprane, Haworth, Three Horses, Lothersdale Athletic + reserve sides of: Cowling, Steeton, Cross Hills, Keighley Lifts & Oxenhope Recreation.
Division 3: reserve sides of: Silsden, Haworth & Cyprane.

183

Chasing Glory

WHARFEDALE SUNDAY LEAGUE

Premier Division	P	W	D	L	F	A	Pts
MAGNET	18	14	2	2	44	13	30
Baildon Athletic	18	9	4	5	52	38	22
Bolton Woods	18	10	2	6	49	45	22
Old Otliensians	18	10	2	6	35	34	22
Ventus United	18	9	3	6	35	30	21
Sportsbag Cav.	18	8	4	6	40	34	20
SILSDEN WHITE S	18	9	0	9	44	46	18
SILSDEN	18	5	2	11	36	44	12
Owlet Hall	18	3	1	14	28	51	7
Cullingworth	18	2	2	14	28	57	6

Guiseley Factory Workers w/d
other local sides include: Haworth Comm C, Silsden (res), Airedale Hospital, Kensington, Green Gables (+ res), Busfeild Arms, Royal Hotel & Low Mill Lane.

1982-83

KEIGHLEY & DISTRICT CUP FINAL
Keighley Town 2   Keighley Shamrocks 0 (after abandoned game, score 1-1)

KEIGHLEY SUNDAY CUP FINAL
Silsden   2   Magnet   1

WEST RIDING COUNTY AMATEUR LEAGUE

Premier Division	P	W	D	L	F	A	Pts
KEIGHLEY TOWN	30	23	4	3	87	26	50
Dudley Hill Athletic	30	18	6	6	67	35	42
Gascoigne United	30	15	10	5	48	28	40
Littletown	30	12	11	7	64	40	35
Eccleshill United	30	13	8	9	57	38	34
Crag Road United	30	15	4	11	52	49	34
Yeadon Celtic	30	15	3	12	69	49	33
Ventus	30	13	7	10	57	63	33
Lower Hopton	30	12	5	13	55	51	29
Ovenden W.R.	30	12	4	14	56	55	28
Grange Moor	30	10	6	14	61	59	26
Trinity Athletic	30	8	9	13	47	52	25
Salts	30	9	6	15	46	54	25
Manningham Mills	30	9	6	15	40	64	24
Rawdon Old Boys	30	8	7	15	39	55	23
Civil Service	30	0	0	30	27	155	0

Division One: Keighley Shamrocks **Reserve Division:** Keighley Town (reserves)

WHARFEDALE SUNDAY LEAGUE

Premier Division	P	W	D	L	Pts
MAGNET	18	13	3	2	29
Bolton Woods	18	12	1	5	25
Baildon Athletic	18	8	5	5	21
SILSDEN WHITE S.	18	10	0	8	20
Old Otliensians	18	8	3	7	19
Bradleys	18	6	4	8	16
Ventus United	18	5	6	7	16
SILSDEN	18	4	4	10	12
Wrose Albion	18	5	2	11	12
Sportsbag Cav.	18	4	2	12	10

other local sides include: Raiseprint, Silsden (res), Green Gables (+ reserves), Kensington, Busfeild Arms, Airedale Hosp, Royal Hotel, Reservoir Sports & Low Mill Lane.

Tables

CRAVEN & DISTRICT LEAGUE

Premier Division	P	W	D	L	Pts
Gargrave	26	24	1	1	49
Steeton	26	19	4	3	42
Cononley Sports	26	13	4	9	30
Cross Hills	26	11	6	9	28
Skipton Town	26	13	2	11	28
Keighley Lifts	26	13	2	11	28
Rock Rovers	26	10	7	9	27
Cowling	26	11	5	10	27
Settle United	26	10	6	10	26
Silsden	26	8	6	12	22
Oxenhope Rec	26	7	5	14	19
Trawden C (Res)	26	7	5	14	19
Mansfield (Res)	26	4	2	20	10
Ilkley	26	3	2	21	8

Division 1: Cyprane, Bradley & Cononley (res) **Division 2:** Haworth, Lothersdale Ath, Airedale Heifer + reserve sides of: Steeton, Cross Hills, Cowling & Oxenhope Rec. **Division 3:** reserve sides of: Silsden, Cyprane, Haworth & Keighley Lifts.

KEIGHLEY SUNDAY ALLIANCE

Jeff Hall Trophy Final: Phoenix 1 Cull'worth 0

Division 1	P	W	D	L	Pts
Timothy Taylors	14	12	0	2	24
Skipton B.R.	14	9	2	3	20
Kly West Yorks	14	8	1	5	17
Keighley News	14	7	2	5	16
Phoenix	14	7	2	5	16
Cullingworth	14	6	1	7	13
Blue Bell (Res)	14	1	2	11	4
Reservoir Sp (Res)	14	1	0	13	2

Division 2: Shoulder, Juventus, Parkwood United, Silentnight, Devonshire Park, Snooker Centre, Victoria Hotel

1983-84

KEIGHLEY & DISTRICT CUP FINAL

Keighley Town   4   Keighley Shamrocks   0

KEIGHLEY SUNDAY CUP FINAL

Bradleys   3   Silsden   1

WEST RIDING COUNTY AMATEUR LEAGUE

Premier Division: Top	P	W	D	L	F	A	Pts
Dudley Hill Athletic	30	20	6	4	64	33	46
Littletown	30	21	2	7	71	33	44
KEIGHLEY TOWN	30	18	8	4	58	22	44

Division 1: Keighley Shamrocks, Silsden **Reserve Division:** Keighley Town (res)

KEIGHLEY SUNDAY ALLIANCE

Jeff Hall Trophy Final: Phoenix   2   Skipton BR.   0
Division 1: Skipton B.R. (champions), Timothy Taylors, Cullingworth, Phoenix, Juventus, Keighley News, Shoulder, Hope & Anchor, Lord Rodney w/d
Division 2: Snooker Centre, Parkwood United, Baildon Rangers, Green Gables, Woolpack, Victoria Hotel, Devonshire Park, Lord Rodney (res) w/d, Timothy Taylors (res), Silentnight w/d pre-season

WHARFEDALE SUNDAY LEAGUE

local sides: **Premier Division**: Magnet, Silsden, Silsden White Star w/d pre-season other divisions: Kensington, Silsden (res), Low Mill Lane, Busfeild Arms, Kensington, Royal, Reservoir Sports, Raiseprint & Airedale Hospital.

CRAVEN & DISTRICT LEAGUE

Premier Division	P	W	D	L	Pts
Gargrave	26	24	1	1	47
Steeton	26	14	7	5	35
Cross Hills	26	13	4	9	30
Colne United	26	12	6	8	30
Cyprane	26	13	4	9	30
Oxenhope Rec	26	13	2	11	28
Cowling	26	12	4	10	28
Skipton Town	26	12	4	10	28
Settle United	26	10	4	12	24
Rock Rovers	26	9	6	11	23
Trawden Celt (Res)	26	7	5	14	19
Cononley Sports	26	7	4	15	18
Bingley Juniors	26	6	2	18	16
Silsden (Reserves)	26	2	3	21	4

other local sides Division 1: Haworth, Bradley + reserve sides of Steeton & Cononley Sports. **Division 2**: Lothersdale Ath, Airedale Heifer + reserve sides of Cross Hills, Cowling, Oxenhope Rec & Cyprane. **Division 3**: Haworth (res). Keighley Lifts (+ reserves) w/d pre-season

WHARFEDALE TRIANGLE

Silsden White Star (reserves)

1984-85

KEIGHLEY & DISTRICT CUP FINAL

Silsden 3 Cross Hills 1

KEIGHLEY SUNDAY CUP FINAL

Silsden 1 Magnet 0

WEST RIDING COUNTY AMATEUR LEAGUE

Premier Division: Keighley Town (+ res, div 2) **Division 1**: Silsden (+ reserves), Keighley Shamrocks **Division 1A**: Cyprane w/d pre-season

KEIGHLEY SUNDAY ALLIANCE

Jeff Hall Trophy Final: Green Gables 2 Keighley News 1

Division 1	P	W	D	L	F	A	Pts
Highfield	14	11	2	1	47	14	24
Keighley News	14	9	2	3	58	30	20
Skipton B.R.	14	8	2	4	44	30	18
Bronte Lifts	14	6	2	6	31	33	14
Phoenix	14	4	4	6	38	32	12
Parkwood United	14	5	1	8	39	43	11
Cullingworth	14	2	3	9	25	64	7
Juventus	14	3	0	11	19	55	6

Division 2: Hope & Anchor, Green Gables, Kly Shamrocks, Keighley Lifts, S.T. Autoparts, Woodhouse, I.S. Calder, Timothy Taylors

WHARFEDALE TRIANGLE

Silsden Town, Airedale Hospital

Tables

CRAVEN & DISTRICT LEAGUE

Premier Division	P	W	D	L	F	A	Pts
Barnoldswick Utd	24	13	6	5	64	41	32
Gargrave	24	13	6	5	44	31	32
Haworth	24	12	7	5	68	43	31
Cowling	24	10	9	5	53	41	29
Cross Hills	24	11	6	7	48	37	28
Cononley Sports	24	11	6	7	53	50	28
Oxenhope Rec	24	11	5	8	55	48	27
Trawden Celt (Res)	24	10	6	8	48	44	26
Steeton	24	7	7	10	41	50	21
Rock Rovers	24	5	6	13	29	45	16
Colne United	24	6	4	14	51	69	16
Skipton Town	24	6	3	15	41	51	15
Settle United	24	4	3	17	37	82	11

Cyprane (reserves) w/d pre-season
other local sides Division 1: Grafton Garage, Bradley & reserve sides of Steeton & Cross Hills, **Division 2:** Airedale Heifer, Lothersdale Ath & reserve sides of Haworth, Cowling, Cononley Sports and Oxenhope Recreation. **Division 3:** reserve sides of Airedale Heifer and Bradley.

WHARFEDALE SUNDAY LEAGUE

Premier Division	P	W	D	L	Pts
Baildon Athletic	20	14	3	3	31
MAGNET	20	14	3	3	31
SILSDEN	20	12	3	5	27
Regent Victoria	20	10	6	4	26
Bolton Woods	20	9	5	6	23
Ilkley Dynamo	20	7	6	7	20
Wrose Albion	20	7	5	8	19
Owlet Hall	20	6	6	8	18
Sun	20	4	2	14	10
Old Otliensians	20	3	3	12	9
Bradleys	20	1	4	15	6

Ventus/Yeadon w/d
other local sides: Royal, Kensington, Low Mill Lane, Reservoir Spts & Silsden (res)

1985-86

KEIGHLEY & DISTRICT CUP FINAL
Keighley Town 3   Haworth   1 (a.e.t.)

KEIGHLEY SUNDAY CUP FINAL
Bradleys   5   Silsden Town   0

WEST RIDING COUNTY AMATEUR LEAGUE
Premier Division: Keighley Town   **Division 1:** Silsden (+ reserves)
Division 1A: Steeton (+ reserves)

KEIGHLEY SUNDAY ALLIANCE
Jeff Hall Trophy Final: Keighley News   6   Campion Bell Dean   3

Division 1	P	W	D	L	F	A	Pts
Highfield	18	14	3	1	78	19	31
Keighley News	18	11	4	3	61	30	26
Kensington	18	12	2	4	66	37	26
Druids	18	9	5	4	43	29	23
Cullingworth	18	6	6	6	47	46	18
Shoulder	18	7	3	8	38	43	17

Chasing Glory

Hope & Anchor	18	6	2	10	45	55	14
Green Gables	18	6	2	10	30	40	14
Juventus	18	3	1	14	25	64	7
Parkwood United	18	0	4	14	31	101	4

Division 2: Campion Bell Dean, Wrose, I.S. Calder, Northern, Kly Shamrocks, Timothy Taylors, Golden Fleece, S.T. Autoparts, Cowling, Royal (Denholme)

BRADFORD RED TRIANGLE

Division 2: Grapes

WHARFEDALE TRIANGLE

Silsden Town, Airedale Hospital

CRAVEN & DISTRICT LEAGUE

Premier Division	P	W	D	L	F	A	Pts
Colne United	22	13	6	3	52	30	32
Haworth	22	13	3	6	61	39	29
Barnoldswick Utd	22	9	10	3	50	28	28
Cross Hills	22	10	6	6	48	35	26
Grafton Garage	22	10	5	7	48	39	25
Trawden Celt (Res)	22	9	5	8	53	46	23
Rolls Royce	22	6	9	7	36	40	21
Cononley Sports	22	8	3	11	46	60	19
Rock Rovers	22	6	6	10	41	53	18
Oxenhope Rec	22	6	4	12	47	62	16
Cowling	22	5	6	11	31	48	16
Gargrave (Res)	22	4	3	15	41	74	11

other local sides Division 1: Airedale Heifer, Bradley & Cross Hills (reserves), **Division 2**: Lothersdale Athletic & reserve sides of Haworth, Oxenhope Rec and Cowling. **Division 3**: reserve sides of Cononley Sports & Bradley.

WHARFEDALE SUNDAY LEAGUE

Premier Division	P	W	D	L	Pts
MAGNET	18	13	4	1	30
Bolton Woods	18	13	2	3	28
Baildon Athletic	18	12	2	4	26
Bradleys	18	9	0	9	18
Regent Victoria	17	7	4	6	18
Wrose Albion	18	6	2	10	14
ROYAL HOTEL	17	5	2	10	12
Ilkley Dynamo	18	4	3	11	11
SILSDEN	18	4	3	11	11
Star Athletic	18	3	4	11	10

other local sides include: Reservoir Sports, Baileys, Silsden (res), Busfeild Arms & Cononley Sports.

1986-87

KEIGHLEY & DISTRICT CUP FINAL

Cross Hills   2   Silsden   1

KEIGHLEY SUNDAY CUP FINAL

Silsden Town   2   Magnet   1

WEST RIDING COUNTY AMATEUR LEAGUE

Premier Division	P	W	D	L	F	A	Pts
Ovenden W.R.	22	14	3	5	55	25	31
Birkenshaw Rovers	22	11	6	5	48	38	28

Tables

	P	W	D	L	F	A	Pts
Crag Road United	22	10	5	7	43	37	25
Dudley Hill Athletic	22	10	4	8	53	43	24
Littletown	22	8	7	7	39	33	23
Fields	22	9	5	8	40	43	23
SILSDEN	22	8	6	8	35	40	22
Ventus/Yeadon Celt	22	8	4	10	34	41	20
Trinity Athletic	22	9	0	13	34	43	18
Gascoigne United	22	7	4	11	34	44	18
Salts	22	7	4	11	34	47	18
KEIGHLEY TOWN	22	5	4	13	25	40	14

Division 2: Haworth, Steeton (+ reserves)

WHARFEDALE SUNDAY LEAGUE

Premier Division	P	W	D	L	F	A	Pts
Bolton Woods	16	12	2	2	51	20	38
Regent Victoria	16	11	1	4	56	19	34
MAGNET	16	11	1	4	42	19	34
Baildon Athletic	16	10	2	4	36	21	32
Wrose Albion	16	8	1	7	37	38	25
Bradford United	16	6	2	8	33	43	20
Yeadon Westfield	16	3	2	11	28	59	11
BLACK HORSE	16	3	1	12	36	57	10
Star Athletic	16	1	2	13	26	69	5

other local sides include: Highfield, Druids Arms, Busfeild Arms, Cononley Sports, Baileys & Silsden.

WEST YORKSHIRE LEAGUE

Division 4: Highfield Shamrocks

BRADFORD RED TRIANGLE

Division 1: Grapes, Grafton Garage

WHARFEDALE TRIANGLE

Silsden Town

CRAVEN & DISTRICT LEAGUE

local sides Premier Division Cross Hills (+ res, div 2) champions, Cowling (+ res, div 3), Haworth (reserves), Oxenhope Rec (+ res, div 2), Cononley Sports (+ res, div 3) **Division 1** Silsden (reserves), Bradley (+ res, div 3), Airedale Heifer **Division 2** Lothersdale Athletic

KEIGHLEY SUNDAY ALLIANCE

Jeff Hall Trophy Final: Campion Bell Dean 6   Hope & Anchor   2

Division 1	P	W	D	L	F	A	Pts
Keighley News	14	11	3	0	46	10	25
Green Gables	14	8	4	2	40	17	20
Cullingworth	14	6	4	4	39	26	16
Hope & Anchor	14	7	2	5	32	38	16
Kensington	14	6	2	6	38	33	14
I.S.Calder	14	4	3	7	33	27	11
Wrose (Reserves)	14	2	3	9	19	58	7
Villa Roma	14	1	1	12	16	54	3

Division 2: Kly Shamrocks, Parkwood United, Timothy Taylors, Campion Bell Dean, Northern, Royal, Golden Fleece. **Division 3:** S.T.Autoparts, Phoenix, Sandy Lane, Cowling, Kly News (Res), Woodlands, Cullingworth (Res), New Inn Rangers.

Chasing Glory

1987-88

KEIGHLEY & DISTRICT CUP FINAL
Cross Hills   3   Silsden   1

KEIGHLEY SUNDAY CUP FINAL
Silsden Town   2   Black Horse   1

WEST RIDING COUNTY AMATEUR LEAGUE
Premier Division: Silsden   **Division 1:** Keighley Town
Division 2: Steeton (+ reserves), Haworth
Division 3: Keighley Borough w/d pre-season

KEIGHLEY SUNDAY ALLIANCE
Jeff Hall Trophy Final: Green Gables 2   Keighley Shamrocks 1

Division 1	P	W	D	L	F	A	Pts
Cullingworth	14	10	2	2	48	30	32
Keighley News	14	10	0	4	58	21	30
Green Gables	14	7	3	4	37	21	24
Kly Shamrocks	14	6	3	5	37	25	21
Parkwood Utd	14	4	3	7	39	50	15
Hope & Anchor	14	4	1	9	37	51	13
Timothy Taylors	14	4	1	9	20	35	13
Bridge	14	2	1	11	26	59	7

Fox & Pheasant w/d
Division 2: Golden Fleece, Sandy Lane, Cowling, Weider, Royal, New Inn Rngrs, Boons, Woodlands, Brown Cow, Cull'worth (Res), Northern

WHARFEDALE TRIANGLE
Silsden Town

CRAVEN & DISTRICT LEAGUE

Premier Division	P	W	D	L	F	A	Pts
Cross Hills	26	23	2	1	81	28	48
Rock Rovers	26	20	2	4	73	31	42
Settle United	26	18	2	6	77	41	38
Trawden Celt (Res)	26	16	2	8	65	52	34
Oxenhope Rec	26	16	1	9	65	51	33
Skipton Town	26	10	5	11	51	49	25
Barnoldswick P.R.	26	11	3	12	59	63	25
Colne United	26	9	5	12	46	52	23
Rolls Royce	26	7	5	14	54	63	19
B'lick United (Res)	26	7	5	14	47	78	19
Haworth (Res)	26	5	8	13	56	73	18
Brierfield	26	6	5	15	44	57	17
Embsay	26	6	5	15	38	65	17
Cowling	26	1	4	21	36	89	6

other local sides Division 1: Cononley Sports, Bradley, Airedale Heifer & reserve sides of Cross Hills & Oxenhope Rec. **Division 2:** Lothersdale Ath & reserve sides of Silsden and Cowling. **Division 3:** reserve sides of Cononley Sports & Bradley.

WHARFEDALE SUNDAY LEAGUE

Premier Division	P	W	D	L	F	A	Pts
Bolton Woods	14	11	1	2	52	14	34
BLACK HORSE	14	10	4	0	42	14	34
AIREDALE MAGNET	14	9	2	3	35	17	29
Baildon Ath	14	7	3	4	26	26	24

Tables

Baildon Town	14	4	2	8	31	35	14
Stanley Road	14	4	1	9	21	35	13
Star Athletic	14	2	1	11	16	47	7
Wrose Albion	14	2	0	12	18	56	6

other local sides include: Thwaites Brow, Beeches, Druids Arms, Highfield & Silsden.

BRADFORD RED TRIANGLE
Division 1: Eastwood Tavern

1988-89

KEIGHLEY & DISTRICT CUP FINAL
Steeton   1   Cross Hills   0

KEIGHLEY SUNDAY CUP FINAL
Silsden Town   2   Black Horse   0

KEIGHLEY SUNDAY ALLIANCE

Jeff Hall Trophy Final: Keighley Shamrocks 4 Green Gables 2

Division 1	P	W	D	L	F	A	Pts
Beeches	22	19	2	1	113	29	59
Parkwood United	22	17	2	3	96	34	53
Green Gables	22	16	2	4	89	32	50
Kly Shamrocks	22	11	6	5	74	32	39
Cowling	22	10	4	8	74	46	34
Cullingworth	22	11	1	10	79	61	34
Sandy Lane	22	7	5	10	61	79	26
Hope & Anchor	22	6	4	12	40	92	22
Royal Oak	22	7	0	15	55	78	21
Turkey	22	5	4	13	54	78	19
Weider	22	5	2	15	35	65	17
Royal	22	1	0	21	21	173	3

Division 2: Timothy Taylors, Phoenix, Aire Valley Gas, New Inn Rangers, M.U.S.C., Woodhouse & SB, Woodlands, Northern, Cullingworth (Res), Brown Cow.

WEST RIDING COUNTY AMATEUR LEAGUE
Premier Division: Silsden (+ reserves) both w/d
Division 2: Steeton (+ reserves), Haworth

WHARFEDALE TRIANGLE
Silsden Town

CRAVEN & DISTRICT LEAGUE

Premier Division	P	W	D	L	Pts
Cross Hills	24	21	3	0	45
Rock Rovers	24	17	4	3	38
Settle United	24	16	5	3	37
Oxenhope Rec	24	15	3	6	33
Waddington	24	14	4	6	32
Skipton Town	24	13	4	7	30
Bar'lick Utd (Res)	24	7	5	12	19
Embsay	24	7	2	15	16
Trawden Celt (Res)	24	6	4	14	16
Colne United	24	5	6	13	16
Haworth (Res)	24	6	2	16	14
West Bradford	24	5	0	19	10
Barnoldswick P.R.	24	2	0	22	4

Chasing Glory

other local sides **Division 1:** Cononley Sports, Cowling, Bradley & reserve sides of Cross Hills and Oxenhope Rec. **Division 2:** Lothersdale Athletic, Cross Roads & reserve side of Cowling. **Division 3:** reserve sides of Cononley Sports & Bradley.

WHARFEDALE SUNDAY LEAGUE

Premier Division	P	W	D	L	F	A	Pts
Bolton Woods	16	13	1	2	59	24	40
Stanley Road	15	10	3	2	45	25	33
Baildon Athletic	15	9	1	5	43	23	28
BLACK HORSE	16	8	3	5	49	31	27
Wrose Bull	16	8	3	5	37	22	27
AIREDALE MAGNET	16	9	0	7	36	23	27
Star Athletic	16	4	1	11	30	46	13
Bolton Woods Social	16	3	0	13	29	72	9
Wrose Albion	16	1	0	15	23	74	3

other local sides include: Silsden, Busfeild Arms, Grapes & Beeches.

BRADFORD RED TRIANGLE

Premier Division (top three)	P	W	D	L	F	A	Pts
Pile Bar	19	18	1	0	98	21	55
EASTWOOD TAVERN	19	15	0	4	83	42	45
Ring O'Bells	20	10	4	6	72	59	34

1989-90

KEIGHLEY & DISTRICT CUP FINAL

Haworth   2   Cross Hills   1

KEIGHLEY SUNDAY CUP FINAL

Airedale Magnet   4   Keighley Star   1

WEST RIDING COUNTY AMATEUR LGE

Division 1: Steeton (+ reserves)   **Division 2:** Haworth

KEIGHLEY SUNDAY ALLIANCE

Jeff Hall Trophy Final: Beeches   3   Sandy Lane   2
Division 1: Red Pig (champions), Beeches, Keighley Shamrocks, Phoenix, Knowle Arms, Market Arms, Cullingworth, Sandy Lane, Cowling, S.T. Autoparts, Timothy Taylors, Hope & Anchor. **Division 2:** Dennys, Aire Valley Gas, Sutton, Woodlands, New Inn, Belgrade, Great Northern, Royal Clarets, St. Annes Celtic, Brown Cow. Cullingworth (reserves) w/d

CRAVEN & DISTRICT LEAGUE

Premier Division	P	W	D	L	F	A	Pts
Rock Rovers	24	18	2	4	66	30	38
Waddington	24	17	3	4	87	34	37
Cross Hills	24	15	6	3	86	32	36
Settle United	24	14	5	5	61	21	33
Oxenhope Rec	24	12	5	7	65	35	29
Haworth (Res)	24	9	6	9	54	48	24
Foulridge	24	9	5	10	49	46	23
Grassington United	24	8	7	9	63	54	21
Skipton Town	24	7	7	10	58	64	21
Bar'lick Utd (Res)	24	9	2	13	63	54	20
Embsay	24	8	3	13	37	57	19
Trawden Celt (Res)	24	2	1	21	22	110	5
Colne Utd (Res)	24	2	0	22	20	145	4

Tables

other local sides **Division 1**: Bradley, Cononley Spts, Cowling & reserve sides of Cross Hills and Oxenhope **Division 2**: Cross Roads, Lothersdale Ath, Keighley Lifts & reserve side of Cowling **Division 3**: reserve sides of Cononley Sports and Bradley.

WHARFEDALE SUNDAY LEAGUE

local sides include **Premier Division**: Airedale Magnet, Silsden & Grapes
other divisions: Busfeild Arms

WHARFEDALE TRIANGLE

Silsden Town   Keighley Star

BRADFORD GRATTAN LEAGUE (ex Red Triangle)

Rodney

1990-91

KEIGHLEY & DISTRICT CUP FINAL

Cross Hills   3   Haworth   1

KEIGHLEY SUNDAY CUP FINAL

Airedale Magnet   2   Druids Arms   1

WEST RIDING COUNTY AMATEUR LEAGUE

Division 1: Steeton (+ reserves)   **Division 2**: Haworth

KEIGHLEY SUNDAY ALLIANCE

Jeff Hall Trophy Final: Keighley Shamrocks   6   Sutton   2
Division 1: Kly Shamrocks (champs), Phoenix, Druids Arms, Rycroft, Knowle Arms, Cowling, Sandy Lane, Cullingworth, Sutton, Bingley WMC, Woodlands, Cricketers Arms
Division 2: Craven Clarets, Brewers Arms, Northern, Phoenix (reserves), Belgrade, S.T. Autoparts, Royal, Hope & Anchor, St.Annes Celtic

BRADFORD GRATTAN LEAGUE

Division 1: Welcome Inn

CRAVEN & DISTRICT LEAGUE

Premier Division	P	W	D	L	Pts
Cross Hills	24	21	1	2	43
Oxenhope Rec	24	19	1	4	39
Settle United	24	19	1	4	39
Waddington	24	17	3	4	35
Rock Rovers	24	13	3	8	28
Foulridge	24	11	4	9	26
Band Club Rangers	24	6	6	12	18
Bar'lick Utd (Res)	24	6	5	13	17
Embsay	24	7	2	15	16
Haworth (Res)	24	6	4	14	16
Skipton Town	24	5	4	15	14
Cowling	24	3	6	15	12
Grassington United	24	1	4	19	6

other local sides: Division 1: Cross Roads, Cononley Spts, Lothersdale Ath, Bradley and reserve sides of Cross Hills & Oxenhope Rec. **Division 2**: Keighley Lifts & reserve side of Cowling. **Division 3**: reserve sides of Bradley, Cononley Spts, Keighley Lifts & Lothersdale Ath + 'A' team of Haworth.

Chasing Glory

WHARFEDALE SUNDAY LEAGUE

Premier Division	P	W	D	L	F	A	Pts
Star Athletic	18	13	3	2	83	36	42
AIREDALE MAGNET	18	12	2	4	56	31	38
Stanley Road	18	10	5	3	50	30	35
Wrose Albion	18	9	5	4	52	26	32
Whitakers Arms	18	8	4	6	48	43	28
SILSDEN	18	7	5	6	42	45	26
RED PIG	18	4	6	8	37	41	18
GRAPES	18	5	3	10	36	45	18
Thornhill Arms	18	4	0	14	30	60	12
Bull Hotel	18	1	1	16	30	107	4

other divisions : Timothy Taylors

WHARFEDALE TRIANGLE

Premier Division	P	W	D	L	F	A	Pts
Station Victoria	18	14	1	3	70	21	43
Baildon Athletic	18	13	2	3	74	23	41
Wrose Bull	18	11	6	1	64	17	39
Horsforth C.C.C.	18	10	3	5	63	25	33
SILSDEN TOWN	18	8	3	7	47	40	27
KEIGHLEY STAR	18	8	2	8	47	35	26
Park Rangers	18	8	0	10	36	53	24
The Drop	18	3	2	13	36	88	11
Rawdon	18	2	2	14	22	90	8
Woolpack	18	2	1	15	25	93	7

1991-92

KEIGHLEY & DISTRICT CUP FINAL

Denholme United　2　Steeton　1

KEIGHLEY SUNDAY CUP FINAL

Star Athletic　3　Keighley Shamrocks　2

WEST RIDING COUNTY AMATEUR LEAGUE

Division 1: Steeton (+ reserves)　　**Division 2:** Haworth w/d pre- season
Division 3: Phoenix

KEIGHLEY SUNDAY ALLIANCE

Jeff Hall Trophy Final: Market Arms　3　　Cullingworth　1
Division 1: Knowle Arms (champions), Market Arms, Cullingworth, Great Northern, Keighley Shamrocks (reserves), Craven Clarets, Bingley WMC, Brewers, Sutton　**Division 2:** Phoenix, Commercial, Boltmakers, Druids Arms (reserves), St.Annes Celtic, Royal, Keighley & District Transport, Crows Nest, Sandy Lane, Strachans, Wask, Green Lane

WHARFEDALE TRIANGLE

Premier Division	P	W	D	L	F	A	Pts
AIREDALE MAGNET	18	15	1	2	82	19	46
Star Athletic	18	12	2	4	74	35	38
Wrose Bull	18	12	0	6	59	34	36
Regent Victoria	18	11	2	5	45	20	35
KEIGHLEY STAR	18	11	1	6	67	37	34
SILSDEN TOWN	18	8	3	7	46	37	27
Tarn Rangers	18	8	1	9	49	54	25
Clothiers	18	4	1	13	31	48	13
Yeadon Westfield	18	3	1	14	20	74	10
Hawkhill	18	0	0	18	8	123	0

Tables

CRAVEN & DISTRICT LEAGUE

Premier Division	P	W	D	L	Pts
Cross Hills	24	20	2	2	42
Oxenhope Rec	24	17	4	3	38
Settle United	24	17	1	6	35
Haworth	23	16	3	4	35
Embsay	24	12	5	7	29
Waddington	24	10	5	9	25
Skipton Town	24	10	4	10	24
Cross Roads	24	10	3	11	23
Foulridge	24	10	2	12	22
Band Club Rangers	24	6	3	15	15
Rock Rovers (Res)	23	4	4	15	12
Bar'lick Utd (Res)	24	3	2	19	8
Barnoldswick P.R.	24	1	0	23	2

other local sides Division 1: Lothersdale Ath, Cononley Spts, Cowling, Bradley & reserves of Cross Hills and Oxenhope Rec **Division 2:** Keighley Lifts and Cowling (res) **Division 3:** reserves of Cononley Sports, Bradley, Haworth, Lothersdale Ath and Keighley Lifts.

WHARFEDALE SUNDAY LEAGUE

Premier Division	P	W	D	L	F	A	Pts
SILSDEN	14	10	2	2	53	28	32
DRUIDS ARMS	14	10	2	2	35	18	32
Wrose Albion	14	8	4	2	42	27	28
KLY SHAMROCKS	14	7	1	6	23	25	22
Owlet Hall	14	4	3	7	36	40	15
Whitakers Arms	14	4	2	8	30	39	14
Horsforth C.C.C.	14	3	2	9	24	32	11
Sandy Lane	14	1	2	11	15	49	5

GRAPES and Coach & Horses w/d
other divisions: Keighley Juniors

BRADFORD GRATTAN LEAGUE

Division 1: Welcome Inn

1992-93

KEIGHLEY & DISTRICT CUP FINAL

Steeton   1   Cross Hills   0

KEIGHLEY SUNDAY CUP FINAL

Star Athletic   2   Druids Arms   0

WEST RIDING COUNTY AMATEUR LEAGUE

Division 1: Steeton (+ reserves)

Division 3	P	W	D	L	F	A	Pts
PHOENIX	30	22	7	1	112	22	51
Allerton	30	21	8	1	113	42	50
Wibsey (Res)	30	19	6	5	111	44	44

& Haworth

EAST LANCASHIRE LEAGUE

Division 2: Cross Hills

Chasing Glory

KEIGHLEY SUNDAY ALLIANCE

Jeff Hall Trophy Final: Knowle Arms 4　Bingley WMC 0

Division 1	P	W	D	L	F	A	Pts
Cavendish Hotel	18	15	2	1	72	20	47
St.Annes Celtic	18	14	2	2	59	16	44
Knowle Arms	18	14	1	3	80	27	40
Cullingworth	18	10	0	8	40	35	30
Great Northern	18	9	2	7	47	42	29
Commercial	18	8	0	10	37	46	24
Phoenix	18	5	2	11	44	60	17
Bingley W.M.C.	18	5	1	12	42	59	16
Boltmakers	18	2	2	14	20	65	8
Gargrave Clarets	18	2	0	16	21	92	6

Division 2: Bell Dean, Sandy Lane, Brown Cow, Kly & Dist. Trnspt, Wask, Kings Arms, Sutton, Kly Juniors (Res), Three Horses, Green Lane

BRADFORD GRATTAN LEAGUE

Premier Division: Phoenix (Reserves)　**Division 1:** Welcome Inn

CRAVEN & DISTRICT LEAGUE

Premier Division	P	W	D	L	F	A	Pts
Gargrave	22	18	3	1	101	35	39
Embsay	22	14	5	3	79	34	33
Skipton Town	22	12	6	4	63	40	30
Oxenhope Rec	22	10	3	9	61	46	23
Band Club Rangers	22	11	3	8	50	50	23
Foulridge O.B.	22	8	5	9	49	45	21
Cononley Sports	22	8	5	9	44	51	21
Settle United	22	8	3	11	48	59	19
Cross Hills (Res)	22	7	5	10	41	54	19
Waddington	22	6	3	13	46	77	15
Rolls Royce	22	7	2	13	58	64	14
Haworth (Res)	22	1	1	20	23	108	3

other local sides Division 1: Cowling, Bradley & Oxenhope Rec (res) **Division 2:** Keighley Lifts, Lothersdale Athletic & reserve sides of Cowling and Cononley Sports **Division 3:** reserve sides of Keighley Lifts, Bradley & Lothersdale Ath.

WHARFEDALE SUNDAY LGE

Premier Division	P	W	D	L	F	A	Pts
SILSDEN	18	15	0	3	59	28	45
DRUIDS ARMS	18	13	3	2	52	35	42
Wrose Albion	18	13	2	3	56	22	41
Milestone	18	10	1	7	54	40	31
Owlet Hall	18	7	2	9	38	36	23
KLY SHAMROCKS	17	6	1	10	31	28	19
Thackley Shoulder	18	6	1	11	32	40	19
Ferrands Arms	16	6	1	9	31	55	19
Sandy Lane	17	4	1	12	34	47	13
New Inn Baildon	18	1	2	15	17	83	5

other divisions: Keighley Shamrocks (reserves), Keighley Juniors, Druids Arms (reserves).

Tables

WHARFEDALE TRIANGLE

Premier Division	P	W	D	L	F	A	Pts
Star Athletic	18	15	1	2	65	17	46=
Regent Victoria	18	15	1	2	59	11	46=
KEIGHLEY STAR	18	15	0	3	67	21	45
AIREDALE MAGNET	18	10	2	6	59	45	32
Wrose Bull	18	7	2	9	53	51	23
White Horse	18	7	2	9	34	35	23
Tarn Rangers	18	7	2	9	45	50	23
Horsforth Rangers	18	5	0	13	27	68	15
New Beacon	18	1	3	14	19	63	6
Ilkley Dynamo	18	1	1	16	20	87	4

1993-94

KEIGHLEY & DISTRICT CUP FINAL

Phoenix   2   Steeton   0

KEIGHLEY SUNDAY CUP FINAL

Keighley Star   2   Keighley Shamrocks   0

WEST RIDING COUNTY AMATEUR LEAGUE

Division 1: Steeton (+ reserves)

Division 2: (Top)	P	W	D	L	F	A	Pts
PHOENIX	26	21	3	2	85	19	45
Ardsley Celtic	26	21	3	2	93	32	45
Golcar United	26	16	4	6	69	48	36

Division 4: Phoenix (reserves)

KEIGHLEY SUNDAY ALLIANCE

Jeff Hall Trophy Final: Timothy Taylors   3   St.Annes Celtic (Res)   1

Division 1	P	W	D	L	F	A	Pts
St.Annes Celtic	18	14	4	0	58	10	46
Grapes	18	13	2	3	44	28	41
Knowle Arms	18	13	0	5	62	27	39
Market Arms	18	10	1	7	63	36	31
Basement Club	18	10	2	6	47	34	29
Cullingworth	18	8	2	8	54	40	26
Great Northern	18	5	4	9	44	46	19
Boltmakers	18	4	0	14	38	75	15
Bingley W.M.C.	18	4	0	14	33	49	12
Phoenix	18	1	1	16	27	131	4

Division 2: Chews Bar, Timothy Taylors, Kings Arms (Haworth), Gargrave Clarets, Wask, Sutton, Golden Fleece, White Bear, Brown Cow, Goats Head
Division 3: Harrison & Clough, Kings Arms (Silsden), St.Annes Celtic (Res), Girlington, Victoria Hotel, Kensington, Eastburn, New Inn, Green Lane

CRAVEN & DISTRICT LEAGUE

Premier Division	P	W	D	L	Pts
Gargrave	20	17	2	1	36
Oxenhope Rec	20	16	3	1	35
Embsay	20	15	3	2	33
Cononley Sports	20	12	1	7	25
Carleton	20	10	2	8	22
Skipton Town	18	5	2	11	12

Chasing Glory

Cross Hills (Res)	20	6	2	12	12
Foulridge O.B.	20	6	0	14	12
Waddington	18	5	1	12	11
Cowling	20	3	2	15	8
Earby Punch Bowl	20	3	2	15	8

other local sides Division 1: Haworth, Bradley, Keighley Lifts & Oxenhope Recreation (res) **Division 2:** Lothersdale Athletic & Bronte Wanderers
Division 3: reserves of Cononley Sp, Keighley Lifts & Cowling
Division 4: reserves of Bradley & Lothersdale Athletic.
Welcome Inn (**Division 2**) w/d

WHARFEDALE SUNDAY LEAGUE

local sides Premier Division: Silsden (champions), Keighley Shamrocks, Druids Arms
other divisions: Druids Arms (reserves), Keighley Juniors (+ reserves).

WHARFEDALE TRIANGLE
Premier Division: Keighley Star (champions)

EAST LANCASHIRE LEAGUE
Division 2: Cross Hills

1994-95

KEIGHLEY & DISTRICT CUP FINAL
Cross Hills   3   Phoenix   1

KEIGHLEY SUNDAY CUP FINAL
Keighley Star   1   Silsden   0

WEST RIDING COUNTY AMATEUR LEAGUE
Division 1: Phoenix (+ reserves), Steeton (+ reserves)
Division 3: Keighley Shamrocks

EAST LANCASHIRE LEAGUE
Division 1: Cross Hills

KEIGHLEY SUNDAY ALLIANCE

Jeff Hall Trophy Final: Knowle Arms 1   St.Annes Celtic 0

Premier Division	P	W	D	L	F	A	Pts
St.Annes Celtic	14	11	2	1	56	14	37
Knowle Arms	14	12	1	1	57	22	37
Rose & Crown	14	8	2	4	46	30	29
Great Northern	13	5	3	5	25	32	15
Yorkshire Lifts	14	3	3	8	27	31	12
Reservoir	14	4	3	7	23	40	11
Boltmakers	14	2	1	11	25	53	7
Cullingworth	13	2	1	10	26	62	7

Grapes w/d
Division 1: Old Swan Clarets, Masons Arms, White Bear, St.Annes Celtic (Res), Harrison & Clough, Kings Arms, White Horse, Golden Fleece. Wask w/d.
Division 2: Victoria Hotel, Phoenix, New Inn, Stanbury Pk Rngrs, Kensington, Villa Roma, A.K.E. Club, Kings Arms (Res). Metro Taxis w/d

Tables

CRAVEN & DISTRICT LEAGUE

Premier Division	P	W	D	L	F	A	Pts
Skipton Bulldogs	20	12	8	0	63	15	32
Cross Hills (Res)	20	14	2	4	56	32	30
Embsay	20	12	5	3	65	23	29
Oxenhope Rec	20	10	7	3	41	27	29
Earby Punch Bowl	20	6	8	6	48	50	20
Keighley Lifts	20	7	5	8	41	40	19
Cononley Sports	20	4	9	7	32	43	17
Carleton	20	4	7	9	37	62	15
Nelson/F'ridge OB	20	5	3	12	48	81	13
Skipton Town	20	3	4	13	46	59	10
Cowling	20	3	2	15	34	79	8

other local sides Division 1: Haworth, Bradley Oxenhope Rec (res)
Division 2: Lothersdale Athletic, Bronte Wanderers and Keighley Lifts (res)
Division 3: Eastburn Rangers & reserves of Cononley Sports and Cowling
Division 4: reserves of Haworth, Bradley & Lothersdale Ath.

WHARFEDALE SUNDAY LEAGUE

Premier Division	P	W	D	L	F	A	Pts
DRUIDS ARMS	16	10	5	1	61	25	35
KEIGHLEY JUNIORS	16	10	4	2	51	26	34
SILSDEN	16	10	3	3	42	28	33
Sandy Lane	16	10	1	5	38	28	31
Bay Horse	16	6	5	5	34	33	23
Ferrands Arms	16	6	0	10	26	33	18
Windhill C.C.	16	4	3	9	36	43	15
Thackley Shoulder	16	2	6	8	21	34	12
Halfway Wdrs	16	0	1	15	13	72	1

other divisions: Keighley Juniors (reserves), Druids Arms (reserves).

WHARFEDALE TRIANGLE
Premier Division: Keighley Star (champions)

1995-96

KEIGHLEY & DISTRICT CUP FINAL
Cross Hills   2   Haworth   1

KEIGHLEY SUNDAY CUP FINAL
Silsden   1   St.Annes Celtic 0

WEST RIDING COUNTY AMATEUR LEAGUE
Division 1: Phoenix (+ reserves)   Division 2: Steeton (+ reserves)
Division 3: Keighley Shamrocks

EAST LANCASHIRE LEAGUE
Division 1: Cross Hills

KEIGHLEY SUNDAY ALLIANCE
Jeff Hall Trophy Final: Knowle Arms 3 Phoenix 2 (after 3-3 draw)

Premier Division	P	W	D	L	F	A	Pts
St.Annes Celtic	16	14	0	2	70	18	42
Knowle Arms	17	11	1	5	76	26	34
Boltmakers	18	11	1	6	48	41	34

199

Chasing Glory

Skipton	18	7	3	8	58	49	25
Old Swan Clarets	18	5	1	12	30	42	16
Cullingworth	17	4	2	11	22	70	14
Market Arms	18	4	2	12	33	91	14

Reservoir, Yorkshire Lifts & Great Northern all w/d pre-season. Masons Arms also w/d

Division 1: St.Annes Celtic (Res), Phoenix, Victoria Hotel, Golden Fleece, Gas Club, Bocking W.M.C., White Horse, Craven Athletic, Stanbury Pk Rngrs, New Inn.

CRAVEN & DISTRICT LEAGUE

Premier Division	P	W	D	L	F	A	Pts
Skipton Bulldogs	20	12	8	0	66	19	32
Oxenhope Rec	20	13	4	3	54	25	30
Cononley Sports	20	13	3	4	65	31	29
Embsay	20	12	4	4	71	25	28
Keighley Lifts	20	10	4	6	42	31	24
Cross Hills (Res)	20	6	5	9	30	42	17
Earby Town	20	7	3	10	39	48	17
Carleton	20	6	3	11	40	62	15
Haworth	20	6	3	11	47	69	15
Barnoldswick P.R.	20	3	3	14	28	65	9
Nelson/F'ridge OB	20	2	0	18	14	79	4

other local sides Division 1: Bradley, Bronte Wanderers, Cowling & Oxenhope Recreation (res)
Division 2: Lothersdale Athletic & Keighley Lifts (res)
Division 3: Eastburn Rangers & reserve sides of Cononley Sports and Cowling
Division 4: reserve sides of Haworth, Bradley & Lothersdale Athletic.

WHARFEDALE SUNDAY LEAGUE

Premier Division	P	W	D	L	F	A	Pts
KEIGHLEY JUNIORS	16	13	2	1	58	21	41
Bay Horse	16	12	2	2	49	16	38
SILSDEN	16	10	3	3	50	32	33
DRUIDS ARMS	16	8	3	5	44	27	27
Shipley Town	16	4	3	9	26	43	15
Thackley Shoulder	16	4	2	10	23	39	14
Windhill	16	3	5	8	27	52	14
Idle Cock	16	3	3	10	32	48	12
Sandy Lane	16	2	3	11	27	58	9

Keighley Star w/d
other divisions: Druids Arms (reserves), Silsden Kings Arms (+ reserves)

1996-97

KEIGHLEY & DISTRICT CUP FINAL
Cowling 3 Oxenhope Recreation 2

KEIGHLEY SUNDAY CUP FINAL
St.Annes Celtic 1 Boltmakers Arms 0

KEIGHLEY SUNDAY ALLIANCE
Jeff Hall Trophy Final: Craven Athletic 2 Skipton 1

Premier Division	P	W	D	L	Pts
Three Horses	26	23	1	2	70
Skipton	26	21	1	4	64
Aire Valley S.C.	26	19	1	6	58

200

Tables

	P	W	D	L	F	A
Phoenix	26	18	2	6	56	
Stanbury Pk Rngs	25	13	5	7	44	
Midland (Bingley)	25	13	3	9	42	
St.Annes Celtic (Res)	26	13	2	11	41	
Craven Athletic	25	11	2	12	35	
New Inn Rangers	26	8	6	12	30	
Golden Fleece	26	7	5	14	26	
Bocking Rangers	25	7	3	15	24	
Brown Cow	26	4	4	18	16	
Knowle Arms	26	2	3	21	9	
Silsden Bridge Inn (Res)	26	2	2	22	8	

CRAVEN & DISTRICT LEAGUE

Premier Division	P	W	D	L	F	A	Pts
Skipton Bulldogs	22	21	0	1	82	20	42
Oxenhope Rec	22	16	3	3	66	28	35
Cowling	22	11	5	6	47	29	27
Haworth	22	10	6	6	54	43	26
Cononley Sports	22	9	6	7	51	43	24
Embsay	22	10	4	8	48	40	24
Keighley Lifts	22	7	6	9	48	43	20
Cross Hills (Res)	22	6	6	10	27	48	18
Skipton L.M.S.	22	6	4	12	38	54	16
Skipton Town	22	5	6	11	32	48	16
Rimington (Res)	22	3	4	15	24	70	10
Carleton	22	0	6	16	28	79	6

other local sides Division 1: Bradley, Bronte Wanderers and reserve sides of Oxenhope Rec & Keighley Lifts **Division 2:** Eastburn Rangers & Silsden **Division 3:** reserve sides of Haworth, Cowling & Cononley Sp, **Division 4:** Sutton, Lothersdale Athletic (*) & Bradley (res).

(*) = *Lothersdale Athletic resigned from* **Division 2** *pre-season & replaced their reserves in* **Division 4**.

WEST RIDING COUNTY AMATEUR LEAGUE

Division 1: (Top)	P	W	D	L	F	A	Pts
Hemsworth M.W.	30	21	6	3	112	38	48
Aberford Albion	30	20	6	4	75	25	46
PHOENIX	30	16	8	6	65	26	40

Division 2: Steeton, Keighley Shamrocks **Division 4:** Phoenix (reserves), Steeton (reserves)

EAST LANCASHIRE LEAGUE

Division 1: Cross Hills

WHARFEDALE SUNDAY LEAGUE

Premier Division	P	W	D	L	F	A	Pts
KEIGHLEY JUNIORS	18	15	0	3	66	24	45
ST. ANNES CELTIC	18	13	3	2	61	19	42
DRUIDS ARMS	18	12	3	3	58	25	39
SILSDEN KINGS ARMS	18	10	4	4	55	35	34
SILSDEN	18	10	2	6	44	33	32
Thackley Shoulder	18	6	2	10	27	39	20
Bay Horse	18	5	2	11	34	37	17
Sandy Lane	18	3	3	12	29	66	12
Idle Cock	18	3	2	13	28	64	11
Shipley Town	18	2	1	15	24	84	7

other divisions: Boltmakers Arms, Royal, Keighley Juniors (res), Druids Arms (res), Silsden Bridge Inn.

1997-98

KEIGHLEY & DISTRICT CUP FINAL
Phoenix   1   Sandy Lane   0 (a.e.t.)

KEIGHLEY SUNDAY CUP FINAL
Craven Athletic   3   Keighley Juniors   2 (a.e.t.)

WEST RIDING COUNTY AMATEUR LEAGUE

Division 1: (Top)	P	W	D	L	F	A	Pts
PHOENIX	30	23	5	2	90	23	51
Pontefract Boro'	30	21	1	8	86	43	43
Campion	30	16	11	3	75	40	43

Division 2: Steeton, Keighley Shamrocks
Division 3: Phoenix (reserves)   **Division 4:** Steeton (reserves)

EAST LANCASHIRE LEAGUE

Division 1	P	W	D	L	F	A	Pts
CROSS HILLS	22	15	4	3	66	38	49
Oswaldtwistle	22	14	4	4	73	44	46
Rimington	22	12	3	7	55	51	39
Trawden Celtic	22	11	4	7	65	48	37
Worsthorne	22	10	4	8	69	49	34
Settle United	22	10	4	8	57	40	34
Stacksteads St.Jos	22	9	5	8	46	48	32
Gargrave	22	7	4	11	54	47	25
Colne United	22	7	1	14	54	79	22
Bar'lick Utd (Res)	22	6	3	13	35	55	21
Hurst Green	22	5	5	12	38	47	20
Mill Hill St.Peters	22	5	1	16	24	90	16

Whalley Rangers w/d

WHARFEDALE SUNDAY LEAGUE

Premier Division	P	W	D	L	F	A	Pts
ST. ANNES CELTIC	12	10	2	0	48	6	32
SILSDEN	12	8	2	2	43	13	26
KEIGHLEY JUNIORS	12	5	3	4	28	23	18
Sandy Lane	12	6	0	6	26	37	18
DRUIDS ARMS	12	5	1	6	37	30	16
BOLTMAKERS ARMS	12	1	3	8	25	61	6
Thackley Shoulder	12	1	1	10	9	46	1

several clubs, inc. Silsden Rangers w/d
other divisions: Royal, Silsden Bridge Inn, Keighley Juniors (res) & St.Annes Celtic (res).

CRAVEN & DISTRICT LEAGUE

Premier Division	P	W	D	L	F	A	Pts
Embsay	22	16	4	2	77	23	36
Skipton Bulldogs	22	16	3	3	86	37	35
Oxenhope Rec	22	12	5	5	76	32	29
Keighley	22	13	3	6	71	40	29
Haworth	22	11	4	7	60	47	26
Cross Hills (Res)	22	8	7	7	39	39	23
Addingham	22	9	3	10	61	60	21
Cononley Sports	22	6	7	9	47	60	19
Colne C.C.	22	7	4	11	35	60	18

Tables

Cowling	22	4	5	13	44	67	13
Skipton L.M.S.	22	4	1	17	30	88	9
Skipton Town	22	2	2	18	43	116	6

other local sides Division 1: Silsden, Bradley & reserve sides of Oxenhope Rec and Keighley **Division 2**: Bronte Wanderers, Eastburn Rangers & Haworth (reserves) **Division 3**: reserve sides of Cowling & Cononley Sports, **Division 4**: Sutton, Lothersdale Athletic & reserve sides of Silsden and Bradley.

KEIGHLEY SUNDAY ALLIANCE

Jeff Hall Trophy Final: Craven Athletic 5 Crown 3

Premier Division

	P	W	D	L	Pts
Craven Athletic	16	12	1	3	37
Skipton (+3)	15	11	0	4	36
Three Horses	16	11	2	3	35
Phoenix	16	11	0	5	33
Stanbury Pk Rngs	16	8	1	7	25
Bngly White Horse	16	5	1	10	16
Aire Valley S.C.	16	5	1	10	16
New Inn (-3)	15	3	1	11	10
Golden Fleece	16	1	1	14	4

Fleece (Cullingworth) w/d pre-season

Division 1: Crown, Lord Rodney, Old Swan Clarets, Brown Cow (Bly), Knowle Arms, Sils. Bridge Inn (Res), Robbo's, Aireworth Rangers w/d

KEIGHLEY SOCCER - WINNERS LIST
Saturday competitions

KEIGHLEY & DISTRICT LEAGUE   **KEIGHLEY LEAGUE VICTORY SHIELD**

1946-47	Haworth	Cullingworth
1947-48	Guardhouse	Guardhouse
1948-49	Guardhouse	Guardhouse
1949-50	St.Annes	Guardhouse
1950-51	Guardhouse	St.Josephs
1951-52	Oakworth Albion	Oakworth Albion
1952-53	No competition	
1953-54	Grippon Sports	Central Youth Club
1954-55	Steeton	Silsden (reserves)
1955-56	Worth Village	Worth Village
1956-57	Keighley Shamrocks	Keighley Shamrocks
1957-58	Keighley Shamrocks	Parkwood Amateurs
1958-59	Parkwood Amateurs	Parkwood Amateurs
1959-60	Keighley Grinders	Keighley Grinders
1960-61	Parkwood Amateurs	Carleton (reserves)
1961-62	Keighley Grinders	Keighley Central (reserves)
1962-63	Parkwood Amateurs	

KEIGHLEY & DISTRICT F.A. CUP

1946-47 Sutton United	1973-74 Silsden
1947-48 Sutton United	1974-75 Silsden
1948-49 Sutton United	1975-76 Silsden
1949-50 Guardhouse/St.Annes	1976-77 Silsden
1950-51 Haworth	1977-78 Silsden
1951-52 Silsden	1978-79 Cross Hills
1952-53 Worth Village	1979-80 Cross Hills
1953-54 Wilsden	1980-81 Keighley Town
1954-55 Wilsden	1981-82 Keighley Town
1955-56 Silsden	1982-83 Keighley Town
1956-57 Cullingworth Rovers	1983-84 Keighley Town
1957-58 Keighley Shamrocks	1984-85 Silsden
1958-59 Eldwick	1985-86 Keighley Town
1959-60 Keighley Central	1986-87 Cross Hills
1960-61 Eldwick	1987-88 Cross Hills
1961-62 Keighley Central	1988-89 Steeton
1962-63 Keighley Central	1989-90 Haworth
1963-64 Keighley Central	1990-91 Cross Hills
1964-65 Silsden	1991-92 Denholme United
1965-66 Oxenhope Rec	1992-93 Steeton
1966-67 Keighley Central	1993-94 Phoenix
1967-68 Keighley Central	1994-95 Cross Hills
1968-69 Keighley Shamrocks	1995-96 Cross Hills
1969-70 Keighley Central	1996-97 Cowling
1970-71 Silsden	1997-98 Phoenix
1971-72 Silsden	
1972-73 Westfield Rovers	

Tables

KEIGHLEY SOCCER - WINNERS LIST
Sunday competitions

	KEIGHLEY SUNDAY CUP	KEIGHLEY SUNDAY ALL.	JEFF HALL TRPHY
1961-62		Victoria Star	Victoria Star
1962-63		Victoria Star	Woodside Rovers
1963-64		Bradford Moor	Dean Smith & Grace
1964-65		Clifton Driving School	Dean Smith & Grace
1965-66		Dean Smith & Grace	Dean Smith & Grace
1966-67		Dean Smith & Grace	Dean Smith & Grace
1967-68		Dean Smith & Grace	Dean Smith & Grace
1968-69		Ventus United	Ventus United
1969-70		Dean Smith & Grace	Westwood
1970-71		Dean Smith & Grace	Dean Smith & Grace
1971-72		Ventus United	Magnet
1972-73	Magnet	Magnet	Ventus United
1973-74	Magnet	Magnet	Magnet
1974-75	Magnet	Magnet	Magnet
1975-76	Magnet	Magnet	Magnet
1976-77	Magnet	Magnet	Magnet
1977-78	Magnet	Keighley Grinders Magnet	
1978-79	Magnet	*unfinished* (Burlington)	Magnet
1979-80	Magnet	Keighley Grinders	Settle United
1980-81	Magnet	Robin Hood '80	Robin Hood '80
1981-82	Magnet	Timothy Taylors	Phoenix
1982-83	Silsden	Timothy Taylors	Phoenix
1983-84	Bradleys	Skipton B.R.	Phoenix
1984-85	Silsden	Highfield	Green Gables
1985-86	Bradleys	Highfield	Keighley News
1986-87	Silsden Town	Keighley News	Bell Dean
1987-88	Silsden Town	Cullingworth Sports	Green Gables
1988-89	Silsden Town	Beeches	K'ley Shamrks
1989-90	Airedale Magnet	Red Pig	Beeches
1990-91	Airedale Magnet	K'ley Shamrks	K'ley Shamrks
1991-92	Star Athletic	Knowle Arms	Market Arms
1992-93	Star Athletic	Cavendish Arms	Knowle Arms
1993-94	Keighley Star	St.Annes Celtic	Timothy Taylors
1994-95	Keighley Star	St.Annes Celtic	Knowle Arms
1995-96	Silsden	St.Annes Celtic	Knowle Arms
1996-97	St. Annes Celtic	Three Horses	Craven Athletic
1997-98	Craven Athletic	Craven Athletic	Craven Athletic

205

ABOUT THE AUTHOR

Rob Grillo teaches P.E. and History, amongst other things, at Woodside Middle School in Bradford. Brought up in Keighley, he has a Degree in Sociology from Loughborough University, where he also did his teacher training. Only a tragic lack of ability has prevented him from becoming a top soccer player and long-distance runner!

He is very interested in local history and sports history, having contributed to a number of magazines and books over the past few years as well as writing bits and pieces for the Keighley News. He lives in Keighley with his girlfriend Sue, two mad border collies and several cats (not to mention the fish). *Chasing Dreams* is his second book.

ALSO AVAILABLE FROM EMPIRE PUBLICATIONS

Cups for Cock-ups - The Extraordinary story of Manchester City F.C. by Ashley Shaw – photographs by Michael Clarke

Paperback - £8.99 inc p&p
ISBN: 1 901746 04 6

"*IF CUPS WERE AWARDED FOR COCK-UPS THEN YOU WOULD NOT BE ABLE TO MOVE IN CITY'S BOARDROOM*"

So said Francis Lee during his first spell at the club. How ironic it is that the man who uttered those very true words, was, in the eyes of many, to be responsible for multiplying the club's problems during a nightmare four-year stint as chairman.

"*Cups for Cock-ups by Ashley Shaw claims that the club hosts a malevolent force, the much-vaunted Fifth Column*"

Mark Hodkinson, The Times.

Three Curries and a Shish Kebab – and other spicy tales from a sports writer's notebook by Richard Bott

Paperback - £7.99 inc p&p
ISBN: 1 901746 02 X

The Sunday Express's former chief soccer writer's wry and humorous look at his 40 years in sports writing - with a foreword by Alex Ferguson.

"*Very funny.....difficult to fault*" Total Sport
"*Whatever you do don't take it to the loo to read, I fell off the seat laughing*" Les Barlow, Rochdale Observer
"*A warts and all picture of a sports writer's life*"

Richard Frost, Manchester Evening News

S.F. Barnes - His Life and Times by Andrew Searle

Hardback - £14.95 inc p&p
ISBN: 1 901746 00 3

The extraordinary story of the legendary cricketer Sydney Francis Barnes, who played for Saltaire and Keighley in the Bradford League.

"*A superbly constructed biography*" Robin Marlar, The Cricketer
"*A good, angry read*" Alistair McClellan, Inside Edge
"*Compulsive reading for anyone interested in the history of the game of cricket*" Ross Reyburn, The Birmingham Post

All available from Empire Publications Ltd, Empire House, 62 Charles Street, Manchester M1 7DF
Make cheques payable to Empire Publications Ltd.

Special Offer for readers of this book!

If you have not yet bought "Chasing Glory", The Story of Association Football in Keighley Volume 1, by Rob Grillo, you can order it direct from the publisher for the special price of just **£6.95** (including UK p&p).

Make Cheques payable to "Empire Publications", and write to Chasing Glory Offer, Empire Publications, Empire House, 62 Charles Street, Manchester M1 7DF